American Cities and the Politics of Party Conventions

American Cities and the Politics of Party Conventions

Eric S. Heberlig, Suzanne M. Leland,
and David Swindell

On the cover: Vice President Joe Biden speaks on the final night of the DNC in Charlotte, North Carolina, September 6, 2012. Photograph by Todd Sumlin (Sumlin-tsumlin@charlotteobserver.com). Courtesy of the *Charlotte Observer.*

Published by State University of New York Press, Albany

© 2017 State University of New York

For information, contact State University of New York Press, Albany, NY
www.sunypress.edu

Production, Dana Foote
Marketing, Michael Campochiaro

Library of Congress Cataloging-in-Publication Data

Names: Heberlig, Eric S., 1970– author. | Leland, Suzanne M., 1971– author. | Swindell, David, 1966– author.
Title: American cities and the politics of party conventions / Eric S. Heberlig, Suzanne M. Leland, and David Swindell.
Description: Albany : State University of New York Press, 2017. | Includes bibliographical references and index.
Identifiers: LCCN 2016045128 (print) | LCCN 2017007997 (ebook) ISBN 9781438466385 (paperback : alk. paper) 9781438466392 (hardcover : alk. paper) | ISBN 9781438466408 (ebook)
Subjects: LCSH: Political conventions—United States—Planning. | Political conventions—Social aspects—United States. | City planning—United States.
Classification: LCC JK2255 .H43 2017 (print) | LCC JK2255 (ebook) | DDC 324.273/156—dc23
LC record available at https://lccn.loc.gov/2016045128

10 9 8 7 6 5 4 3 2 1

Contents

Preface

The origins of this project should be easy to guess. On February 1, 2011, the Democratic National Committee announced that Charlotte would host the 2012 Democratic National Convention. Having just lived through North Carolina's new status as a competitive state in the 2008 presidential election, and the media attention that came with it, the potential to add the media saturation of a party convention on top of it seemed overkill. How could we get any academic research done? We couldn't study the convention since conventions don't "matter" anymore, according to the conventional wisdom in political science. Then Gene Alpert of The Washington Center provided the direction we needed when he observed that no one had studied conventions from the city's perspective. Indeed, cities do a tremendous amount of work to recruit and implement presidential nominating conventions, and parties have developed extensive site selection processes to choose the best host. The parties and the cities partner to make themselves look good in the national and international media and to avoid repeats of the 1968 Chicago Democratic National Convention. We sought to understand how and why parties and cities developed their partnerships during the conventions and the implications for understanding how cities operate.

Our vision from the beginning was that this project would be of interest to multiple audiences, and our academic backgrounds reflect that multidisciplinary approach. Heberlig studies political parties, elections, and campaign finance. Leland studies public administration, city planning, and intergovernmental relations. Swindell studies urban policy and economic development, particularly with regard to sports.

This book will appeal to those interested in urban management, policy and planning, economic development, party politics, interest groups, and general public administration. It should also be of interest to community leaders such as members of the chamber of commerce, city council members, county commissioners, mayors, city and county staff, and reporters who wonder: "Why did the convention end up there? How does a city pull this off? Is it really worth it for our city to do this?"

We owe our thanks to numerous people who have contributed to this project. First, we thank Rye Barcott and Elizabeth Terry of Duke Energy for supporting local universities' engagement with the 2012 DNC and for generously providing the funds for us to partner with Winthrop University's Social and Behavioral Research Lab and its director, Scott Huffman, to survey residents of Mecklenburg County, North Carolina, about their experiences with the convention. The analyses of the citizens' views on paying for mega-events, the political effects of conventions, and residents' evaluations of mega-event development strategies in chapters 3, 5, and 7 are made possible with this survey data. We thank the University of North Carolina at Charlotte, especially Chancellor Phil Dubois, Provost Joan Lorden, Special Assistant to the Chancellor Betty Doster, and Dean Nancy Gutierrez for their consistent and enthusiastic support of the 49er Democracy Experience that engaged UNC Charlotte students (and their faculty leaders!) with the convention. We thank the many officials of the Democratic National Convention Committee, the Charlotte in 2012 Host Committee, and the city of Charlotte, who participated in classes and other academic forums, provided documents, and sat for interviews (often multiple interviews) about the convention. A full list of interviewees is provided in appendix 1. In particular, we thank former mayor Anthony Foxx, two of his chiefs of staff, Tracy Montross and Kevin Monroe, city attorney Bob Hagemann, and assistant to the city manager Carol Jennings for opening doors for us. And we thank the many graduate students who assisted with interviews and searched through countless NewsBank articles, especially MPAD 6184 fall 2012 students. Finally, we thank our Charlotte Research Scholars, Mark Shields and Justin McCoy, undergraduates who gathered much of data for the site selection and mayoral advancement, respectively, sections of the book. Shields was a coauthor of "The Disruption Costs of Post-911 Security Measures and Cities' Bids for Presidential Nominating Conventions," published in the *Journal of Urban Affairs*, an earlier version of parts of chapter 2. McCoy was a coauthor of "Mayors, Accomplishments, and Advancement," published in *Urban Affairs Review*, parts of which form the "Mayor's Careers" and "Do They Win?" sections of chapter 5. Finally, we thank our families for their patience with this (seemingly) never-ending book project. We dedicate this book to them:

Tracy, Colin, Mena, and Ellie

—Eric

Dan and Max

—Suzanne

Jennie and Alex

—David

1

Who Wants Circus *Politicus*?

> The political convention . . . demands organizational skill and manipulative genius—both of which qualities are exceeding useful in democratic government.
>
> —Pendleton Herring, 1965

Professor Herring was referring to presidential candidates in this quote, but its relevance to them has declined as presidential nominating conventions have largely ratified decisions made by primary and caucus voters since the reforms of the 1970s. Today, we argue the quote more aptly applies to the cities that host the conventions. Cities develop bid strategies and compete with one another to entice the national party committees to choose them. Cities are at the center of complex intergovernmental and public-private networks to plan and implement political conventions. Cities decide how much to invest in infrastructure to attract tourism generally and mega-events specifically as part of their economic development efforts. When presidential nomination conventions or other mega-events come to town, cities can benefit from the short-term boost in delegate spending and the longer-term reputational benefits brought by the national and international media attention. While the potential benefits of mega-events are relatively clear, how and why cities weigh the costs and benefits of pursing them change over time, how they implement these strategies differently than a normal tourism promotion strategy, and how local politicians (as opposed to the city collectively) can benefit from them are more open questions.

1

Political scientists have devoted little recent attention to presidential nominating conventions. As the preeminent scholar of conventions, Byron Shafer (2010: 264) puts it, "[C]onventions are widely overlooked—marginalized, even disrespected—as research sites for understanding partisan politics in the United States." This marginalization is understandable. Since the reforms of the presidential selection process in the 1970s, party nominating conventions no longer decide who the party's presidential nominee will be.[1] Voters in state primaries and caucuses have made that decision; the convention makes their selection official. We argue that the politics of the convention is now outside the conventional hall. The story of contemporary presidential nominating conventions is less about the nomination of presidential candidates than about the partnership between the parties and the cities to capture the media attention and advance their own goals. Conventions "inseparably linked a city and a political party in their quests for national respect" (Sack, 1987a).

A Partnership: Cities and Parties

In the process of recruiting and implementing a political convention, the host city develops many organizational partnerships and faces the critical task of coordinating them. The most important of these partnerships is with the national party committee that seeks a city as its agent to implement its convention. The party's goal for the convention is to motivate its delegates to work hard to elect the party nominee and to create a weeklong infomercial for viewers to persuade them to vote for the party nominee. The party seeks a partner in the host city to whom it can delegate the logistics and transaction costs so it can keep its attention (and that of the media) on the party's message of unity, accomplishment, and promise. The party needs the city to entertain the delegates and media representatives, keep demonstrators out of the news, and fix inevitable glitches quickly and competently so that the only story occurs on the podium.

Cities' Goals

The city uses its success in the party's site selection process and accepts the grunt work of implementing the convention to take advantage of the party's media spotlight to signal the city's qualities to multiple audiences simultaneously. The city signals to business leaders with the goal of attracting and retaining companies to bolster the local economy and protect or strengthen its existing tax base (Spence, 1973; Preuss and Alfs, 2011).

The convention site selection process is a key means by which a city signals its desirable qualities. For cities, the site selection process is an Olympic competition of assets and entrepreneurialism. The city chooses to put itself in a contest with other cities to demonstrate to the party that it has the capacity and can-do spirit to merit hosting the nominating convention. Selection as host by an outside judge verifies the victor's claims regarding the city's merits, adding to the credibility of its marketing claims: "We are a World Class city—an attractive location for conventions, businesses, tourists, and new residents." The victory allows the city to get the attention of audiences who otherwise wouldn't consider the city or to gain an advantage over direct competitors for an organizational convention[2] or business relocation decision. Winners have shown that they are desirable locations.

Cities are constantly attempting to signal their qualities to maintain existing residents and businesses, and to recruit new ones. They want to let people know that they offer the infrastructure, amenities, and opportunities that lead to a better quality of life. They signal through active advertising campaigns and targeted recruitment efforts. The challenge for any individual city is that the recruitment environment is competitive. Many cities have very similar packages of assets and amenities, and all engage in recruitment and advertising efforts. A business or resident considering relocation thus faces a cacophony of messages from suitors with few clear differences to distinguish one from another. The city has to figure out how to get its signal recognized in an environment where all its competitors are sending similar messages. How can Charlotte distinguish itself from Charlottesville and Charleston? Hosting the Democratic National Convention (DNC) signals that it has more capacity. How can Charlotte distinguish itself from forty-two other major-league cities? Hosting the DNC signals it has the entrepreneurialism. The value of a mega-event is the strength of the signal. It temporarily overrides the competing signals in the environment and allows a city to reach domestic and international audiences who otherwise would be less likely to receive its message. Would the average American know anything about Sochi, Russia, had it not hosted the 2014 Winter Olympics?

The city, of course, cannot control either the size of the television audience or the way the media and social media will report on the city. Viewers are obviously tuning in to hear news coverage about the conventions and to hear party luminaries speak directly. Indeed, the Nielson ratings of party conventions since 1984 show that viewership of both party conventions track together, regardless of their locations or even the competitiveness of the election.[3] The city tries to supply positive stories about itself to the media during the week, and head off or mitigate negative stories that would damage the city or take the focus off the party nominees.

Beyond the television audience, the participants in attendance at a political convention make particularly good targets for cities to disseminate their messages. The largest single group of visitors during the convention is actually not the delegates; it's the thousands of national and international reporters who will cover the convention. National news reporters will set up broadcasting booths, and convention coverage will be during prime time on all of the major networks. Months before the convention even comes to town, reporters write stories about the city and its preparations. Hosting the Republican or Democratic national convention is one of the biggest publicity opportunities that a city can achieve.

Furthermore, while the delegates themselves are often influential party activists in their hometowns, the influence quotient of the elected and unelected national and state leadership of the party, corporate leaders, and domestic and international media can hardly be equaled. As observed by Bill Langkopp, director of the Greater New Orleans Hotel and Motel Association, "Everybody is a big shot. At most conventions everybody thinks they are big shots but they are not. Here, you do have governors and senators" (quoted in Roth, 1991). These elites come with expectations of being treated well, can make lots of noise when they don't think they are being treated well, and can draw lots of attention whether they complain in private or in public, especially in the age of social media. Cities desire positive word of mouth from the attendees of any convention, but attendees at most conventions do not have the same level of clout and visibility as political conventions attendees.

Charlotte Chamber of Commerce president Bob Morgan explains the specific value of the signaling opportunity provided by political convention:

> Usually we are going out to sell the Charlotte story and trying to find people who will listen. This week they're coming to us.[4] . . . This was a chance to be seen by millions of people who had never been to Charlotte before. . . . Media was here for a year and a half—trade journals, broader publications from New York, DC, Europe, Asia. The media is here for the whole week [of the convention], but they're really interested in Thursday night. We're feeding them stories Monday, Tuesday, and Wednesday about Charlotte. . . . I got to do a thirty-minute show on C-SPAN to talk about Charlotte. All softball questions. I'm talking like I'm talking to a corporate executive [who might be persuaded to move]. . . . What is all that worth? You can't put a price on it.[5]

For cities, conventions and other mega-events provide a branding opportunity that cannot be duplicated by traditional marketing and business recruitment campaigns.

Motivations

Certainly, the potential benefits of signaling via mega-events are real for any city. But there is likely to be variation among cities in terms of the specific goal they desire to achieve with this strategy. We consider three types of cities and their motivations: 1) the global city; 2) the redeveloping city; 3) the emerging city. Of course, there are also cities that would not follow a mega-event signaling strategy because they have not invested in the tourism infrastructure to do so effectively.

The megacities of the United States already have domestic and international reputations as centers of business and tourism. They may be traditional megacities (New York City, Chicago, Los Angeles, San Francisco, Boston) or large, tourism-oriented cities (New Orleans, San Antonio, San Diego, Miami). They have long had the size and infrastructure to host political conventions, sports championships, and other mega-events. They bid for conventions because they can. They have the infrastructure, which was created in part for purposes such as these, so they might as well use them and get some additional economic payoff from them. Because they have established reputations, the signaling benefits of a political convention are low compared to other cities. In fact, there may even be reputational risks in the partisan message of a convention or in security breakdowns (for example, the pitched battles at the 1968 Chicago DNC between police and anti–Vietnam War protesters). For these cities, attracting a political convention is part of their ongoing efforts to maintain their visibility and promote their images as world-class cities. But as the costs of conventions increase, whether from the disruption to commerce caused by post-9/11 security measures or having to risk already strong tourism and convention business for a political convention, these cities are more likely than others to drop out of the competition for political convention bids (Heberlig et al., 2016).

Older industrial cities (Baltimore, Detroit, Philadelphia, Minneapolis, Indianapolis, St. Louis, Cleveland) have invested in tourism infrastructure as redevelopment strategies (Frieden and Sagalyn, 1989; Judd, 2003). They seek to replace the loss of manufacturing jobs with downtowns of office towers, festival malls, convention centers, atrium hotels, sports stadia, redeveloped waterfronts, aquariums, and other amenities to attract the spending of middle-class employees and tourists. Redeveloping cities need conventions and mega-events as the strong signal for their audience to update and revise their image of the city from one of decay to one of vibrancy and culture. Philadelphia's victory in the 2000 contest for the Republican National Convention (RNC) was hailed as a "rare bit of cachet, and capped the mayor's relentless eight-year effort to turn [Philadelphia] from a nearly bankrupt husk into a worthy rival of the nation's great urban centers" (Nicholas, 2000).[6]

Emerging cities use bids for conventions (and obtaining major-league sports teams) to signal their status to a world that may not know much about them (Dallas, Atlanta, Houston in the 1970s and 1980s, Denver, Charlotte, Tampa, Salt Lake, Phoenix in the 1990s and 2000s). They may not (yet) be the New Yorks or Chicagos, but their bids show that they have the infrastructure to be players in this arena. Denver invested heavily in sports infrastructure and other amenities as "part of a conscious effort to position Denver in the emerging global urban hierarchy" (Clarke and Saiz, 2003: 174), and its multiple bids for political conventions fit securely within that strategy. The 1984 RNC was Dallas's chance to move away from the legacy of the Kennedy assassination, and shift its image from the "scandalous oilmen" of the 1980s television show *Dallas* and the "scantily clad Dallas cowboy cheerleaders" to "one of culture, class, and clout" (McCartney, 1984). The chief of staff to Charlotte's mayor argued that the 2012 DNC gave Charlotte "a new brand. Now people see Charlotte as a metropolitan city rather than a small town. . . . A modern, new American city."[7]

Particularly for the emerging and redeveloping cities, bidding for conventions is a means for city leaders to share the vision for what they want the city to be with residents and potential residents. In this sense, any concrete economic benefits may be beside the point to leaders of these cities (Judd, 1999: 51–52). The site selection process, and later if the city is selected, the implementation process of the convention gives residents a common cause around which to rally. Being selected as host not only advertises a city's vision to meeting planners and businesses, but it is also a powerful civic validation of the leaders and residents of the city. Particularly for cities that do not have widely recognized historical or cultural assets, iconic structures, or resort-like physical locations (Fainstain and Judd, 1999), mega-events may be part of the city's strategy to attract visitors to pay off its investments in tourism infrastructures.

Not a Shriners Convention and Not the Olympics

While attracting tourism and convention business is a standard city development strategy, the presence of the dignitaries and attendant security precautions and national and international media attention change the nature of convention implementation for political conventions. Core elements are the same: assuring that delegates have hotels, food, transportation, and entertainment.[8] But political conventions also carry much higher risks of terrorism and disruptions from demonstrators, who also take advantage of the media presence to magnify their messages. The intensive security precautions and large security perimeters surrounding the arenas to deal with them can potentially disrupt existing city business, particularly post-9/11. Cities may prefer their typical in-house planning process, but when the Secret Service is protecting national leaders, it's going to be a top-down operation (chapter 4). Likewise, cities must draw upon thousands of additional police from other cities and integrate them effectively into the local force for a week. Nor do ordinary conventions spur revisions of ordinances on parades and use of public spaces to keep demonstrators from blocking commuters and delegates. And as the city implements its extensive security perimeter, it must communicate with local businesses and residents so that they can adjust their routines accordingly. During the convention, the city must continue to provide routine services to residents while providing world-class treatment to visiting dignitaries, putting a premium on coordination between city departments that do not regularly need to coordinate.

Unlike the Olympics, political conventions cannot be used by local leaders to redevelop sections of the city or to bring in substantial intergovernmental capital revenues (Preuss, 2004). The parties want cities with assets in place. Yet conventions are credit-claiming opportunities that local leaders can use to boost residents' evaluations of the effectiveness of city government and provide a platform for seeking higher office (chapter 5).

Seeking political conventions can fit squarely within cities' broader strategies of tourism-oriented economic development and national and international branding efforts. Certainly the large numbers of attendees make political conventions inviting targets to implement such strategies. At the same time, the intense media coverage and high profiles of the attendees create additional risks to go with the potential rewards for cities. How cities evaluate the risk-reward trade-off is a key to understanding the city politics of convention activities. Additionally, unlike implementing most other types of conventions, political conventions require the city to achieve its goals while simultaneously promoting the objectives of the national party whose main event it is hosting.

Party Goals

If staging a successful nominating convention is important to cities competing for attention, it is critically important to the national party committees.

The convention is one the core functions of the national party committees, and it is the only aspect of the presidential nomination campaign over which they exert substantial control. Presidential conventions and debates are the few campaign events to which a large proportion of the population will pay attention, thereby providing parties with the opportunity to activate their own supporters, remind weak supporters why they typically vote for the party, and frame issues and candidate qualifications in a way that will appeal to persuadable voters. The convention acceptance speech is one of the best opportunities for the nominee to communicate the party's message to the public. Indeed, depending on the election, 15% to 30% of voters claim to make their vote choices during the conventions in the American National Election Studies (Shafer, 2010: 274). Analyses of convention effects on public opinion not only find a short-term "convention bump" for the candidate (Campbell, 2001; Campbell, Cherry, and Wink, 1992; Cera and Weinschenk, 2012; Gelman and King, 1993; Hagen and Johnston, 2007; Hillygus and Jackman, 2003) but also a longer-term effect on candidate support (Atkinson et al., 2014; Erickson and Wlezien, 2012; Shaw and Roberts, 2000; Stimson, 2004). If the national parties are to contribute to the election of their party's presidential nominee, the best way to do it is by controlling the media's message and image about the party and its nominee by executing a competent convention. As presidential elections scholar James W. Davis (1983: 154) argues, "[A] smooth and well-run convention offers the public evidence of the party and the candidate's capacity to manage the government."

The "out" party is particularly dependent on a smooth nominating convention as evidence of its competence, since it does not control the machinery of government to show its skills in policy development and implementation. Mismanaged scheduling of speakers, a partially plagiarized speech from the nominee's wife, technical problems in the arena, allowing Senator Ted Cruz to speak without endorsing the nominee, and repeated off-message comments by the nominee (including attacks on the governor of the host state), led to headlines questioning Donald Trump's managerial capabilities in 2016 (e.g., Henneberger, 2016; Peoples and Colvin, 2016; Politico, 2016; Stokol, 2016). In fact, a post-convention Gallup poll found that 51% of respondents were less likely to vote for Trump based on what they saw or read about the GOP convention compared to 36% who were more likely to vote for him, the only negative net rating the firm has ever measured following the conventions (Jones, 2016).[9] In contrast, the smoothly managed DNC produced a net positive rating of 4 points for Hillary Clinton in the Gallup polls.

Cotter and Hennessy (1964) describe the twofold task of the national committees during the convention: "It is a function of the national committee to make possible one of the most important decisions in Western democracy, namely, the nomination of a candidate for president of the United States. But it is also the committee's task to be sure that the nomination takes place in a context in which there are enough sheets and enough telephones for all" (109). Our research question is how the parties achieve both these convention goals—nominating a candidate and handling the logistics—simultaneously. Our theoretical starting point is that the parties seek to prioritize their energy on their first and most important goal of nominating the candidate and controlling the message through the media by delegating achievement of the second goal—the sheets, telephones, and quartering of troops—to the host cities. The party needs a partner with the assets to make its production feasible, the amenities and energy to give the attendees an enjoyable convention, and the ability to fix the glitches. Snafus inevitably happen during conventions, "[b]ut when hotels are roach-infested, burglarized, or located in inconvenient places, the party's image suffers" (Smith and Nimmo, 1991: 85). The challenge of the site selection process is to develop a way to entice competent host cities to bid, and to distinguish the competent hosts from the bidding cities that talk a good game. Once the host is selected, the party can retain its control over the aspects of the convention that are most critical to the dissemination of its message—the renovation of the arena and negotiations with the media—then delegate many of the other logistical tasks of implementation to the city.

The Party Signal

The parties use conventions to send multiple signals. The verbal signals, which are often supplemented by visuals such as films, introduce the nominee and establish themes for the general election campaign. The nonverbal signals are also critical, and thus are also subject to considerable planning and attention to execution by the party: who speaks, unity of delegates, and the physical environment.

The parties' extensive efforts to script the conventions as infomercials for the media to disseminate are well established (see especially Panagopolous, 2007; Smith and Nimmo, 1991). In the infomercial convention, the primary role of delegates is less to select the nominee or ratify the platform than to be the "cheering section for the nominee."[10] Delegates are provided "homemade" signs—and, in fact, are prohibited from bringing their own—and are led in cheers and chants at designated times (Panagopolous, 2007: 7; Polsby et al., 2012: 137). Though members of the media establishment may complain about the scripted, no-news nature of contemporary conventions, Polsby and colleagues conclude (2012: 136): "[C]onventions are now judged by pundits on how well they are organized as advertisements. Any intrusion of substantive debate (such as platform disagreements) into the convention is considered a breach of unity and therefore a sign of weakness in the party. More serious still is poor entertainment." Even Donald Trump's promise to create a more interesting, Hollywood-style convention ended up as the standard podium-oriented speaker convention fare. As *The Cook Political Report*'s Amy Walter observed, "The most disruptive candidate in modern history has done nothing to dismantle or redefine the party convention" (2016).

The choreography of delegates promotes the convention's core message of unity: the party is united and enthusiastic about its nominee (Wayne, 2011). The party must introduce its nominee to the voter in a way that mobilizes the party's traditional supporters to work on behalf of the candidate during the election while simultaneously appealing to swing voters. The party wants to place the nominee in the context of the rich legacy of heroes and accomplishments of the party while simultaneously charting the nominee's vision for the future of the nation. In essence, the convention serves as the bridge between the nominee's primary campaign and a general election campaign appealing to a more diverse electorate.

The party will present its convention message both directly through speeches, and indirectly through choices of imagery and visuals—including the selection of who speaks and provides entertainment (Philpot, 2008). Who the party strategically choses to speak is critical because the media decides which speakers to cover. So much so that Don Fowler, former chair of the Democratic National Committee, has asserted the party's choice of "the messenger is more important than the message" (quoted in Smith and Nimmo, 1991: 64). Even the demographic mix of delegates itself provides visual, social group cues to the audience (Green, Palmquist, and Schickler, 2002). The convention will mix consensual issues and imagery (how many flag images can be packed into each camera angle; condemning terrorism and praising fiscal responsibility), with messages that will contrast one party effectively with the other: emphasizing issues "owned" by the party (Petrocik, 1996), critiques of the other party, and repetitive talking points for supporters (to increase the likelihood that viewers who are only watching short snippets are exposed to the core points).

In addition to determining who speaks, the other key facet of the party's message control is the creation of the visual environment that viewers will see. The stage itself is part of the party message: the height and shape of the stage, the style of the podium and chairs, the backdrop, the colors, the lighting, are all planned to achieve an objective such as making the candidate stand out, to project calmness and confidence, and to reassure the audience about the nominee on an emotional level.[11] In fact, the major expense to the party of producing the convention is to reconstruct the city arena as a production stage for the party message. In 1988, New Orleans officials went so far as hiring an architectural consultant just to help them design the delegates' chairs (which cost $805,500 in 2014 dollars) to look good on television (Roth, 1991). The message the viewer expects to receive comes from the content and identity of the speakers, but it is powerfully supplemented by the visual world constructed in the arena.

The parties' message management is more critical than ever given the declining amount of live television coverage in the past several election cycles (Panagopolous, 2007; Shaffer, 2010) and the simultaneous rise of full-time cable news stations devoted to commentary and instant analysis. In this environment, the parties have a smaller margin for error as any "off message" moment has the potential to crowd out a large portion of coverage and marginalize the message the party wants the audience to receive. This challenge is magnified with the growing importance of the new media, many of whose chroniclers never seek to go into the arena or interview any party officials, and the fact that anyone (indeed, everyone) can "report" on convention-related happenings through social media. Anything occurring in the city or by people associated with the convention can now easily find a broader audience.

Thus, despite its best efforts, the party cannot entirely control the message coming out of the convention. The more they attempt to script the media, the more the media will seek stories that are unscripted. Conflict and drama bring the media their audience, and professional journalists resist being used as mouthpieces for the parties. As R. Sam Garrett (2007: 126–27) observes, "[I]n bringing increased political order, modern conventions also open themselves to *message crises* in lack of coverage and lack of interest. Modern conventions can be just plain boring. This causes political journalists and producers to focus on whatever conflict they find, sometimes implying crises based on minor disagreements" [italics in original]. In 2012, for example, considerable media attention was devoted to whether Governor Chris Christie's speech promoted Christie more than GOP candidate Mitt Romney, and what Clint Eastwood was doing in pretending to have a conversation with an empty chair (representing President Obama). Other times, the disagreements are real: Pat Buchanan's culture war speech in 1992, the Democrats preventing Pennsylvania governor Robert Casey from delivering an antiabortion speech in 1992, or Texas senator Ted Cruz's prime-time diss of 2016 GOP nominee Donald Trump as he urged delegates to "vote their conscience." The parties and the nominees thus have considerable incentive to negotiate platform concessions and make other accommodations to losing candidates and party factions to keep them from using the nearby cameras to air their grievances (Malbin 1981). And other times, the media focuses on events outside the hall: the 1968 battle between anti–Vietnam War demonstrators and police in the streets of Chicago, and Hurricane Isaac in Tampa 2012. Often the events of the convention that captivate the audience are the human moments that may have little policy or "political" content. As Ricky Kirschner, executive producer of DNC 2012, observes: "I can tell you what the highlights of the Tony Awards, Super Bowl halftime show are ahead of time because we plan them. I can't tell you what the highlight of the convention will be. Gore kissing Tipper. Obama walking out at Invesco Field. Obama's 2004 convention speech. We couldn't have predicted ahead of time that these would be the memorable events."[12]

Regardless of what events end up receiving lots of media play and making a public impression, there is little doubt that parties try to maximize the messages favorable to them and minimize distracting or incongruent messages. To do this, they need a partner—a host city who will not only relieve the party of many of the transaction costs of putting on the big production (finding hotels and entertaining thousands of delegates and allies, recruiting thousands of volunteers, upgrading telecommunications capacities for the media—and smart phone–using hordes) but who also will competently issue permits to get the arena and hotels renovated on time, raise the funds to pay for the production, protect the dignitaries and contain the demonstrators (without beating them up), fix the inevitable glitches quickly and quietly, and "feed the [media] beast" with positive stories.[13] By selecting a competent host, the party will increase the probability that voters will judge the party to be competent and worthy of support (e.g., Cover, 1986; Peffley, Feldman, and Sigelman, 1987).

Recently, the Democratic Party has made a more concerted effort to use the presence of the convention as a tactic to mobilize local residents (see chapter 5). The city's host committee, which traditionally has focused on entertaining the delegates and visiting dignitaries, organizes festival activities to which local residents are also invited. The party uses the event to register voters, collect contact information, attract campaign volunteers, and buff its image. The city benefits from having the residents experience the perks of hosting a convention while simultaneously subsidizing the party's get-out-the-vote efforts. In this way, the partners benefit on dimensions beyond message control.

The Organizational Chart

Implementing a presidential nominating convention is an organizationally complex task. It involves the national parties, the campaigns of their prospective nominees, the city government, the host committee organized by the city to undertake convention planning, officials from federal, state, and neighboring local governments, private vendors who will provide services during the convention, city residents and businesses whose lives will be temporarily dislocated by the convention, and thousands of volunteers . . . all under the glare of the domestic and international media.

Three key organizations make a political convention happen: the national party committee, the city government, and the host committee. The national party committees are officially responsible for the business of the nominating conventions. Traditionally, their main responsibility has been to conduct the convention to nominate their presidential candidate and approve the party platform. Their direct involvement comes through two different guises: 1) initially the site selection committee, and 2) once the host city is chosen, the Democratic National Convention Committee and the Republican National Committee's Committee on Arrangements (hereafter National Party Convention Committees).

The National Party Convention Committees (NPCC) are responsible for the "business" of the convention—the official program that occurs inside the convention hall. Their programmatic decisions include identifying and scheduling the speakers, entertainers, and video clips, and hiring the consultants to produce them. They handle negotiations with the media regarding camera placement, skyboxes and other physical spaces for the press, technical needs, and scheduling their access to facilities. They also assure that their contract with the city gives them control over renovations of the hall. Controlling the physical space of the hall allows control over the visual backdrop that is a core element of the party messaging effort. The NPCCs coordinate the activities of and serve as the communications channel for the delegates, other party officials, "affiliated groups," (a.k.a. representatives of the interest groups aligned with the parties), and VIPs.[14] They decide who gets credentials—and how many (and since there are never enough, they manage the fallout). They assign hotels to the delegates, media, and affiliated groups, and coordinate transportation from the hotels to the arena and other venues for the delegates. They provide the security within the arena. They solicit bids for and oversee arena construction. They manage contracts, hiring, legal, insurance, and communications. Smith and Nimmo (1991: 43) argue that conventions have become "almost as much of a showcase for managerial as for partisan political skills." The NPCCs must exhibit both managerial and political skill to execute conventions. Importantly, they retain control over the messaging (physical, scheduling, script, onstage personnel) and media management elements of the convention while delegating the hospitality and financing tasks to the host city.

The host city contracts with the national party committee to provide the various resources necessary to conduct the convention, but the main responsibility of the city government is providing security. This includes contracting with police officers and other security personnel from many other cities to expand the city force during the convention, purchasing equipment for them, and working with the Secret Service, FBI, and other federal security agencies to develop and implement security plans for the convention. Chapter 4 will show that these are significant tasks and often require cities to depart from their standard modes of decision-making and operations.

The rest of the convention implementation responsibilities are delegated to the host committee, a nonprofit (typically a 501c3 or 501c6 organization) set up by city leaders to recruit and implement the convention. Officially (that is, legally from the perspective of the Federal Election Commission), the host committee is responsible for activities that promote the host city but are independent of activities inside the conventional hall. The host committee is the bridge between the NPCC, all the city agencies, and private and civic organizations in the city to make the convention happen. The host committee promotes the city to the national party committee during the site selection process and promotes the city to the delegates, dignitaries, and media audience during the convention. They provide the hospitality to assure that convention attendees leave with a positive impression of the host

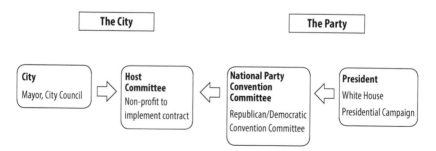

Figure 1.1. The organizational chart.

city. As explained by Kevin Monroe, the chief of staff to Charlotte's mayor, the goal of the host committee is to "Entertain the delegates. You can't just drop them in any city. Charm the media first. . . . Wine and dine the media [before the convention] on their site visits so that their first impressions, and the first impressions they give the audience, of your city are positive."[15] Typically, this hospitality includes a media party and a delegate party promoting local themes, food, and music in the days before the opening gavel. The host committee recruits and trains thousands of volunteers and procures thousands of hotel accommodations for the visiting dignitaries. The host committee coordinates the image and branding activities for the city.

In practice, the host committee is "the father of the bride"[16]—they raise the money for the party convention committees to spend. The NPCCs traditionally have been limited to spending money provided by a portion of the income tax's presidential public financing check-off (Garrett and Reese, 2014), but the parties required the cities to raise substantial funds to supplement them in their requests for proposals (RFPs) and contracts with the host cities. As we will elaborate in chapter 3, fundraising consistently poses a challenge for the host committees even as the demands of the parties and the funding streams available to cities have changed over time.

While the host committee is officially responsible for convention implementation and fundraising activities, the city government often serves as the backstop. The mayor often becomes the chief fundraiser for the committee, and city governments have to develop plans to cover shortages if fundraising falls short. If cities seek conventions to boost their images, that goal is at risk if the host committee stumbles. A city's inability to provide funds undercuts its signal to businesses and event planners that it has the can-do to pull off events of this magnitude and follow through on its commitments. Los Angeles city councilwoman Ruth Galanter described the city's situation when the Los Angeles Host Committee asked the city council for an additional $4 million to cover fundraising shortfalls: "However uncomfortable we may be with this, I don't think we have a whole lot of choices. It is the city that will be hosting all these people. They're not going to turn around and say the host committee didn't do this or didn't do that. They're going to say it was the city of Los Angeles that didn't do something" (quoted in *Daily Breeze*, 2000).

The campaign organization of the party's presidential nominee plays a variable role in the convention decision-making hierarchy. When the incumbent president seeks reelection, the campaign is frequently consulted and makes the decision when it has strong preferences. The chief executive is, after all, also the chief of the party. Dan Murrey, president of the Charlotte in 2012 Host Committee, describes the benefits of planning a convention for the campaign of the president: "Working with an incumbent president decreases the uncertainty. You know all the players. With hurricanes, hot weather, demonstrators, and anarchists, it's nice to have a few things you're certain of."[17] Conventions without incumbents are also more complicated to plan because preparations must be made not only for the nominee but also for the staff and supporters of all the other contending candidates.

A nonincumbent nominee's campaign contributes to decisions regarding the messaging and staging of the convention, but has little input into the key logistical decisions. Most of those decisions must be made by the NPCC before the nominee has won a majority of delegates in state primaries and caucuses through the winter and spring of the convention year. One of the key exceptions was the 2008 decision for Obama to give his acceptance speech in Mile High Stadium in Denver—a different venue from the Pepsi Center where the rest of the convention was planned. The DNC and Denver Host Committee had forty-nine days to develop a process for selecting which members of the public could attend, develop new credentials for the public (to differentiate them from the delegates), develop new transportation and security plans, and design and build a new stage and media production facilities in the new venue.[18]

The challenge of coordinating across organizations is compounded by the fact that presidential nominating conventions are rare events in the sense that they only occur once every four years. The staff members of the NPCCs have experience in party and presidential campaign politics but varying levels of experience with past conventions. Similar to many campaign staffers, they are frequently young and confident beyond their years. The NPCC staffs swoop into town to confront city and host committee staffers who are experienced in hosting large conventions, but who probably have never been involved in a political convention. At best, the city players have talked to their compatriots in previous host cities to get an idea of what worked and didn't work there. The NPCC wants to plan the convention based on their experience with other cities, and the city staffers think they know what will work in their city.[19] We will see in chapter 4 that a similar dynamic occurs between city officials and federal security agencies. The city staff wants to retain control of the convention and conduct the convention in a way that will help brand the city positively and uniquely. The inevitable tension is compounded by generational differences between the young and brash party staffers and the older city staffers who don't appreciate being told how to run their city.

Given the stakes for both the parties and the cities, they learn to work together. They must plan security arrangements and contingency plans for dealing with emergencies with a large number of federal and state security agencies. They must expand the police force with officers from many jurisdictions and train their police forces, who may not frequently deal with mass marches and thousands of demonstrators. They must raise the funds and develop methods of soliciting and screening vendors so that the convention production makes both of them look good. They must communicate with local employers and residents whose ordinary routines will be disrupted by the convention. At the same time, cities must continue to deliver the full array of services to local residents as if a major international event were not in town. If governing is often a balancing act, governing during a mega-event is governing on a high wire.

Cities and Mega-Events

As has been well documented, cities seek mega-events to attract tourism spending and media attention (e.g., Andranovich et al., 2001; Burbank et al., 2002; Eisinger, 2000; Judd and Swanstrom, 2012; Smith, 2014; Strom, 2008). We seek to use the frequency and regularity of presidential nominating conventions to explore the costs and benefits of mega-events more systematically. In examining which cities bid for political conventions and which cities win them, we use the convention as our dependent variable; in examining the political and economic effects of conventions, we use convention activities as an independent variable. And in several chapters, for example, on convention fundraising, we use the host cities to define our population for analysis. Our approach is not to develop and test a theory of political conventions specifically or mega-events generally, but to use conventions as a site to analyze the behavior of numerous political actors who are involved in them. Some of the actors and their activities will be most interesting to political scientists: political parties, fundraisers, voters, and ambitious mayors. Some activities will be most relevant to urban scholars: mega-event strategies and economic development benefits. Other activities will find their audience among public administrators: policy implementation, organizational analysis, intergovernmental relations, and residents' evaluation of government. But in taking more of a cross-disciplinary and multi-methods approach, we intend for the whole of the analysis to provide a compelling exploration of how cities operate and adapt in a competitive economic environment in the U.S. federal system.

In particular, we analyze how changes in the environment affect the cost/benefit evaluations of cities. We develop a database of 131 cities that are potential hosts for political conventions since the 1990s. In chapter 2, we analyze which cities receive Requests for Proposals (RFPs) to assess the qualities that the parties desire in host cities. We then analyze the cities' bids to explain why cities recruit mega-events. We find that the qualities desired by parties has remained consistent over time, yet the disruption costs imposed by post-9/11 security measures have changed the cost/benefit calculation for cities and thus the types of cities willing to bid for conventions. Moreover, despite parties' political incentive to select host cities in states that could provide a boost in the Electoral College vote, our evidence shows that parties' prioritize consideration of cities that can be reliable agents and that will run a competently executed convention.

Not only have the costs and benefits of political conventions changed over time, but so have the financing methods by which cities pay for conventions. In chapter 3, we show that the legal environment governing convention financing has changed dramatically and as such has affected the types of cities that can bid for conventions and the balance of power between the national parties and the cities. Cities have increasingly succeeded in financing conventions by shifting away from direct appropriations to a combination of federal security grants and private fundraising from an unwieldy coalition of local donors, access-oriented national donors, and party activists. We use Federal Election Commission data on host committee donors to analyze the amounts and timing of donations to explain the dynamics of convention fundraising.

We also explore the political benefits of political conventions (chapter 5) in addition to the economic benefits (chapter 6). Parties have recently attempted to use conventions to engage local residents and mobilize them to affect the Electoral College outcome in the host state. We use a post-2012 election survey of Charlotte residents to measure the results of these efforts. We find that conventions can have modest effects on campaign voluntarism, efforts to persuade others, campaign interest, and vote choice, mostly for those who follow convention coverage closely in the local media. Convention effects are especially large for Democrats who would be most likely to be energized by the local presence of the DNC.

But the political benefits of conventions may be more valuable to local government officials than to the national parties. Our survey data shows that conventions have significant effects on how residents evaluate local government and local officials. The evaluations of "out-partisans" are especially susceptible to influence when they believe the event has been successful. Finally, we show that host city mayors think they are the beneficiaries of political conventions. Having a high-profile accomplishment spurs them to seek higher office at rates significantly higher than other mayors—though voters do not seem to be impressed by this particular accomplishment.

While the mega-events literature has given substantial attention to why cities promote them, it has given less attention to the public management issues that are critical to implementing them. City governments, host committees, party committees, federal security agencies, and local stakeholders all must coordinate. Typically, as we show in chapter 4, they do not have any experience coordinating with one another, and must develop plans in an environment that maximizes uncertainty. Given the security issues at stake, cities must adapt their traditional decision-making and planning activities to federal security agencies' authority. Regardless of the economic benefits, cities benefit by deepening their capacity to work across city agencies, working with other organizations across government and the private sector, developing and practicing emergency management plans, engaging with civic organizations and citizens to do something constructive together, and earning trust in a polarized political environment.

The mega-events literature has typically focused on the decision making of local economic and political elite. Key players in the local "regime" believe investments in tourism infrastructure are necessary for the city's economic development, and they develop and execute the city's marketing strategy. Often these investments are made using financial strategies that do not require the approval or direct financial commitment of residents to avoid backlash against regime decisions.[20] Political conventions are no different. Still, we know little about how citizens evaluate mega-events or cities' investments in them or the conditions under which citizens would be more or less willing to financially support attracting mega-events. In chapter 7, we use our survey data to analyze residents' commitment to mega-events as economic development and reputation-building strategies.

In our final chapter, we also return to the question about which parties, city officials, and residents should care most: What makes a successful convention? We use our 2012 Charlotte survey to assess how residents evaluate the success of a convention. We use our interviews and case studies to present best practices for public administrators. For potential bid cities, we discuss why would/should a city host a convention (or not). For residents of the rest of the nation, we discuss whether contemporary conventions are "worth it." For scholars, we discuss what the changing politics of convention siting and implementation tells us about party and city politics. Merely because the selection of the nominee has become a foreordained conclusion, this doesn't mean that there is no politics at party conventions. The politics has left the hall; the politics is out in the cities.

2

Matchmaking

The Politics of Site Selection

When the Republican National Committee announced that Cleveland would host the 2016 Republican National Convention over Dallas, the Associated Press framed the story as a selection of a politically competitive state over a solidly Republican state: "The move reflects the role Ohio—and its 18 electoral votes—plays in presidential campaigns. 'As goes Ohio, so goes the presidential race,' said [National Republican] Party Chairman Reince Priebus" (Elliot and Peoples, 2014). Then Columbus mayor Michael Coleman doubled down on the electoral competition hypothesis, arguing that, with the RNC in Cleveland, the Democrats would be ceding Ohio to the GOP if his city were not chosen as the host of the DNC (Cheney, 2014).

Indeed, political competitiveness has to be the explanation for the Republicans' selection of Cleveland, doesn't it? For years, Cleveland has epitomized the struggles of the Rust Belt. Dallas is larger, has more hotels, and much greater fundraising capacity. It is a place more people want to go as indicated by its higher population growth and its larger tourism sector. But what Dallas did not have was a willingness to make its arena available for the six weeks that the Republican National Committee required for renovations nor the willingness to make its arena available in June, when the GOP wanted to hold its convention (Doran and Fernandez, 2014; Goldstein, 2014).[1]

Twenty years earlier, in a mirror-image situation, the Bush White House wanted to go San Diego for the 1992 RNC for political reasons (McDonald, 1991). George H. W. Bush had won California narrowly in 1988 and thought the convention would help secure that state for his reelection and two U.S. Senate races. Houston, the main competition, was already an electoral lock for Bush. But San Diego wouldn't commit to raising additional funds for the convention and wanted to split the convention between two sites, its convention center for the delegate meetings and the football stadium for President Bush's acceptance speech. GOP officials didn't like the logistics of managing two venues and worried about bad weather spoiling the television visuals. Despite the political advantages of San Diego, Houston hosted the 1992 RNC because it had the logistical advantages.

The Cleveland and Houston cases illustrate the evidence we will present in this chapter showing that the national parties consistently weight logistical considerations more heavily than electoral ones in their choices of host cities. It is intuitive that politics, especially the presidential competitiveness of the state, should matter in the site selection for conventions. It is so intuitive, in fact, that it has been promoted as a key rationale for the national parties' site selection choices for decades. Bibby and Alexander (1968: 37–38) noted the claim during the 1960s, then dismissed its importance after reviewing conventions going back to the 1920s. In many recent cases, cities in noncompetitive states have been chosen—New York City (twice), Los Angeles, San Diego, Houston, and Chicago—while in other years, all the finalists were in competitive states, providing no advantage to any of the bid cities. Since 2008, parties have chosen cities in more competitive states as they simultaneously have staged convention activities to engage local residents.

Whatever qualities parties may desire in the ideal host city, they are constrained in obtaining them by the limited number of cities who submit bids. We will show that as the cost/benefit ratio of hosting conventions (as exemplified by the increased security costs and disruptions after 9/11) has changed, the number and types of cities that bid have changed as well.

We argue that politics makes a difference in which cities are selected by the parties to host conventions, but not in the simplistic way that it is most often considered. Politics matters in how cities organize, lobby, and build coalitions in support of their bids. It matters in whether the host city is unified behind the bid and whether the state government can be counted on to be supportive. The national parties have constructed their site selection processes to induce cities to demonstrate that they have the assets necessary to accommodate the party's logistical needs, as well as the skills and enthusiasm necessary to be a good partner with the party. The city's job is to help the national party pull off the convention and make it look easy—to help focus the national and international media's attention on how the strengths of the city illustrate the party agenda, rather than on protesters run amok, delegates stuck in traffic, or local businesspeople who are losing money because of security concerns.

In this chapter, we analyze the qualities that help cities advance through several stages of the site selection process—from the "invisible primary" pre-invitation and pre-bid politics through site visitations through the party's final selection. We also tell the stories of some bid cities to illustrate how and why some cities succeed and others fail.

The Site Selection Process

Stage 1—The Pre-bid Phase: "The Invisible Primary"

The "invisible primary" of a presidential campaign occurs as the potential candidate surveys party officials, interest group allies, and donors for potential support. The candidate seeks to determine whether he or she has a core of support to mount a viable campaign for the nomination and a strategically plausible path to victory.

A similar process unfolds for cities that are interested in hosting a party convention between the end of the previous presidential election and the official beginning of the site selection process. City representatives consult party officials about what assets are likely to be required to determine whether they have a chance and to see if they get any encouragement about their prospects. They assess their own level of excitement for a long and potentially grueling campaign. They monitor who else is considering a bid. They start to build coalitions to support a bid within the city and within the party in case the decision is to go for it.

The key actor in the invisible primary stage of site selection is an entrepreneur. The entrepreneur invests his or her time and energy to encourage the city to make a bid. Recruiting a convention is a collective good—everyone benefits from the city's enhanced stature. Yet because the benefits of the convention are widely disbursed across the city, no one individual has much personal incentive to invest in developing the bid and coordinating all the participants (Olson, 1965). This is particularly true when the probability of attaining the collective good is uncertain—the city could invest in a bid only to lose to a competitor. So, for most city officials, the incentive is to focus on the activities that have helped them succeed in getting where they are rather than taking a risk on a costly, uncertain adventure.

Entrepreneurs are critical to solving collective action problems because they are willing to take the risk of investing their time and resources to mobilize others (Bianco and Bates, 1990; Salisbury, 1969; Schneider and Teske, 1992). If the bid progresses, they may be rewarded with a job and its salary and benefits on the host committee, increased contacts and status in the community, and an enhanced media profile. They are also motivated by their commitment to the cause—they think it a good thing for the city, and many are willing to pay the costs of entrepreneurship regardless of whether others "free ride" off their efforts.

The role of an entrepreneur is illustrated by the late Susan Burgess, a Charlotte city councilwoman and a North Carolina member of the Democratic National Committee.[2] As early as 2000, Burgess thought that hosting the DNC was something Charlotte should do. Promoting Charlotte to businesses, conferences, and potential residents was something she did constantly based on her position on the city council and her genuine passion for her adopted home city. Charlotte bid for the RNC in 2000, but Burgess thought that the city did not yet have the assets in place. In fact, the lack of hotel rooms was a key reason why the city's 2000 bid came up short.[3] By the 2008 Denver DNC, Burgess thought Charlotte was ready and started to talk up the opportunity to other members of the North Carolina delegation. Her plan was twofold: convincing the Democratic National Committee to choose Charlotte, and convincing Charlotte that a bid for the DNC would be good for the city.

As part of the internal Charlotte campaign, Burgess used her contacts as a longtime city councilwoman. Early on, she teamed up with Tim Newman, CEO of the Charlotte Regional Visitors Authority (CRVA), to put together promotional material and to recruit others to back the effort. She enlisted the support of the chamber of commerce and, with Newman, recruited Jim Rogers, CEO of Duke Energy, to be the lead organizer of the business community. With the assistance of Don Fowler, a South Carolinian who was former chair of the Democratic National Committee, she and Newman retained consultants who had been involved in previous DNCs to assist with the bid. She asked fellow city councilmember Anthony Foxx, a candidate for mayor, to make bidding for the DNC a priority if he won.

Burgess's status as a member of the Democratic National Committee helped with the campaign to win the party's support. At Obama's 2009 inaugural, she talked up Charlotte with other national committee members and handed a letter to then DNC chair Tim Kaine stating Charlotte's interest. She brought Newman with her (or sent him as her representative once her cancer made her too ill to travel) to regional and national Democratic National Committee meetings to promote Charlotte's candidacy. Through her service as a board member of the National League of Cities, she knew Mayor Tom

Menino of Boston and Mayor John Hickenlooper of Denver, the previous two DNC hosts, and she contacted them to get their advice on developing a bid and to seek their support for Charlotte's bid.

In short, Burgess's entrepreneurialism not only initiated the idea that Charlotte should bid for the DNC but also built the coalition to make it a reality. She identified the people who would make the decision within the city and within the party, and identified what information or what contacts were necessary to influence them.

We searched NewsBank from 1980 through 2016 for "back stories" to identify the entrepreneurs in other cities' bids to assess whether Burgess's case is generalizable or whether the city's mayor is generally the entrepreneur. The regime literature, for example, argues that leaders of the business community often make key economic development decisions and the mayor is brought into the process later (Logan and Molotch, 1987), and if that is the case regarding the recruitment of political conventions, mayors may not play a leading role. Many cities' media do not cover this element of the story, and when it is covered, politicians have an incentive to inflate their roles, so our findings must be taken as tentative.

We found sufficient information on eighteen cities to make an assessment of credit. In one-third of the cities, a government official other than mayor is the entrepreneur. Nearly as often, a local party officer is the entrepreneur (31%). Business leaders are the convention entrepreneurs in 19% of the cities (and in all cases, the business leaders were well connected in the party). In only three cities (17%) is there clear attribution of the mayor as the originator and primary organizer of the convention bid (Menino in Boston, 2000/2004; Whitmire in Houston 1988, 1992; and Rendell in Philadelphia 2000). Mayors play a prominent role in lobbying the national party to accept the bid, in raising the funds, and in overseeing planning and implementation, but they rarely seem to be initiating the idea of hosting a convention as a legacy accomplishment. More frequently, the news coverage indicates that the mayor initially was skeptical and had to be convinced that bidding was in the city's interest. And given that mayors attract the bulk of the coverage and have every incentive to claim credit for the reputational and economic boost for their city, it is telling that mayors are not publicly credited more often as the primary convention entrepreneurs.

The initial organizational step for a city is to establish a host committee, usually a 501c3 (charity) or 501c6 (business league) that allows the city to raise funds and hire staff to promote the city through the bid and convention process. A private organizational entity allows the city to solicit private contributions[4] rather than committing existing city funds and allows the city to avoid public meeting and document laws. The host committee recruits business and political leaders to serve on its board to signal the breadth of local support for the convention. Strategically, organizers often make it a point to recruit members from both political parties and geographical locations across the state and neighboring states to signal widespread support for the bid.[5]

The host committee staff works with city staff and representatives of private organizations to develop the strategy for promoting the city as a contender and to write and package the bid proposal. A variety of organizations are involved in developing the bid as the bid itself covers a wide range of topics: fundraising, budget, facilities, security, lodging, transportation, things to do in the city, legal protections, insurance, and so on. The committee needs experts in each of those areas to contribute to a credible bid.[6]

In some respects, the bid for a political convention is like a city's bid for any other large convention. As Bill McMillan of the Charlotte Regional Visitors Authority put it, "Whether the convention is for 10 or 100, the logistics are the same. Get 'em here, get 'em rooms, feed 'em, transport 'em, get 'em home. It's just how many rooms do you need?"[7] There are several critical differences, however. Most other conventions are centered on the city's convention center; political conventions are centered on the city's arena. Most other convention planners are keenly interested in the other tourist activities to entertain their attendees outside of the convention; "fun stuff" is a lower priority for the parties since the delegates will be involved in delegation and caucus meetings during the day, the convention and receptions at night. And other conventions aren't federally designated National Special Security Events, involving current and past presidents and vice presidents, members of the cabinet, and members of Congress. That means extensive security plans that aren't relevant for typical business or fraternal meetings. It also means that, "You have the [director of the airport] and the chief of police assisting with the RFP [request for proposal] and the site selection visit rather than mid-level personnel."[8]

Given that political convention bids vary in their content from the typical convention, the host committee may hire consultants to assist in developing and promoting the bid. Cities, except perhaps New York City, which bids nearly every cycle, don't have the institutional memory of what it takes to recruit a political convention nor the requisite contacts in D.C. to find out. When Charlotte started the process of bidding for the 2012 DNC, City Councilwoman Susan Burgess, Tim Newman, and former Democratic National Committee chair Don Fowler recruited a team of consultants who had worked for the Democratic Party and/or the 2008 Obama campaign. Kevin Monroe, the mayor's chief of staff, described them as an "A-Team of consultants . . . as inside as inside can get . . . [and thus they were] respected by TAG [Technical Advisory Group, the Democratic National Committee's site selection committee]."[9] Monroe noted that their experience "helped us do convention/DNC-speak. . . . They knew what the TAG was going to ask. It allowed us to be preemptive."[10] For example, the Democratic National Committee required a convention headquarters hotel of 1,000 rooms. Charlotte didn't have one, which had inhibited previous bids for the DNC (it had bid for the RNC in 2000). Monroe noted, "It was their idea to pitch the Hilton and the Westin as convention headquarters hotels to bookend Time Warner Arena. That gave them 1,500 rooms rather than the 1,000 required by the DNC."[11]

The CRVA's Tim Newman also noted that the consultants brought attention to political sensitivities that the local host committee hadn't identified:

> They made us aware of political issues we weren't attuned to. Unions for example. Denver didn't have any union hotels but was able to organize one during the convention. North Carolina law prevented us from doing that. So we had to look for opportunities to assuage union concerns. Our second round of buttons was made at a union shop and included the union seal. They also urged us to make it a broad, diverse, regional effort. So we brought in Jim Clyburn [the House Democratic Whip from South Carolina] and [former North Carolina Governor] Jim Hunt for the site visit. They let us know about various events with the President so we could get the Mayor or another representative to attend to promote Charlotte.[12]

As Newman's final comment indicates, the consultants were also critical in developing Charlotte's lobbying strategy. First, merely by hiring them, Charlotte "sent the signal that we were serious, that we knew what we were doing."[13] Moreover, they helped the Charlotte in 2012 Host Committee identify the key people in the Obama campaign and Obama White House to influence.[14] Charlotte in 2012 Host Committee director Will Miller described the process: "We had a map of who we knew that they listened to and worked those connections. We sought people who said they could talk to them; some could, some couldn't. We pursued everyone. The mayor periodically talked to them directly."[15] In fact, Mayor Foxx lobbied President Obama frequently enough that the president preempted, "I know you want the convention," as Foxx approached him at a Council of Mayors meeting.[16] The consultants themselves used their personal connections and put together the network and got information and talking points to its members.[17] They further worked with the public relations firm hired by the host committee to do the marketing of Charlotte's bid and Charlotte itself during the DNC.

Cities also lobby at regional and national party meetings. They set up tables to distribute promotional material, give away trinkets, and provide free food and drink to entice party officials to talk with local representatives. Mayors and prominent city council members may attend to help with the schmoozing process. Later in the process, mayors may make formal presentations to party officials to promote their bids. Showing the city's flag at party meetings is important as a way of assessing interest and getting feedback from party officials from across the country and also as a way of the city identifying its competition and how they are marketing themselves. These are critical pieces of intelligence as the city makes its final decision to commit to a bid.

As with the invisible primary for candidates, the pre-bid phase is a critical one for cities. Like competitive candidates during this phase, cities gather information about themselves and their competition, assess their strengths and weaknesses, get their team organized, and assess their level of support within the city and within the party. They put themselves in the position to run a competitive campaign for the party's bid if the final decision is to "go."

Stage 2—The Party Invites: The Request for Proposal

The national party committees issue official requests for proposals (RFPs) for their conventions two-and-a-half to three years before the conventions.[18] The issuance of the RFPs is the culmination of an informal process of consultation with potential bid cities. The party site selection committees have distributed bid criteria to cities, adapted them based on feedback, and drafted rosters of potential candidates. The site selection committees issue open invitations for cities to attend DNC and RNC planning meetings to allow prospective candidates to gain information about the process and the bid criteria, as well as to express their interest.

The party signals the qualities of cities it prioritizes in the RFP. The RFP sets the party's requirements for hotel rooms, venue capacity and characteristics, technology, fundraising, insurance, and so on. The parties differ somewhat in how the RFPs are framed: the Democrats' are written as requirements; the Republicans couch their RFP in terms of listing their needs and priorities while encouraging cities to "show us what you've got."[19] But essentially, the parties are asking for fifteen thousand to twenty thousand hotel rooms; hotels with the capacity for breakfast, lunch, and dinner meetings for delegation caucuses; a centrally located convention headquarters hotel; a convention hall

Table 2.1. City population size and convention assets, 2010

	Infrastructure			Fundraising Capacity		
	Air hub	Air passengers	Arena capacity	Time since arena renovation	Fortune 500 companies	Campaign donations	Median income
Population size	.65**	.58**	.15*	-.18*	.83**	.69**	.10

Note: N = 130. Coefficients are Pearson r. **p < .05; *p < .10 two-tailed test.

Data sources: Airline passengers: Federal Aviation Administration; Arena capacity and renovation: Obtained from Samuel Bassett of the University of Illinois, Chicago, based on web and NewsBank searches; Fortune 500 companies: *Fortune* magazine; Campaign donations: The Center for Responsive Politics; Median income: The U.S. Census Bureau. Details are available in endnote 26 and appendix 2A.

of fifteen thousand seats—and, more recently, luxury boxes—and working space for the media.[20] The RFP signals that, all things being equal, parties prefer larger cities to host because they have more capacity: large arenas, full-service hotel rooms, hub airports, fundraising potential, "things to do," etc.[21]

Table 2.1 illustrates how city size is an effective indicator of many of the more specific attributes that the parties desire. In particular, population size in 2010 is strongly correlated with airline capacity (hub status and number of airline passengers in 2010) and fundraising capacity (number of Fortune 500 companies and total contributions to federal candidates in 2010).[22] Population size is weakly correlated with arena capacity and the length of time since the city's arena has been renovated (the negative sign on the correlation shows that the larger the city, the less amount of time has elapsed since a renovation or new construction). Larger cities tend to have larger and more modern arenas, but their advantage over smaller cities is small since smaller cities can invest in arenas to attract sports teams, concerts, and other major events. By focusing their recruitment efforts on the largest cities, the national parties can obtain many of their desired assets in one-stop shopping.

Hotels are a particularly important concern for the parties. A city with larger hotels in close proximity makes planning much easier for the party because it takes fewer hotels to house all the delegates and thus a less complicated transportation plan to get the delegates from their hotels to the arena.[23] Moreover, the party is not just looking for fifteen thousand ordinary hotel rooms. It is particularly desirous of full-service rooms, that is, rooms with round-the-clock staffing, which is usually available only at high-end hotels. Delegates often return from convention business and receptions in the wee hours of the morning and need staff availability.

The parties' requests for a "convention hall" primarily mean an arena. Dallas's failure to assure the RNC's access to its arena, the American Airlines Center, during June 2016 was a key factor in its loss to Cleveland, as noted in the chapter introduction. The last presidential nominating convention to occur in a convention center was the 1996 RNC in San Diego; the last DNC in a convention center was San Francisco in 1984. Convention centers are typically not well suited for political conventions because they tend to have less seating capacity and less sophisticated lighting and sound systems than arenas. Convention centers tend to be wide and have low ceilings and thus fewer appealing angles for television coverage. They do not have skyboxes or luxury boxes for television anchors, big donors, and other dignitaries.

Though 4,700 (Democrats) to 2,400 (Republican) delegates attend, the parties seek arenas of fifteen thousand or more. Substantial numbers of seats are lost to the elaborate stage and many more are used for media work space. Other seats are needed for VIPs and party donors. More seats mean fewer conflicts for credentials between the parties and the seat demanders. More seats mean more people can get in before the fire marshal declares the building to have met capacity and locks everyone else out. The limited capacity of Atlanta's Omni in the 1988 DNC led to coverage of media personalities and Martin Luther King III being locked out, and keynote speaker Ann Richards having to wait (Smith and Nimmo, 1991: 113 and 150–51).

Airport hubs are important for the ease of getting delegates in and out of the city. Delegates come from every state in the union, and the more delegates who can reach the convention city on a direct flight, the better. Moreover, if a flight is canceled, hub airports are more likely to provide additional flights later the same day so the delegate does not miss convention activities.

To illustrate and analyze the dynamics of the site selection process, we gathered data on a list of 131 cities. We chose cities to investigate based on whether their population was equal to or greater than the smallest city that had received an invitation to bid for a convention during our period of study (Salt Lake City).[24] Salt Lake was also the smallest city to submit a bid. Smaller but rapidly growing cities were added to our data set in election cycles in which they passed Salt Lake's population size; shrinking cities were excluded when they dropped below Salt Lake's population. The list of cities and their participation in the site selection process is provided in table 2.2 on page 32.

We identified cities' participation in the site selection process by using NewsBank searches of major metropolitan newspapers.[25] Articles about one city often contained a list of other potential applicants in their reports. Each city, even if speculated as a potential bidder, was searched using the same parameters for each convention cycle.[26] The applicants' local newspapers often reported on their city's progress up to any failed stage of advancement. In table 2.2, we italicize the names of cities that participated in the site selection process from 1992 to 2016 and identify the cities that hosted a convention during the period.

In table 2.3, we provide a comparison of some descriptive characteristics of the cities in each stage of the bid process. Discussion of the measurements and data sources can be found in the Measurement Appendix. Here, we are interested in the characteristics of the cities that the parties invite to bid for their conventions compared to all the cities that meet Salt Lake City's threshold size requirement (columns 1 vs. 2). On all size-related dimensions, the median characteristics of the cities invited to bid by the parties are larger than the rest of the cases. Invitees are double in size, have larger arenas, are

Table 2.2. List of cities participating in political convention site selection and comparison cities, 1992–2016

Akron, OH	Long Beach, CA
Albuquerque, NM	*Los Angeles, CA*—2000 DNC
Amarillo, TX*	Louisville, KY
Anaheim, CA	Lubbock, TX
Anchorage, AK	Madison, WI
Arlington, TX	*Memphis, TN*
Atlanta, GA	Mesa, AZ
Augusta, GA	*Miami, FL*
Aurora, CO	*Milwaukee, WI*
Aurora, IL*	*Minneapolis, MN*
Austin, TX	Mobile, AL
Bakersfield, CA	Modesto, CA
Baltimore, MD	Montgomery, AL
Baton Rouge, LA	Moreno Valley, CA*
Birmingham, AL	*Nashville, TN*
Boise City, ID*	*New Orleans, LA*
Boston, MA—2004 DNC	*New York, NY*—1992 DNC; 2004 RNC
Buffalo, NY	Newark, NJ
Chandler, AZ*	Norfolk, VA
Charlotte, NC—2012 DNC	North Las Vegas, NV*
Chesapeake, VA*	Oakland, CA
Chicago, IL—1996 DNC	*Oklahoma City, OK*
Chula Vista, CA*	Omaha, NE
Cincinnati, OH	*Orlando, FL*
Cleveland, OH—2016 RNC	Oxnard, CA*
Colorado Springs, CO	*Philadelphia, PA*—2000 RNC, 2016 DNC
Columbus, GA	*Phoenix, AZ*
Columbus, OH	*Pittsburgh, PA*
Corpus Christi, TX	Plano, TX*
Dallas, TX	*Portland, OR*
Dayton, OH*	Providence, RI*
Denver, CO—2008 DNC	Raleigh, NC
Des Moines, IA	Reno, NV*
Detroit, MI	Richmond, VA
Durham, NC*	Riverside, CA

El Paso, TX
Fayetteville, NC*
Fontana, CA*
Fort Wayne, IN
Fort Worth, TX
Fremont, CA
Fresno, CA
Garland, TX
Gilbert, AZ*
Glendale AZ*
Glendale, CA
Grand Rapids, MI
Greensboro, NC
Henderson, NV*
Hialeah, FL
Honolulu, HI
Houston, TX—1992 RNC
Huntington Beach, CA
Huntsville, AL*
Indianapolis, IN
Irvine, CA*
Irving, TX*
Jackson, MS*
Jacksonville, FL
Jersey City, NJ
Kansas City, MO
Laredo, TX*
Las Vegas, NV
Lexington, KY
Lincoln, NE
Little Rock, AR

Rochester, NY
Sacramento, CA
Salt Lake City, UT
San Antonio, TX
San Bernardino, CA
San Diego, CA—1996 RNC
San Francisco, CA
San Jose, CA
Santa Ana, CA
Scottsdale, AZ*
Seattle, WA
Shreveport, LA
Spokane, WA
St. Louis, MO
St. Paul, MN—2008 RNC
St. Petersburg, FL
Stockton, CA
Syracuse, NY*
Tacoma, WA
Tampa, FL—2012 RNC
Toledo, OH
Tucson, AZ
Tulsa, OK
Virginia Beach, VA
Washington, D.C.
Wichita, KS
Winston-Salem, NC*
Worcester, MA*
Yonkers, NY

Note: Table 2.2 includes 131 incorporated places in the United States with populations equal to or greater than Salt Lake City (the smallest city to bid or be invited to bid) at any point from 1992 to 2012. Starred cities (*) fell below the population threshold for one or more cycles. The 44 italicized cities received or solicited an invitation and/or submitted a bid during a convention cycle between 1992 and 2016. The host cities are specified.

Data source: NewsBank searches by the authors.

substantially more likely to be airline hubs, and have somewhat larger percent-ages of their population employed in tourism. These are the key assets that parties need to host successful conventions, so it is not surprising that they identify cities that have them and encourage them to bid.

About half the cities on the invitation list are cities that have bid in one or both of the previous two election cycles. It makes sense for the parties to invite them to bid again as they have already demonstrated their interest. By bidding previously, they at least think they meet all or most of the key requirements of the RFP so the party can see if they've improved their assets in the intervening years, or are more competitive with a different mix of bid cities. At the very least, the party avoids offending local officials who have previously invested in the process.

The differences in cities' infrastructure are more apparent than their electoral differences for invited and non-invited cities. Invited cities are in states that were only slightly more competitive in the previous presidential election and have only a few more Electoral College votes than non-invited cities. In fairness, of course, Electoral College votes and presidential outcomes are based on statewide results compared to the infrastructure measures that are city-specific. Nevertheless, the results do not indicate that electoral considerations are a primary consideration when parties decide who should receive an RFP.

Setting high standards in the RFPs limits the number of bids the party receives. Creating high costs of entry in the site selection competition limits the party's ability to foment a "bidding war." But it also screens out the less

Table 2.3. Characteristics of cities that participated in the site selection process, 1992–2012

	All	Invited to bid	Bid	Host
Population size (median)	287,858	566,221	512,277	1,296,600
Tourism employment	5.4%	6.2%	5.7%	5.4%
Arena size (median)	13,595	19,023	19,094	19,068
Airline hub	23%	62%	64%	75%
Previous bid	13%	48%	66%	83%
Presidential difference$_{x-1}$ (median)	11	9	9	11
Electoral College votes	15	18	18	16

Data sources: Authors' calculations from the following sources. Population size: U.S. Census Bureau; Tourism employment: U.S. Census Bureau's Economic Census; Arena size: Obtained from Samuel Bassett of the University of Illinois, Chicago, based on web and NewsBank searches; Previous bid: NewsBank searches by authors.

qualified contenders who would likely place more transaction costs on the party to achieve a successful convention. More importantly, higher costs of entry limits bids to those cities that want it the most. The party wants a demonstration of commitment because those cities will be the party's most enthused partners in implementation. Having a competent partner helps the party focus its attention on internal party coalition building and external messaging rather than the transaction costs of putting on the event. Successful conventions will attract more cities to bid in future cycles.

The parties invite a similar number of cities—on average, twenty-five—to bid in each election cycle. Many of the cities are invited by both parties, though there are a few cities that tend to receive invitations from only one of the parties. Between 1992 and 2016, the Democratic National Committee most frequently invited Chicago, Cleveland, Detroit, Minneapolis, New Orleans, New York City, and Philadelphia. Houston, Indianapolis, Miami, New Orleans, New York City, and Orlando regularly received the Republican RFPs. Both the fundraising and the space requirements to hold the RNC are smaller each convention cycle, while the more expensive DNC tacks on additional labor obligations to its contracts. Despite stricter DNC requirements, the number of proposals received by both planning committees is roughly the same. The stringent, federally mandated security requirements are similarly outlined between proposal requests.

The cities that receive invitations remain stable in most election cycles, which is not surprising given that the number of cities that can meet the parties' facilities requirements are not likely to change dramatically from one election cycle to the next. Several growing cities have received invitations to bid only in recent election cycles: Anaheim, Austin, Columbus, Oklahoma City, and Salt Lake, for example. Other cities traditionally have received invitations but have recently dropped off one or both parties' lists: Boston, Milwaukee, Los Angeles, and Washington, D.C. Other cities that rank in the top twenty in population size have never received invitations: El Paso, San Jose, Jacksonville, and Fort Worth.

In table 2.4, we analyze the characteristics of cities that are invited to bid for conventions by the national parties. We use a technique called "logit," which allows us to examine the factors related to dependent variables that have only two values, as in our case (invited or not). Statistical techniques like logit allow us to separate the effects of several different independent variables on the probability of receiving an invitation.[27] This allows us to assess whether all of the variables have an influence on invitations, and how much of an influence each variable has. To assess the magnitude of each variable's impact on the likelihood of receiving an RFP, we estimate the change in the dependent variable from one standard deviation above the mean to one standard deviation below the mean for each continuous variable or from minimum to maximum value for dichotomous variables while all other variables are held at their mean (or mode).

Table 2.4 shows that many of the variables affect a city's likelihood of receiving an invitation in the way we predicted. Specifically, a city's infrastructure is critical to receiving an invitation. The parties are significantly more likely to invite cities with larger populations (and all the assets, such as hotels and financial capacity, that population represents), larger arenas, and airport hubs. Parties also invite cities with moderate levels of tourism employment, as shown by the positive linear term and the negative squared term for tourism employment. The

Table 2.4. Cities receiving requests for proposals (RFPs) for presidential nominating conventions, 1992–2012, logit

	Coefficient	SE	Probability change
Capacity			
Population (nl)	2.89***	.363	.26
Arena size	.0002***	.00003	.21
Airline hub	1.21***	.437	.14
Tourism	.705***	.116	
Tourism^2	−.015***	.002	.14
Median income	−.005	.034	−.002
Politics			
Hometown	.964	.651	.02
Presidential margin$_{x-1}$	−.061***	.014	−.07
Electoral College votes	.001	.020	.002
Local Government			
Previous bid	3.19***	.613	.13
Mayoral turnover	−.522**	.222	−.04
Mayor/Council government	1.01**	.467	.06
Mayor/Governor of same party	−.399	.377	−.02
Constant	−46.37***	5.35	
Number =	604		
−2* Log-likelihood =	244 (Chi^2 = 115, p < .01)		
Pseudo R^2 =	.67		

Note: ***p < .01; **p < .05

parties want cities with "enough" to do, and enough tourism infrastructure to handle their event, but they are not seeking resorts. Local politics matters too. Parties are more likely to invite cities that have bid for conventions in previous cycles. They are less likely to invite cities in which mayoral turnover is frequent, as these cities are riskier partners to implement a bid. Parties exhibit a preference for cities with a mayor/council form of government, probably because electorally accountable mayors have greater incentive to partner with the party to make the convention a visible success for which the mayor can claim credit. Parties are also more likely to invite cities in states that have close presidential elections (the negative coefficient shows that the electoral margins are smaller in states that receive invitations). Parties do not disproportionately invite cities that are the hometowns of the national party chairs or the president. Likewise, a state's bounty of Electoral College votes will not increase the likelihood that its cities will be invited to bid.

Stage 3–Bid Submission

The RFPs signal what the parties want in host cities, but the parties are ultimately dependent on which cities volunteer. The host committee assembles a bid book that encompasses the city's ability to go above and beyond minimal compliance with the RFP's requirements. The host committee lists details regarding arena, meeting, and media spaces, hotel rooms, and transportation. The bid includes fundraising plans to provide for the convention budget. The bid books also include the conventions' security and emergency response plans in cooperation with local and federal law enforcement agencies.

Table 2.5 shows that submitting a bid is a relatively rare event. On average, each party receives six (6) bids per convention cycle. Many are invited,

Table 2.5. Presidential nominating convention invitations and bids, 1992–2012

	DNC	RNC	Overall
Average # invited per cycle	25.5	23.5	29.0
Average # of bids per cycle	6.3	6.0	12.3
% Invited who placed bids	24.7	25.5	31.0
Pre-9/11 bid average per cycle	8.3	7.0	15.3
Post-9/11 bid average per cycle	5.0	3.3	8.3
# Occurrence of multiple bids	—	—	17.0
Pre-9/11 multi-bid avg. per cycle	—	—	4.0
Post-9/11 multi-bid avg. per cycle	—	—	1.7

Data source: Authors' calculations.

but only about one-third of the invitees respond to either party (with some cities submitting bids to both parties). Table 2.5 also shows that bids have decreased by more than one-third in the post-9/11 era, including a drop-off of more than 50% for the RNC. The average number of cities bidding for both party conventions in the same year also dropped in half after 9/11. We will explore the impact of 9/11 security measures on cities' decisions to bid in more detail below.

The characteristics of the cities who submit bids was presented along with the characteristics of invitees in table 2.3, so we now turn our attention back to understand the differences between the cities that the parties invite and the cities that actually respond with a bid. Table 2.3 shows that the median bid city is slightly smaller and less tourism-oriented than the cities invited by the parties, but has equivalent arena and airport hub capacity. We'll discuss the physical assets first and then discuss the tourism industry.

SIZE

Table 2.3 shows that bid cities are much larger than the size of the median city in our data set, indicating the importance of having a wide variety of assets and resources that accompany population size. But bid cities are not quite as large as the median city invited by the parties. Clearly bid cities understand the importance of having the assets to meet the criteria in the RFPs, but not all cities with the right size and assets (from the parties' perspective) are motivated to bid every year.

Critically, the size of the cities bidding for political conventions has changed in important ways in the two decades of our data. The increase in the disruption costs imposed on a city due to post-9/11 security requirements (see chapter 4) and cities' decreased willingness to risk further disruption to their economies during the 2008–10 recession changed the cost/benefit calculation for cities (Heberlig, Leland, Shields, and Swindell, 2014). The largest cities—with the largest economies and most established brands—had less need for political conventions to establish their reputations than smaller cities. Smaller cities might have had similar risks from a terrorist attack or the economic disruptions from security measures as large cities, but the branding effects of a political convention would have larger positive effect on their status quo. Larger cities therefore were less likely to submit bids after 9/11 relative to smaller cities. Indeed, table 2.6 shows that parties continued to invite larger cities to bid after 9/11, but the median size of cities submitting bids declined by more than one hundred thousand after 9/11.

Table 2.6. Pre- and post-9/11 differences between bid and host cities

	Bid cities		Host cities	
	Pre-9/11	Post-9/11	Pre-9/11	Post-9/11
Population	533,000	410,000	2,200,000	558,000
Tourism employment	55,000	29,900	108,200	46,800
Arena capacity	18,500	19,500	19,000	19,100

Note: Cells contain the median value (rounded).

Data source: Authors' calculations.

Specific examples are also instructive. The largest city in the United States, New York City, has bid for one or both (usually both) conventions in every year in our data set, except 2012, when Madison Square Garden was undergoing renovations (Sandomir, 2010). The second- through fifth-largest U.S. cities (Los Angeles, Chicago, Houston, and Philadelphia) submitted twelve bids between 1992 and 2000 and frequently bid for both conventions. Each city, in fact, hosted a convention during this period, as did New York. Between 2004 and 2012, however, these four megacities submitted zero bids. Philadelphia was the first to reenter the competition with a bid for the DNC in 2016. Phoenix—the sixth-largest city—was the next-largest city to bid after 9/11, bidding for both conventions in 2012. After Phoenix, the next-largest cities to bid after 9/11 include Charlotte in 2012 (ranked seventeenth in population 2012) and Detroit in 2004 (ranked eleventh in 2004).

INFRASTRUCTURE

Table 2.3 shows that bid cities have larger arenas and are more likely to be airline hubs than comparison cities. These assets are critical requirements of the RFPs. The importance of arena capacity is further demonstrated in the findings in table 2.6, which shows that while the median population size of bid cities has dropped since 9/11, the median capacity of the city's arenas has not. Regardless of their total mix of assets, cities understand that they need a large arena to host a presidential nominating convention.

The role of such physical assets is different in political convention bids than those for bids for other mega-events, such as the Olympics, that afford similar branding opportunities to cities. A successful Olympic bid is often used by city leaders as an opportunity to build assets and change the physical structure of a city (Preuss, 2004). In part, this is due to the number and kinds of sports-related facilities that are needed, but host cities also have used the Olympics to leverage substantial changes in development and transportation patterns in their cities. In contrast, bids for political conventions rely on exiting assets, not the promise that they will be built by the time the convention occurs.[28] The party does not want to take the risk that the mud holes the host committee is showing them during the site selection visit will be actual hotels in a year. They want guarantees that their delegates, "affiliated groups" (a.k.a., party-aligned interest groups, lobbyists, party activists, and celebrities), and media personnel will have beds.

In our review of NewsBank articles, fourteen cities declined to bid or withdrew bids due to large downtown revitalization projects. In these cases, city officials did not want the resource demands of the convention to impinge on the resources (such as voters' support for bonds) necessary to complete the development project (e.g., Appleman, 2004). Others expressed an unwillingness to risk the city's image by bringing in large numbers of tourists while sections of the city were under heavy construction.

New arena construction can be major assets for bid cities, be it new facilities or major renovations once completed. An arms race of investments in tourism and sports infrastructure is a central dynamic of cities' efforts to compete for tourism business (e.g., Judd and Fainstein, 1999.) The National Football League and Major League Baseball, for example, award Super Bowls and All-Star Games to cities that have invested in stadium projects as incentives for these physical subsidies for their teams. Such construction is an indicator of a city's overall investment in its tourism infrastructure and its effort in recruiting convention business. It is thus likely that a city that makes such investments will be more likely to bid. We find this is the case: the median number of years from new construction or renovation of their arena for bid cities is seven years, almost half the median of thirteen years since renovation for non-bid cities.

TOURISM EMPLOYMENT

Beyond physical assets, table 2.3 also shows that bid cities have somewhat smaller tourism industries than invitees. This fact points to an interesting dynamic in the site selection process. One would expect that cities with larger tourism industries should be more likely to seek political conventions. A larger tourism industry should mean more infrastructure for hosting a convention of this size. It also means a politically potent group of employers and employees who will be pleased by the city attracting a lucrative project for them.

But cities with the largest tourism industries also face disincentives in seeking political conventions. Because political conventions are disruptive to a city's normal functioning, cities that can count on a constant flow of tourists or who are consistently successful in attracting major business meetings—which often are booked two to three years in advance (well before the parties' site selection process unfolds)[29]—face high opportunity costs and are unlikely to risk sacrificing their existing business for the uncertain possibility of landing a political convention. For example, as part of the bid, the parties require that sufficient hotel rooms be set aside and held until the party disqualifies the city. Local hoteliers thus cannot rent these rooms to others during the prospective convention period until the party has released the rooms. In addition, cities that have already booked major meetings during the same time as the political conventions have to reschedule them. Each alternative imposes high risks and substantial transaction and opportunity costs on the bid city. Moreover, cities with a successful tourism industry already have a strong brand that is unlikely to be significantly enhanced by an "off-brand" partisan message brought by a political convention.

Our review of NewsBank coverage of convention bids shows that sixteen cities have cited the need to relocate or reschedule other conventions as a reason for dropping out or not bidding between 1992 and 2012. The *Orlando Sentinel* frequently editorializes in favor of a bid, but city officials have consistently demurred because of the impact on their existing commitments. After being invited to host a 2000 convention, an unidentified Orlando official reported that a convention would hurt tourism business. "We already have plenty of business booked during that time that we would displace, and [political] conventioneers don't visit our other attractions" (quoted in Guerra, 1998). Therefore, we argue that citizens with "medium-size" tourism industries are more likely to bid: a city's tourism industry must be large enough to provide the capacity to host, yet not be so large that a political convention would disrupt existing business.

ECONOMICS

Cities must raise the funds to host the conventions and increasingly such funding has come from solicitation of private sources (see chapter 3). Mayor Michael Nutter of Philadelphia describes the economic trade-off for cities: "Obviously it would be a lot easier if the DNC would guarantee that it would not cost the city a dime. We still have a city to run. This all has to be weighed in the balance of all the near-term things that we care to do" (Lucey, 2010). Cities that have higher per capita incomes are more likely to have the financial capacity to host conventions and therefore will be more likely to submit bids.

PREVIOUS BIDS

Convention planners believe that multiple bids are usually necessary to land major conventions, including the party nomination conventions: an initial bid puts a city on the site selection committee's radar; later bids demonstrate one's seriousness and tenacity.[30] Moreover, it is easier to revise a past year's bid and integrate feedback from a previous round than to develop a bid from scratch. Indeed, table 2.3 shows that more than two-thirds of bids come from cities that bid in one or both of the previous two election cycles. Tampa, for example, greatly impressed GOP officials during their 2006 site visit. Although the 2008 RNC was awarded to St. Paul, party officials strongly encouraged Tampa to bid for the 2012 RNC.

Though the RFPs for each party are somewhat different, the marginal costs for a city to modify one bid into two bids to bid for both parties' conventions simultaneously are relative low. Bidding for both conventions doubles a city's opportunity to get one and signals the intensity of a city's desire. Bidding for both conventions is not uncommon: seventeen cities did so from 1992 to 2012, accounting nearly one-half (47.9%) of total bid submissions.

POLITICS

As noted in the introduction, many politicians and pundits focus on the potential electoral consequences of a particular city hosting a convention. Table 2.3, however, shows that bid cities have the same median competitiveness and number of Electoral College votes as the cities the parties have invited.

Just as the median values for city population obscured important differences before and after 9/11, the median electoral values also obscure important changes over time. From 1992 to 2000, the median bid city's presidential margin was 10.5 percentage points and its median number of Electoral College votes was twenty-two; from 2004 to 2012, the median presidential margin dropped to 5 percentage points and the median number of Electoral College votes declined to sixteen. In other words, over time, cities in smaller and more politically competitive states have been bidding for conventions. Whether or not the parties believe their rhetoric about selecting states that will help their candidate win Electoral College votes, it seems that more cities in those competitive states are willing to ask the parties to choose their state on that basis. As we will see in chapter 5, the parties, particularly the

Democrats, have become more intentional about engaging the residents of the host city to influence the election outcome, and cities in competitive states seem increasingly willing to use their competitive status as a selling point.

Cities may be more likely to bid when the mayor and/or governor are the same as the party for whose convention they are bidding on (David et al., 1960). Since mayors of large cities tend to be Democrats, the partisanship of the governor probably matters more. A "match" between the local/state officials and the party is likely to increase the probability of a bid because officials likely anticipate that the party is more willing to reward a member of their own party with the prize and economic benefits of a convention. Having a governor and mayor of the same party provides additional support for the bid and signals the national parties that there is a high probability that any intergovernmental assistance that is necessary will be forthcoming.

Local political structure likely matters too. If parties are looking for cities to be their agents, they will look for indicators that a city can deliver on its commitments. As mayors can reap political credit for successful bids, cities with a mayoral (rather than a council-manager) form of government are more likely to bid. The national parties are likely to prefer cities with a mayoral form of government as the process of bargaining over contracts and the implementation of decisions have lower transaction costs when dealing with a less diffuse system of local decision making. The mayor has substantial incentive to be responsive to the need to head off mishaps, because he or she is the representative of government most likely to be seen by residents as accountable for snafus during the convention.

Another way in which politics could make a difference in the willingness of cities to bid is if they have an insider connection, for example, if they are the hometown of the president or a national party chair and believe their connections will advantage their bids. Our evidence shows some additional willingness to bid: 8.6% (five) of bid cities could claim hometown status, nearly triple the 2.9% of the cities overall who were home to the president or a national party chair.

Which cities are more likely to bid for political conventions? We analyze which city characteristics are related to bid submission using logit analysis. As with invitations, our dependent variable again has two values (bid or did not bid). We present two version of the model; the second includes a variable measuring amount of time since the city opened a new arena or made a major renovation to an existing arena. We estimate two models because there are a large number of cases on which we do not have data on arena renovations. It is important to show that the other independent variables are related to bids when the maximum number of city/years are included.

Table 2.7 shows that there are many similarities with the invitation model—that is, not surprisingly, cities bid when they have the character-istics that are desired by the parties. City leaders thus believe it is worth their effort to bid when they have a chance to succeed. Table 2.7 confirms the importance of city and arena size. Arena size is more important than population size, according to the one standard deviation change in predicted probabilities. Relatedly, model 2 shows that cities with recently renovated

Table 2.7. Cities submitting bids for presidential nominating conventions, 1992–2012, logit

	Model 1			Model 2		
	Coeff.	SE	Prob. change	Coeff.	SE	Prob. change
Capacity						
Population (nl)	.579**	.277	.03	.547**	.265	.04
Arena size	.00009***	.00003	.05	.00008**	.00003	.06
Time from renovation	—			−.024*	.013	−.04
Airline hub	.686	.432	.03	.601	.426	.04
Tourism	.447	.296		.391	.278	
Tourism^2	−.021	.014	−.08	−.108	.013	−.20
Median income	−.011	.034	.005	−.014	.033	.01
Politics						
Hometown	1.09	.73	.01	1.12	.708	.03
Presidential margin$_{x-1}$	−.026	.019	−.02	−.028	.020	−.04
Electoral College votes	−.008	.014	−.01	−.008	.013	−.02
Local government						
Previous bid	1.92***	.463	.05	1.90***	.447	.08
Mayoral turnover	−.830***	.320	−.04	−.865**	.342	−.06
Mayor/Council gov't	1.06**	.453	.04	1.05**	.456	.06
Mayor/Governor party match	−.103	.134	−.01	−.103	.133	.02
Constant	−14.04***	3.56		−12.79***	3.38	

Number =	604	523
−2* Log-likelihood =	232 (Chi^2 = 130, p < .01)	228 (Chi^2 = 126, p < .01)
Pseudo R^2 =	.38	.36

arenas are significantly more likely to bid, providing evidence that cities seek a payoff from their investment in mega-event infrastructure. They may also believe that the parties will find newer facilities appealing. The magnitude of the relationship between population size and bids is modest compared to other variables in part because the largest cities have been less willing to bid after 9/11 (Heberlig, Leland, Shields, and Swindell, 2015).[31]

In contrast to the capacity variables, the political variables are unrelated to cities' convention bids. While the parties are more likely to invite cities in competitive states, the most politically desirable cities fail to help the parties by submitting bids, thus limiting the overall electoral impact of conventions.

Instead, city government characteristics are important to explaining which cities bid. Bidding in the previous two convention cycles creates the largest estimated effect on whether a city submits a bid in the current cycle. Cities with mayoral turnover during the convention cycle are significantly less likely to bid. A change in mayor potentially disrupts the coalition that seeks the convention and the lobbying effort to attain it. Turnover also creates uncertainty for the convention coalition and the party as to how reliable and effective the new mayor will be implementing a complex mega-event. Mayor-council governments also are significantly more likely to bid than council-manager governments. Mayors have an incentive to land high-profile accomplishments for which they can claim credit; city managers don't. Importantly, the magnitude of changes in predicted probabilities of these three local government variables rival or surpass the effect of city arena and population size.

The role of local government varies, however, when we estimate the bid models separately by party. Table 2.8 shows that local government structure matters for Democratic bid cities, while partisanship matters for Republican bid cities. Specifically, mayor/council city governments and governments without mayoral turnover are significantly more likely to bid for the DNC. In contrast, RNC bids disproportionately come from cities that have Republican mayors and governors. This suggests that cities see the Republican National Committee as likely to reward co-partisan allies or to trust that they will deliver the necessary resources.[32]

A few other partisan differences are apparent in table 2.8 on page 46 as well. First, the GOP has more repeat players: submitting bids in previous cycles has twice the effect on RNC bids as DNC bids. Second, cities with larger arenas are significantly more likely to bid for the DNC, while the coefficient falls just short of significance for GOP bids. The difference is likely due to the fact that the DNC has substantially more delegates and alternates. Thus, cities with smaller arenas would not be competitive for the DNC yet might still be competitive for the RNC.

Table 2.8. Republican vs. Democratic convention bids, 1992–2012, logit

	Republicans			Democrats		
	Coeff.	SE	Prob. change	Coeff.	SE	Prob. change
Capacity						
Population (nl)	.999***	.385	.03	.886***	.337	.02
Arena size	.0001	.00007	.03	.00009***	.00002	.02
Airline hub	−.249	.586	.03	.926	.616	.01
Tourism	.470	.296		.510	.327	
Tourism^2	−.021	.015	−.08	−.022	.016	−.05
Median income	.016	.050	.005	−.017	.049	−.0005
Politics						
Competitive state	−.022	.027	−.01	−.038	.025	−.01
Electoral College votes	−.003	.016	−.002	−.029	.017	−.01
Local government						
Previous bid	2.11***	.574	.04	1.727***	.584	.02
Mayoral turnover	−.069	.354	−.02	−.903**	.427	−.02
Mayor/Council gov't	.750	.542	.02	1.533**	.753	.01
Mayor/Governor party match	.426**	.181	.03	.029	.162	.01
Constant	−21.95***	4.99		−18.7***	4.58	

Number =	596		596	
−2* Log-likelihood =	158 (Chi^2 = 147, p < .01)		168 (Chi^2 = 89, p < .01)	
Pseudo R^2 =	.40		.41	

Stage 4–Selection of Finalists and Site Selection Visits

Once the party has received the bids, its site selection team reviews them and selects finalists for on-site visits. When few cities apply, the parties keep a high percentage of bidders as finalists. Some cities also drop out prior to the announcement of the finalists, as they decide they cannot deliver the resources and assets they committed in the bid or they realize they will not make the cut to the next round.

In addition to the content of the bid itself, the site selection team assesses the city's ability to host the convention through an on-the-ground view of the city for a day or two. In recent years, the site visitation teams for both parties have included eight to twelve party officials, most of whom have been involved in executing past conventions and are the "experts" in their particular field.[33] Each expert visits the relevant city assets and meets with his or local counterparts. For example, the transportation experts visit the airport and the hotels, the production team visits the arena, and the security experts meet the police. Their job is to analyze the strengths and weaknesses of each city based on their specialization.[34] They evaluate whether the city has the capability of fulfilling the promises it made in its bid.

The site visit is critical to the party's ability to assure that it selects a reliable agent. Cities are less likely to exaggerate (too much) in their bids when they know the party will check their assertions. It allows the party to decline the bids of cities whose bids are too far from the party's needs. It gives the party the time to negotiate solutions to identified areas of concern and include those solutions in the contract with the city before a host is announced.

The host committee plans the site visit to show off the assets they have presented in their bid. They show off the arena, the hotel clusters, the facilities the media will be using, and local amenities and attractions that can be used for delegate parties and receptions. They show the proximity of venues and hotels to one another and how the transportation networks in the city facilitate access to the convention activities. If convention venues and several first-class hotels are clustered, they highlight the possibility of an "Olympic village" during the convention and decreased travel time for delegates.

The visits also give the host committees the opportunity to market their intangible assets. Their goal is to display the unyielding support of political and business leaders, convincing the selection committees that they are capable of procuring facilities, personnel, and funds. Local corporate leaders are given roles to demonstrate that the city has the capacity and commitment to raise the funds. Politicians from outside the city are given roles to show the breadth of regional support for hosting the convention. Representatives from both parties are given roles to show unity and, probably more importantly, to signal to local residents that hosting the convention is an economic development opportunity. Local party activists, and sometimes the public, may be invited to big dinners or celebrations with the site selection committee to show the breadth of excitement for the convention and the host committee's ability to generate volunteers. St. Louis, for example, threw a public concert featuring Chuck Berry and Nelly for the DNC's site selection committee in 2010, hoping the energy would remind officials of a October 2008 Obama rally that drew eighty thousand to one hundred thousand supporters (Wagman, 2011a; Wagman, 2011b).

Like most other corporate or convention recruitment visits, the site visit is the host committee's opportunity to wine and dine party officials, to show them that they and their delegates will enjoy coming to the city. Host committees give packages of city-specific marketing items to site selection members during the visits to reinforce the city's brand and image. This can include tickets to a Cubs baseball game in Chicago, a Broadway show in New York, or a jazz club in New Orleans. During the months surrounding the visit, some cities opt to mail weekly gifts to selection committee members to promote their bids.

The host committees, the city inhabitants, and the local press have to show excitement in anticipation of the two years of planning and fundraising that will take place before the conventions. Los Angeles's bid for the 1976 DNC was rejected, in part, according to political scientist Herbert Alexander (1979: 42), due to "a less than enthusiastic invitation from Governor Brown" (and a lack of hotel space). In *Olympic Politics*, Christopher R. Hill observes, "if a country's government and people are not seen to be behind a bid the IOC [International Olympic Committee] is unlikely to take it seriously" (1996: 180; for specific examples see pp. 73, 108, 114–15). The IOC is even known to commission polls of residents in countries who have bid for the Olympics to assess the levels of public support (Jobling, 2000: 265). A lack of unity during the bid is a problematic signal, for if there are conflicts at this stage, they are only likely to worsen during the harder process of implementation. And once the bid is awarded, the party has to deal with the internal politics of the host city. As Steve Kerrigan, chair of the DNC's 2012 site selection committee, described the process: "There were at least some people in other cities who were not excited. Everyone in Charlotte wanted it. That's important since we'll essentially be married through the convention. We really have to work well together."[35]

Some residents of Minneapolis provide an example of how a lack of fervor—or in this case, a display of antagonism—can hurt a city's bid. There, the DNC's site selection team was greeted by protesters called "No DNC" during the 2010 site selection visit (Gansen, 2010). Some locals were displeased with the violent demonstrations (see chapter 4) and lack of financial benefit for local businesses during the 2008 St. Paul RNC and did not wish to repeat the experience. The fact that St. Paul did not bid jointly with Minneapolis (as they had done several times) surely also signaled an enthusiasm deficit to the site selection committee (Hoppin, 2010).

Given the media-message orientation of modern conventions, the party needs to have a city that will help it reinforce the message from inside the convention hall. New York City, for example, emphasized that the 9/11 attacks on the city and the city's efforts to rebound from them would provide a "good backdrop for President Bush" (Bridges, 2002). At the very least, the party does not want the city to distract from its message. Therefore, cities that might signal a competing message are disfavored in the site selection process. Las Vegas, for example, has been a frequent invitee of both parties since 2000. Despite being a convention capital—with plenty of first-class hotel rooms and all the amenities—the city has consistently rejected convention invitations, in part due to having to sacrifice its existing tourism business but also knowing the risk to the parties' images. With a reputation for gambling, showgirls, and prostitution, Las Vegas projects a brand either party would be cautious to appropriate. When Las Vegas finally bid for the RNC in 2016, social conservatives lobbied hard against it—citing sixty-four pages of escort services in the local phonebook—and it withdrew its bid (Barabak, 2014). The prospect of financial backing for the convention by GOP mega-donor and casino magnate Sheldon Adelson was not sufficient to risk antagonizing a significant part of the GOP base or spending the convention trying to focus the media's attention on fiscal policy rather than local exotics. Similarly, Arizona's controversial immigration law created a burden for Phoenix as pro-immigration groups, and one of its members of Congress, called for a convention boycott of the state (Barron, 2010). New Orleans was sidelined in 1992 due to the risk of a media frenzy over state Rep. David Duke (and future gubernatorial candidate), a former Ku Klux Klan grand wizard (Feeney and Leubsdorf, 1991).

The city's framing of its message to the party is a major component of its lobbying during the site selection visit and it reinforces the city's lobbying message throughout the entire site selection process. The site selection visit is the city's best opportunity to deliver that message to a captive audience. The lobbying process is important not only because it provides information but also because it builds relationships between city and party officials. Through relationships comes trust, which is critical to forming an effective partnership.

Stage 5—Selection of the Host

The site selection committee then provides its assessment of the merits of each of the finalists to the national party chair and, if it is the party of the incumbent president, the president's campaign team as well. The committee further serves as a resource to answer questions while the decision is being made.[36] The site selection team assesses the logistics of each city; the electoral merits for the candidates are the purview of the national party chair and the presidential campaign team. The official decision is made by the chair of the national party committee and ratified by national party committee members, though when the party's candidate is the incumbent president, the White House exercises dominant influence.

In the months leading up to the announcement of the host city, the party negotiates with several of the finalists. The Democrats negotiate contracts with multiple finalists, then sign the contract for the city selected as host; the GOP reaches "a gentleman's agreement" then writes the official contract after the host has been announced.[37] The GOP's traditional eagerness to move before the Democrats assures that it signs its priority city, but limits its bargaining leverage. In 2008, for example, the GOP's weak hand with St. Paul led the Republican National Committee to cover the cost of the police liability insurance policy, which is usually the responsibility of the host city (Hamburger and Hufstutter, 2008). The contract is the legal list of "deliverables" that the host committee and the host city will provide the party during the convention implementation process. The list ranges from office space for party officials and access to the arena for renovation and cleanup, to the number of notebook/tablet computers, transit vouchers, and color plasma television monitors (Harrison, 2011). The Democrats use elements of other cities' bids—and even informal offers—as leverage to entice the other finalists to include similar commitments in their contract.[38] In other words, the Democrats play the cities off one another to extract the best deal for itself. For the GOP, the best deal is getting the city with the major assets and capabilities that it wants, even if that means losing a little on the details.

When discussing convention host cities, the key question for most observers is, "Why did X city get it?" From the perspective of interested cities, the key question is, "What do we need to do to win?" Through this chapter, we've listed a large number of characteristics that are part of the mix of attributes that the parties are looking for and that cities seek to highlight. In analyzing the invitation and bid stages, we used statistical analyses to assess the relative weights that these attributes have on cities receiving invitations or bids. It is not appropriate to follow the same approach when evaluating which cities are selected as hosts because all the cities in our data set are not eligible to be hosts at this stage in the process. Only the cities that have submitted bids are potential winners, and the number of cities submitting bids is fifty-four (seventeen cities bid for both conventions, producing seventy-one total bids), too small a number to do advanced quantitative analysis with a large number of independent variables.

So to evaluate the question of "Why did they win?" we compared key attributes of the cities that bid against one another for each party's convention in the same year. Each convention cycle thus has two lists of competitors: one for the DNC, another for the RNC. We take two approaches to evaluating which attributes matter. The first is to rank each bid city for each party's convention on each attribute. The second approach is to develop a "checklist" of criteria, count the number criteria met by each bid city, and then see if the winner met more of the criteria than its competitors.

Some of the attributes on which we compare the cities are those that we have already used to analyze the invitation and bid stages: population, arena size, airport hubs, and vote margin in the previous presidential campaign. We add two more criteria at this stage: campaign money and "unity." Bibby and Alexander (1968: 43; also see Davis, 1983: 47) assert that the bid city's financial offer was one of the most important elements in site selection in the 1950s and 1960s, and given the importance of resources for implementing an effective convention, we must account for it. Since raising money for conventions is hard, parties are wise not to take the financial commitment in the city's bid at face value, but to evaluate the city's real capacity for producing enough funds.[39] Indeed, in March 2014, Republican National Committee chair Reince Priebus ranked "finances" as the GOP's most important criteria for the 2016 host city (Gillman, 2014). Unity, as we saw in the discussion of the finalist stage, is an important asset that contemporary site selection committees seek in determining who will be an effective partner.

We use data on the amount of money contributed to federal candidates from individuals and organizations (mostly political action committees) from each city provided by the Center for Responsive Politics (CRP). The limitation on these data—and the reason we did not use it to analyze the invitation or bid stages—is that the CRP changes how it groups contributions geographically from 2000 to 2012. In essence, CRP clusters cities differently in different years. In early years, the data are largely organized around metropolitan areas; in later years, most of the cities are presented separately. Since many of the cities in the full data set are smaller, the ability to measure their levels of contributions over time is thus compromised.[40] The additional problem is that CRP's geographic coding of the data only goes back to 2000, and so only allows us to use it with half our convention cycles.

By focusing only on bid cities, we mitigate the problem of inconsistent treatment of the smaller cities, since it is the larger cities that submit bids. The problem of a lack of campaign contribution data during the 1990s still exists, however. We decided it was important to evaluate the importance of a city's capacity for funding a convention. Certainly, this is a critical concern of the party's and leaving it out of our evaluation due to data limitations means we would not be assessing the relative merits of bid cities in the same way as the national parties. For the years 1992 through 2000, we use CRP's data from the 2000 presidential election to illustrate the likely role of campaign money in a city's ability to win a convention. We will not be using the campaign finance data to make a precise statistical estimate of how much each dollar contributed increases a city's probability of attaining a convention.

Second, as discussed as part of the finalist stage, a city's unity is an important criterion for the party. A city that is united about the wisdom of hosting the convention is a safer risk to be a good partner than one that is divided. We reviewed all the NewsBank articles on each city's bid, looking for indications of opposition to the city hosting a convention from key organizations or individuals in city politics. Most commonly, opposition came from some segment of the business community (e.g., they were being asked for money for other major projects too, or the hotel industry did not want to set aside the rooms to take a chance to land the convention). Sometimes the lack of unity came from conflict between the city and the state (governor's office or legislature, e.g., the 2012 Phoenix bid).[41] And there were a couple of other interesting cases such as the "No DNC" protests in Minneapolis and Senator Claire McCaskill's (D-MO) asking President Obama not to select St. Louis because of the concern that protests during the DNC or the partisan nature of the event would complicate her reelection efforts (Zeleny, 2011). We coded evidence of lack of unity in cities involved in thirty-eight bids (44.7%) from 1992 to 2016. This is not to say that there was no conflict in other bid cities, of course, but that their levels of conflict were not sufficiently intense to elicit coverage by the media.

In table 2.9, we present the percentage of times (based on sixteen host cities) that the host city achieved a particular rank for that attribute when compared to competing bid cities for a party's convention in the same election cycle.[42] We present the rankings for population size, arena size, past presidential margin, and campaign money (we don't rank airport hubs or unity since they are binary measures and thus we can't rank the cities). Table 2.9 shows that the parties often fail to select the top-ranked bid city on a particular attribute but often do select one of the top two. The parties, table 2.9 shows, give somewhat greater preferences to the largest cities and those that are more generous to federal campaigns: almost two-thirds of the host cities were ranked first or second on these attributes.

The lessons of table 2.9 are hardly crystal clear as host cities are spread across rankings for all the criteria. A city that ranks first on one of these attributes is not clearly in the driver's seat. Realistically, however, a city does not need to rank first on everything to demonstrate to the party that it can be an effective host. Rather, the party is looking for a host that meets several important criteria simultaneously and meets more of those criteria than its competitors.

To evaluate cities from this perspective, we developed a checklist of several criteria. We developed them by examining the list of attributes of host

Table 2.9. Host attribute rankings compared to other bid cities, 1990–2016

Rank	Population	Arena	Presidential margin	Campaign $
1	29%	21%	21%	29%
2	36%	29%	14%	36%
3	7%	14%	21%	7%
4	21%	21%	29%	14%
5		7%	7%	7%
6		7%		
7	7%		7%	7%

Data source: Authors' calculations.

cities compared to their bid competition and identified a threshold separating most winners from the losers. We then analyzed the criteria in several combinations, and in doing so, have come to the conclusion that the parties follow a two-tiered process for selecting the host city from among its competitors.

For purposes of illustration, we compare two sets of criteria, which we label the "Reliable Agent" criteria and the "Electoral" criteria. The Reliable Agent criteria incorporate the qualities that a party would seek in an effective partner in implementation. The Electoral criteria are those that would help the party advance explicitly political goals. We find that criteria based on agent qualities predict host selection better than criteria based on political criteria. Table 2.10 provides the comparison of each set of criteria and the summary results.

Table 2.10. Reliable Agent vs. Electoral Criteria for selection of host city, 1992–2016

Reliable Agent		Electoral	
Population size	93%	Population size	93%
Campaign $	86%	Governor-party match	79%
Unity	100%	Presidential competitiveness	57%
% of Points	93%	% of Points	76%
Better than competitors	57%		29%
Same as competitors	36%		29%
Worse than competitors	7%		43%

Note: Numbers are the percentage of points obtained by the cities that were selected as hosts.
Data source: Authors' calculations.

The three Reliable Agent criteria are the city's population size, the city's amount of campaign money, and unity. These are the key factors the party needs to assure that, to the greatest extent it can predict, the city has the capacity, resources, and willingness to implement the convention competently. The first criterion is a population size of greater than 450,000.[43] Population size, and all the assets and resources that come with it, matters: the parties do not necessarily choose the largest city that bids, but they do select a city that is large enough. It turns out that arena size and airport hubs are accounted for by population size and do not improve our ability to distinguish host cities from their competitors. For the record, 86% of host cities have arenas with seating capacity of more than eighteen thousand, and 71% have airport hubs.

Campaign money is the second of the Reliable Agent criterion. The vast majority of host cities (86%) have generated more than $20 million for federal candidates in the previous presidential election (again, we use 2000 data for the 1992–2000 cycles). Two of the host cities that did not meet the campaign contributions criterion, San Diego in 1996 and Charlotte in 2012, were the cities that had the most significant problems raising funds for their conventions (see chapter 3). If a community is not used to contributing to candidates, it probably will not suddenly become generous for a party convention.

The final criterion is unity. The unity criterion is both self-evident and underappreciated. None of the host cities evinced media reports on dissention within the city about the desirability of hosting a convention. And none of the cities in which dissension was reported (44.7%) won. If the business community or other politicians voiced public doubts about the convention being there, that was enough for the national parties to doubt whether it should be there too.

If we sum each bid city's scores on only these three criteria (1 = met the criterion, 0 = did not meet the criterion), and then compare the scores for each of the bidders for that party's convention, in eight (8) cases (57%), the host city has a higher score than any of its competitors, in five (5) cases, the host city was tied with one or more competitor, and in only one (1) case (Cleveland 2016 because of its low population) did it score worse.[44] The host cities collectively scored 93% of the points on the three Reliable Agent criteria. In three of the five cases of a tie, multiple cities met all three criteria.

The three Reliable Agent criteria do well in identifying host cities, but leave quite a few ties. A second tier of more explicitly political criteria are the tiebreakers. In three cases, the governor's party identification aligned the party for the host city but not the competitors, and in all three cases, the city with the governor of the "correct" party was awarded the convention. In the other two cases, the governors were of the same party and thus could not serve as a tiebreaker. In one case, Philadelphia's 2000 RNC victory over New York and Chicago, Pennsylvania's status as a competitive presidential state may have tipped the balance. The final case of a tier-one tie is Chicago versus New York City for the 1996 DNC, where it is likely that the chairman of the Democratic National Committee, David Whilhelm, who had worked for Mayor Richard Daley of Chicago, resolved the tie in favor of his adopted hometown (Sweet, 1993). Having relationships in a city is a way to assess whether the city will be a reliable partner in implementing a convention and in ensuring that it follows through. The party, of course, can break ties on whatever idiosyncratic factors are important to the chair or the president in a particular year: the "walkability" of city's downtown for delegates,[45] the synchronicity of the city's and the party's messages, the relationships that have been developed with city leaders, the desire to appeal to certain constituencies by going into a city or region that is demographically or politically difficult for the party.

To illustrate the value of the Reliable Agent criteria, we can compare them to a cluster of Electoral criteria: the competitiveness of the state in the previous election (decided by 10 points or fewer), a match between the governor's partisanship and the party awarding the convention (Polsby et al., 2012: 129), and the population threshold of 450,000. If parties prioritize the host city's ability to affect the electoral outcome, these three criteria should equal or exceed the performance of the Reliable Agent criteria. This is not what we find. Only four host cities scored better than the other cities that bid for the same convention in the same year, four host cities tied their competitors, and five hosts scored less than at least one competitor. All host cities, except Cleveland, met the population threshold. Of the states of host cities, 79% have a governor that matches the party, compared to 49% of the losing cities. Only 57% of host cities are in states in which the previous election was decided by 10 points or less—the same percentage as all the other cases on our data set.

One critical addendum is in order: the parties have recently put more emphasis on politically competitive, medium-size states with a governor of the same party from 2008 to 2016 than since the dawn of the television era. From 1948 through 2004, the mean difference between the presidential candidates in the previous election was 12.3 points and the mean state population ranking was 5.6. From 2008 through 2016, the mean vote gap dropped to 3.1 and the state size ranking dropped to 12.0. As the parties have placed more effort into mobilizing local residents, they have selected states where such mobilization is more likely to affect the electoral outcome.

The comparison of the Reliable Agent and Electoral criteria produce a clear conclusion: the parties prioritize cities that demonstrate that they can be an effective partner over those that can provide a political advantage. Politics certainly matters—but it is the political unity of the host city that matters most. Electoral politics matters as a secondary set of considerations, when multiple bid cities are equally qualified as agents. Then parties have a chance both to win a competitive state and to show their competence to a national audience.

Conclusion

The national parties have designed a multistage process for selecting host cities for their convention to maximize their ability to get the cities with the right assets and the right energy to be a good partner. The invitation allows the party to signal the facilities and capabilities it desires so that it can avoid the transaction costs of evaluating bids from unqualified cities and the political costs of rejecting scores of local officials. The site selection visit allows the party to evaluate the veracity of the bid and to evaluate the people with whom they will work if a city is selected. The contract negotiation stage allows the party to use the competition inherent in the process to leverage the best deal it can get.

Parties also are limited in their choices by the cities that submit bids. Cities' willingness to bid varies over time as the cost/benefit ratio of hosting a convention, as exemplified by the disruption costs of post-9/11 security measures, change. Cities may desire the economic and status benefits of hosting political conventions, but they are clearly not willing to seek those benefits at any cost.

For cities, the goal of the site selection process is to demonstrate that they have the capacity, the unity, and the willingness to be a helpful partner. There are several specific lessons that can be taken from this chapter's analysis for cities that are considering bidding for a convention. First, size and related assets (arena size, airports) matter. Parties prefer larger cities, but medium-size cities (i.e., those with a population between a half a million and one million) stand a greater chance in years when large cities do not bid (for example, after 9/11), as long as they have the arenas and other critical assets in place. Investments in arenas, convention hotels, and so on, put a city in position to be competitive. Second, cities with a solid record of making political contributions are in a better position than cities that are historically stingy with their donations. Not only is political giving a criterion that helps a city win, but being able to raise the funds makes life easier after the city has been selected as host (chapter 3). Third, if there are significant objections to hosting the convention, it is probably not worth the effort to bid. Dissension is a clear signal of trouble to the national party and a clear signal that their lives will be easier somewhere else. Having a governor from the party will help convince the party that the city will have reliable support from the state government, but having a governor from the right party in and of itself is insufficient. Demonstrating that the state government is supportive (regardless of partisanship) is likely more important. A city cannot control the political competitiveness of its state. If your city has the assets and unity, bid even if your state is not competitive. If you are in a competitive state, by all means highlight that fact, but don't expect it to be an ace-in-the-hole; our evidence demonstrates consistently that, regardless of the focus on competitiveness by many pundits (political scientists included), other criteria are more important. Finally, a city needs to have a plan. Submitting a bid, executing a lobbying campaign, and executing a site selection visit are major endeavors that require substantial investments of time and effort. The city needs to demonstrate to the party that it has the facilities, fundraising capacity, and unity that are on par or superior to its competitors. And that's the point—the party wants to see that the city is willing to exert the effort to be a committed host.

3

Paying for Conventions

In May of 2008, the Democratic National Committee publicly rebuked Denver for failing to meet its fundraising deadline (Vaughan, 2008). One month later, candidate Obama's decision to deliver his acceptance speech in Invesco Field allowed the Denver Host Committee to use the stadium's skyboxes as incentives for donors and helped the city meet its fundraising targets (Vaughan and Chacon, 2008). In 1996, San Diego's mayor, Susan Golding, engaged in a public feud with the Republican National Committee over cost overruns and who should pay for them (Braun, 1996a; Braun, 1996b; Braun, 1996c; Crabtree, 1995). In 2000, fundraising for the DNC lagged, so Mayor Richard Riordan, a Republican, fired the head of the host committee, installed one of his aides, and himself took over the job of fundraiser-in-chief (Lelyveld, 2000). Similar fundraising troubles have caused mayors (e.g., Bloomberg of New York 2004 [Smith, 2004], Hickenlooper of Denver 2008 [Chacon, 2008b], Foxx of Charlotte 2012 [Funk and Morrill, 2012]) or leading businessmen (e.g., Bill Edwards of Tampa 2012 [Danielson, Martin, and Cameron, 2012], Robert Wood Johnson of St. Paul 2008 [Hamburger and Huffstutter, 2008]) to take over the role of primary fundraisers late in the game. The Cleveland Host Committee asked GOP mega-donor Sheldon Adelson to cover all of its $6 million shortfall one week before the 2016 RNC (Isenstadt and Goldmacher, 2016). Cities with legendary strong mayors such as Daley in Chicago (1996) and Menino in Boston (2004) have struggled (Silberman, 2003; Gatlin, 2003). Chicago increased city appropriations for the convention, as did Los Angeles (Sweet and Spellman, 1995; *Daily Breeze*, 2000). Menino fought with Governor Romney over who should pay the police before a federal security grant bailed them out (Silberman, 2003b). Atlanta (1998) and Houston (1992) raised their hotel and restaurant taxes to help pay for the DNC and RNC, respectively (Roth, 1991; Sack, 1987b). Chicago (1996) and Philadelphia (2000, 2016) got multimillion-dollar boosts from their state governments (La Torre, 2000; Lowe, 1994; Vargas, 2016a). Charlotte cut its fundraising target by $5 million and still came up $7 million short (Morrill, 2012), forcing it to use a line of credit backstopped by Duke Energy to pay the bills. The presidential candidates themselves have frequently assisted the host committees by providing donor lists and lead fundraisers, headlining fundraising events, allowing mayors to travel with them to meet donors, and most recently, by contributing through super PACs allied with their campaigns (Funk, 2012; Vargas, 2016a; Weissman, 2008: 9). As highly trained social scientists, we sense a pattern: Cities have substantial difficulty meeting their fundraising targets for conventions in a timely manner.

Part of the difficulty is due to the sheer magnitude of the task. Based on our calculations from press reports, the eight host committees between 2004 and 2016 set average goals of $55 million to fulfill their contractual obligations to the national parties and to spend on their own promotional activities. To put the task of raising $55 million in context, it is almost 4.8 times the fundraising for the average U.S. Senate campaign in the 2012 election cycle.[1] Furthermore, senators have six years to raise those sums rather than eighteen months (though host committees have the advantage of soliciting and accepting contributions in unlimited amounts).

For insight into the timing of fundraising by the host committees, we gathered data on their fundraising from 2004 through 2012 from the Federal Election Commission (FEC). We present the cumulative funds raised as a percentage of each committee's goals in figure 3.1. Since host committees raise funds for different time periods, we standardize the fundraising periods as the percentage of days from the first contribution. The final day of the convention is 100 on figure 3.1 (values greater than 100 include post-convention days). The data verify the alarmist reporting of the news media: half the contributions arrive within three months of the convention. By the time the final balloon drops, most host committees have the money in hand, but it is a cliffhanger. To be sure, much of this money is pledged earlier, but the host committee has many contracts to sign and bills to pay prior to the convention. Moreover, the contracts with the national parties typically commit that the city will have the money in the bank at least one month prior to the convention. City and party leaders understandably would be stressed about whether and when the funding targets will be met.

Given cities' enthusiasm for hosting the conventions and the parties' selection of host cities with fundraising capabilities in mind, this struggle is notable. It is based on several factors: 1) the national parties have every

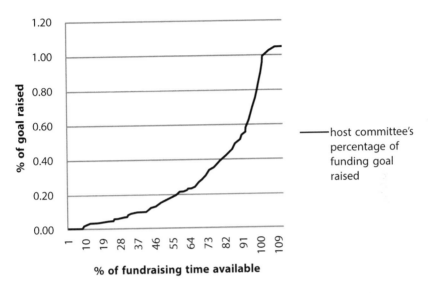

Figure 3.1. The timing of contributions to host committees, 2004–2012. *Data source: Federal Election Commission.*

incentive to spend as much as possible, causing the costs of conventions, and thus the fundraising demands on host cities, to soar; 2) cities increasingly rely on raising private contributions, rather than the city budget, to host conventions; and 3) cities face a collective action problem when fundraising for conventions—local businesses and residents benefit from the convention regardless of whether they contribute to making it happen. Furthermore, the number of people who can directly benefit from a convention (that is, obtain a selective incentive) in exchange for their donation is relatively few. Despite the fact that city leaders promote the conventions as economic development opportunities and donations to them as "community chest" contributions, they are partisan events. Thus, the people and organizations who contribute are highly political donors. They are invested in obtaining access to politicians and/or are promoting the election of the party's candidates.

Who Pays for the Parties' Parties?
The Struggle over Public versus Private Funding

For most of American history, the national parties paid for the conventions themselves (Davis, 1983: 77). They procured the means to do so by seeking pledges from bid cities for direct or in-kind support and sold advertising in convention programs. The remainder came from money raised during the presidential campaign.[2] Thus, conventions have always been paid for with a mix of private and public funds. The host cities historically relied on four sources of funds to fulfill the pledges they made in their bids: (1) municipal, county, and state appropriations; (2) local businesses and individual contributions; (3) state and national business contributions; and (4) revenues from convention programs (Bibby and Alexander, 1968: 48). The second and third sources continue to play critical roles in contemporary convention funding.

The convention program is no longer a source of convention revenue. But its story illustrates some of the broader issues in funding conventions. Similar to souvenir programs sold at sporting or musical events today, convention programs were essentially books containing a variety of information about the party's history, heroes, and accomplishments; its major constituency groups; information about the federal government; and information about the host city. They were sold at the convention and could be ordered by mail by the party faithful around the country. The 1936 DNC program was a compact three hundred pages and sold for $2.50 in paperback, $5 in hardback, and, for a pittance of $100 ($1,714 in 2014 dollars), one could obtain the leather-bound deluxe edition complete with the signature of President Franklin Delano Roosevelt (Webber, 2000: 70).

Importantly, the programs contained advertising. Corporations could not contribute directly to the parties, but they could buy advertisements. And, as a business expense, the ads had the virtue of being tax deductible. The sponsors who advertised in both parties' programs tended to be similar and were dominated by government contractors and heavily regulated industries such as railroads, airlines, and defense contractors (Bibby and Alexander, 1968: 58–60). After heavy media criticism of the 1964 convention programs as barely disguised vehicles for corporations to donate to political parties, Congress removed the tax deduction for the ads (Bibby and Alexander, 1968: 61). The parties worked out an arrangement to keep the paid advertising in convention books in 1972 (Alexander, 1976), where the Democrats made $1 million and the GOP made $1.6 million (Alexander, 1979: 340). Thereafter, convention programs contained no paid advertising, as the Federal Election Campaign Amendments of 1974 put an end to the practice.

The Federal Election Campaign Amendments (FECA) of 1974 overhauled the campaign finance system in response to the abuses uncovered during the Watergate investigations. FECA sought to remove the appearance of corruption from presidential elections by instituting public funding for presidential candidates—the Presidential Election Campaign Fund. By accepting limits on their spending, presidential candidates could accept money from a pool created by income tax check-offs rather than raising it from wealthy donors and interest groups. In doing so, candidates would be removed from making implicit or explicit promises to donors in exchange for contributions but instead could devote their attention to the priorities of the voting public.

The general issue of corruption exposed by the Watergate scandal had one specific connection to convention funding, and it illustrates two larger dilemmas of convention funding. One dilemma is whether giving to a host committee can be truly separate from giving to a party. Another dilemma is whether giving to promote the interests of the host city are necessarily distinct from giving to promote other political goals. The situation involved International Telephone and Telegraph's (ITT) pledge of $400,000 to assist in San Diego's pursuit of the 1972 RNC (Alexander, 1976b: 263–68). At the same time as its pledge, ITT was pursuing an out-of-court settlement to some antitrust charges with the Justice Department. The controversy surrounding the donation focused on whether there was a direct link between the contribution and the favorable settlement by Nixon's Justice Department. ITT argued that the donation was given to San Diego's host committee to promote the city, and ITT had an interest in promoting San Diego because it owned the Sheraton Hotel chain, which had a presence in the city. The Sheraton, in fact, was scheduled to be Nixon's headquarters. Congressional investigations and the Watergate investigation produced conflicting evidence about whether the Justice Department acted because of the contributions (several officials were punished for lying to Congress about it). The controversy—along with delays and cost overruns in renovating San Diego's convention center—caused the Republican National Committee to move the 1972 convention to Miami Beach.

As part of the new system of public funding created by FECA, party conventions would receive some money from the Presidential Election Campaign Fund. (Congress ended this provision in 2014, a point we will elaborate later.) The intention was for the Presidential Election Campaign Fund to pay the bulk of the cost of the "inside the hall" business of the convention, such as renovating the convention site, staff expenses, convention operations and planning, security, biographical films, and selected transportation and entertainment costs (Garrett and Reese, 2014: 4–5). The public funds go directly to the party convention committees, and, by accepting them, the convention committees agree not to raise additional funds. Public funding was never intended to cover the entire cost of the convention (Alexander, 1979: 339) and was not to cover the cost of activities "outside the hall" (other than transporting delegates from their hotels to the hall). Public funding for delegates' travel and hotel expenses, or any expenses of the candidates, was specifically banned. Delegates today continue to pay their own way.

Host committees were permitted to raise funds for the use of the facility (including renovations), providing security and local transportation services, promoting the city, and hosting receptions (CFR 9008.52). The Federal Election Commission allowed host committees to raise money from local corporations as a means of promoting the cities. National corporations with local retail establishments also were allowed to contribute as long as the amount was "commensurate" to the amount the local office could expect to making during the time of the convention (Alexander, 1979: 341).

Cities are also allowed to establish organizations called "municipal funds" to solicit contributions to defray the municipal government's expenses during political conventions, rather than using appropriations. The municipal funds are supposed to be short-term entities for the purposes of conventions only, but several have existed for long periods, essentially as fundraising arms of the visitor's bureau (Weisman, 2008). As we will show in the next section, municipal funds are now a rarely used fundraising mechanism as direct city contributions to political conventions have declined.

Both parties found allocations from the Presidential Election Campaign Fund to be too limiting. Adjusted for inflation from 1974's base of $4 million, they amounted to $18.2 million per convention in 2012. Since the national party convention committees are barred from raising money as a condition of accepting public funds, the parties have used contracts with the bid cities to get cities to raise significantly more money to "supplement" the public funds. The escalating costs of conventions have raised the challenge for cities to produce the desired sums. The genius of the parties is apparent in their ability to shift the costs of their conventions onto local host committees and the federal government.

The Costs of Conventions

Spending on presidential nominating conventions more than quadrupled between 1980 and 2004, even when accounting for inflation as shown in figure 3.2.[3] The most dramatic increase occurred during the 1990s as the Federal Election Commission eased the rules on contributions to host committees and the parties were learning to exploit unlimited "soft money" contributions that supported "party building" activities rather than candidate endorsements. Another change in this time period was to the FEC's requirement that only local retail establishments (or national corporations with local offices) could contribute to host committees. During the 1970s and 1980s,

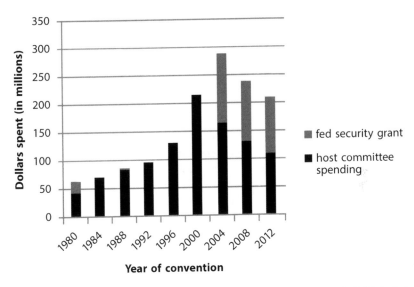

Figure 3.2. Expenditures on presidential nominating conventions, 1980–2012 (inflation adjusted to 2012). *Data source:* Weissman (2008) and Federal Election Commission.

this rule constrained medium-size cities' ability to raise sufficient funds. Dallas's bid for the 1980 DNC, for example, was tripped up when the city council barred the use of city money. The host committee instead pledged to raise $3 million from private contributors statewide (Alexander, 1983: 270). The Democratic National Committee doubted that "statewide" met the FEC's local contribution criterion and doubted that Dallas could raise sufficient private funds locally. The FEC loosened this restriction in 1994 by allowing unlimited contributions from local businesses, organizations, and individuals, and allowing "vendors"—regardless of whether they were retail establishments or locally based—to donate goods and services to host committees (FEC, 1994). The floodgates were open. The FEC removed the requirement that donors have any local presence in 2003 due to the increasingly globalized economy (FEC, 2003: 47398–9). Parties took advantage of the removal of fundraising restrictions on host committees to push them to raise and spend more money.

Host committees are not supposed to raise funds for the official business of the convention. These expenses are to be paid with public funds from the taxpayer check-off. Host committees are, however, allowed to pay for some of the major expenses that occur "inside the hall," namely rent and construction costs. As former FEC commissioner Scott Thomas has argued, "the FEC has not done a very good job of defining what types of expenses can be paid for by a host committee in connection with a presidential nominating convention or how to allocate costs between the host committee, the party's publicly funded convention committee, and the party's other federal and non-federal accounts" (2003: 11). If there are not clear prohibitions against a host committee paying for a particular expense, the parties will shift the expense to them to extend the life of the public funding account. Thus, host committees now pay substantial sums for items that historically were paid for by the parties with the taxpayer check-off funds; spending on promoting the local economy has not increased (Green et al., 2003: 71–73).

National parties have every incentive to seek higher levels of convention spending since the host committees have the task of raising the money. The parties want to produce the most impressive infomercials and have delegates, affinity groups, and media personnel lavishly entertained. Cities are willing to underwrite the whole affair and sign contracts with gold-plated requirements from the parties, thus accepting the attendant fundraising commitments, because of the signaling benefits they receive from a successful convention. The parties have incentive to push the cities for more because they know that the city's reputation is on the line for delivering their commitment. A city that can't follow through undercuts a key component of its signal to potential recruitment targets.

The national parties' efforts to ratchet up convention spending became most apparent in the case of the 1996 San Diego RNC. The money struggle between the city and the Republican National Committee started in the previous convention cycle, when San Diego was the favorite for the convention but ended up losing to Houston in large part because of Houston's willingness to accommodate the Republican National Committee's demands for more spending (McDonald, 1991). After San Diego was chosen to host the 1996 RNC, the National Republican Convention Committee released a budget calling for record spending of between $27.5 and $31.6 million.[4] San Diego officials dismissed that budget as a "wish list" and sought to negotiate the budget down to the $22–$26 million they proposed in their bid. Mayor Susan Golding claimed that officials in Houston and New Orleans, the previous RNC hosts, had warned her that the RNC would attempt to wring more money out of the city. The Republican National Committee retorted that the mayor had promised more than she could deliver. As the convention approached, the city and the Republican National Committee battled publicly over $5 million in disputed costs. At the last minute, city officials covered $1.2 million in cost "overruns" that the host committee couldn't cover. The fact that the San Diego Host Committee raised nearly three times as much as the previous record holder, New York City in 1992, and still could not meet the Republican National Committee's demands lends credence to the interpretation that the party was trying to maximize its gains from its host. The Republican National Committee's immediate lesson from this spat was to put a high priority on a city's fundraising capacity in the 2000 site selection process, seeking assurances from corporate leaders in medium-size cities that money would be available.[5]

Nevertheless, figure 3.2 also shows that the parties' ability to leverage ever-higher spending has reached its limits. Spending retreated after 2004 as larger cities have increasingly declined to bid and medium-size cities have won a larger share of the bids. The recession of 2008–10 also made it more difficult for cities to raise funds or to justify committing city budgets to political conventions. The recession not only put pressure on city's general revenue but also crimped hotel and motel taxes often used to fund convention and tourism activities. Squeezed between the decline in tourism tax money and preexisting commitment of those funds, cities became reticent to devote tourism taxes toward political conventions (Harrison, 2011).

The recent decline in convention spending suggests that while the parties have an incentive to push cities for more money, they also don't have an incentive to throw their partners under the bus. The parties need city and host committee officials to be enthusiastic and cooperative during the convention to keep delegates and media personnel happy, so it is risky to antagonize them too relentlessly over fundraising. Nor do the parties have an incentive to push costs so high that interested cities forgo bids, as happened for a time with the Olympics after Montreal in 1976 (e.g., Levine, 2003) and may be happening again (Axon, 2015; Lauermann, 2015; O'Sullivan, 2014).

An additional part of the story, as shown by the shaded section of the graph in figure 3.2, is that the parties and cities have taken advantage of the $100 million Department of Justice security grants since 9/11 to bolster total convention spending while relieving the cities of some of their fundraising obligations.[6] The security grants reimburse local and state law enforcement for all security planning and training activities, pay overtime for security personnel, and purchase security equipment used during the convention for the local police department (Garrett and Reese, 2014: 5).[7] With the presence of national leaders and international dignitaries at conventions, Congress decided to treat political conventions as "National Special Security Events" (Reese, 2014), rather than local affairs, and provided greater federal technical support and financial assistance, much as the federal government had done for Olympics hosted in the United States (Green et al., 2003: 76).

Indeed, the federal security grant has important implications for fundraising for political conventions. With the federal government now picking up the tab for security, which traditionally has been the major expense of local government (or one for which the host committee had to raise funds to reimburse the city), convention appropriations by local governments have nearly vanished. As figure 3.3 shows, the federal contribution has entirely supplanted state and local funds.

Even suggestions that local governments might contribute directly to funding the conventions have caused considerable consternation. A torrent of public protest stirred up by radio talk shows greeted the Los Angeles City Council in 2000 when their host committee made a request for additional city support when the committee was unable to meet its budget (*Daily Breeze*, 2000). Denver's auditor made some political hay by asking the mayor to reiterate his public commitment that no taxpayer money would be used to fund the convention when Denver lagged in its fundraising (Chacon, 2008a). Three of the four cities in 2008 and 2012 loudly and repeatedly rejected spending taxpayer money on the conventions. Only the Tampa Host Committee received $1.2 million toward the 2012 RNC from nearby counties.

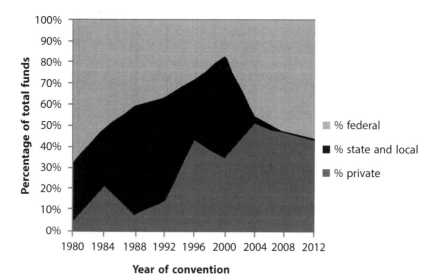

Figure 3.3. Sources of funding of presidential conventions, 1980–2012 (inflation adjusted). *Data sources:* Data for 1980–2004 are taken from Weissman (2008). Data on more recent conventions were collected by the authors from host committee reports to the Federal Election Commission, media reports, and Garrett and Reese (2014).

City officials' wariness of using direct taxes on residents to pay for mega-events is validated by our post-2012 election survey of Charlotteans (see chapter 5 for details). We asked residents to rate five methods of paying for mega-events: hotel and rental car taxes, property taxes, sales taxes, food and beverages taxes, and imposing sales taxes in a special district around the event location.[8] The specific wordings of the questions are available in appendix 3-A. Respondents rated each financing option on a scale of 1 to 10, with 10 being the best way to pay for mega-events and 1 being the worst way to pay for them. Their rankings, as shown in table 3.1, are the same whether we use respondents' average ratings or the option to which they gave the highest ratings. Hotel and car taxes were the most favored option, though the mean of just under 6 shows rather tepid support for even the top option. Twenty-eight percent of respondents did not give any of the options a score higher than 5, which indicates their lack of enthusiasm about paying for (and presumably hosting) mega-events. Creating a special district around the event location was the second-ranked option. Not surprisingly, the two most popular options would shift the costs onto people other than most of the respondents. Food and beverage taxes, sales taxes, and property taxes were less popular options for paying for mega-events. Thus, given residents' ambivalence about person-ally funding mega-events, it is not surprising that when cities do contribute directly to convention costs, it is usually through a tourism bureau funded by tourism taxes rather than directly from the city budget.

City funding probably has never be an easy sell politically. Bibby and Alexander (1968: 46, 50, 71) noted that city and state appropriations in the 1950s and 1960s were limited and typically came from cities that had sepa-rate pots of hotel tax money that was used to attract convention business.

Table 3.1. Preferred methods of paying for mega-events, Mecklenburg County residents, 2012

	Mean	Top-ranked option*
Hotel and car taxes:	5.97	56.0%
Special district:	4.54	31.9%
Food tax:	3.69	13.9%
Sales tax:	3.36	8.8%
Property tax:	2.40	5.5%

Column sums to greater than 100 because ties were counted.

Data source: 2012 Post-Election Survey of Mecklenburg County, North Carolina, residents.

Furthermore, cities' major contributions rarely came through the budget where they could be easily criticized by residents but came in the form of providing city assets and services to the party such as rent-free use of the convention hall, city buses for delegation transportation, and police and emergency services personnel (Davis, 1983: 47). Indirect methods of funding tourism projects are not unusual. Even though city spending on tourism infrastructure, such as convention centers, boomed during the end of the twentieth century, it often was financed "off-budget" by special authorities (Perry, 2003: 41). Hill (1996: 110) observes a similar dynamic in Olympic host cities, wherein local tax money is rarely used, but municipal land is provided for venues and local officials devote substantial amounts of time to planning and execution. Nevertheless, the contemporary polarized political environment makes spending on politicians (by politicians!) even more perilous.

Even with the significant contribution of federal security funds and their relief of the financial impact on city governments, host committees still must raise nearly half the total funds from private contributions. Host committees must identify the local residents willing to chip in on behalf of the collective good, outsiders willing to pay for access to party officials during the convention, and ideologues willing to support their team.

The Fundraising Challenge

Host committees are not party organizations. They are usually 501c3 (charity) or 501c6 (business league) organizations created *to promote the city*. Thus, they are not subject to traditional "source" restrictions regarding who can contribute to candidates or parties. For example, corporations, unions, and other interest groups may contribute directly to host committees but must form political action committees (PACs) to raise voluntary contributions from their members to give to candidates or parties. Foundations may contribute to host committees but not candidates or parties. Nor are host committees subject to limits on the amounts that an individual or PAC can contribute to parties or candidates.

The legal distinction between host committees and political parties is an important point for city leaders who are framing their solicitations to local businesspeople and residents. They promote support of the host committees as contributions that will benefit the city by enhancing its reputation and economic prospects. They pitch it as a collective good that everyone should support as opposed to a political party event, which is more divisive. It is also important because contributions to 501c3 organizations are tax deductible, while political contributions are not. At the same time, political conventions are clearly partisan events. Some potential donors who may be willing to support the city may not want to support an event that promotes the election of a disliked candidate or party. But it may also mobilize donors who want to support that same party or candidate. The quandary over the extent to which conventions are partisan versus civic events was exemplified by the IRS's denial of the 2016 Philadelphia host committee's application to be a 501c3 charitable organization, because some of the spending was deemed to be political (Vargas, 2016c).

Political fundraisers face a collective action problem in soliciting funds (Olson, 1965). Even for supporters of a cause, victory is a collective good. All supporters benefit from having their candidate or party win regardless of whether they contributed time or money (or even showed up to vote!) to produce the victory. Each supporter has an incentive to "free ride" off the efforts of others—which means no one has a personal incentive to contribute. Fundraising is more likely to succeed when the fundraiser can create some individualized benefit for the donor. City leaders can tout the local economic and reputational benefits to residents and businesses as the incentive to contribute. For nonlocal donors, host committees can offer the ideological benefits of supporting their party to partisan donors and the benefits of access to national political leaders to investor donors.

Host committees, then, have the possibility of appealing to at least three groups of donors: local donors, access-oriented investor donors, and partisan donors. To examine who funds conventions and why, we pooled the Federal Election Commission data on contributions to host committees from the 2004–12 convention cities.[9] We also gathered data on all donors' contribution histories—for example, how much the donor contributed in the previous presidential election and the partisanship of the donor's contribution record from the Center for Responsive Politics.[10] We classified donors from the same state as the host city as "local" donors.

Community Chest Contributions from Local Residents and Businesses

All local residents and businesses share in the promotional and reputational value of hosting the convention. Just as local businesses and residents pool their resources to fund other community chest activities, such as sports, the arts, and hospitals, they are asked to contribute towards the community good of hosting a prestigious event. While local residents can still "free ride" off the contributions of their neighbors, they would perceive more incentive to contribute to the host committee than nonlocal donors. Local political leaders will find business leaders to be easier targets of fundraising appeals than ordinary taxpayers. These members of the "growth coalition," after all, benefit most from the city's enhanced image and the opportunity for business recruitment presented by the convention (Logan and Molotch, 1987). Moreover, local giving is enhanced by the social pressure that can be brought to bear in face-to-face solicitations through community organizations (like the chamber of commerce) and social networks.

Many local donors rise to meet the call: our data show that 41% of host committee contributions come from local donors. One donor to Philadelphia's 2000 host committee provided a community chest rationale for his contribution, "If you are a business person or a professional in the Philadelphia region, whenever there is something that is going to help the city, the business community will support it, whether it is the Avenue of the Arts or the Convention Center or anything else" (quoted in Goldstein and Von Bergen, 2000). In Minnesota, nineteen of twenty Fortune 500 companies contributed to the 2008 St. Paul Host Committee. Target's spokeswomen explained, "This wasn't about Target, this was about helping showcase Minnesota. We've never donated to a Host Committee before; we did it this year because one of them was in our hometown" (quoted in Baca, 2008).

Despite the fact that the money is raised from local businesses, much of the total amount is from national and internationals corporations with local offices rather than small businesses. The big contributors tend to be banks and utilities that are heavily regulated and thus have a history of political giving (Grier, Munger and Roberts, 1994). Figure 3.4 shows the variation in host

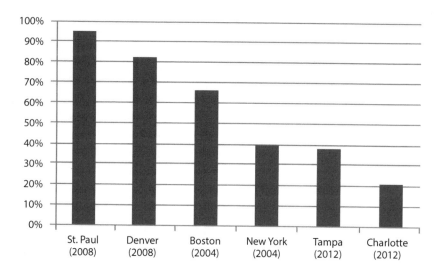

Figure 3.4. Percentage of Fortune 500 companies from host state contributing to host committees. *Data source:* Federal Election Commission.

committee contributions from in-state Fortune 500 companies. St. Paul and Denver lead the pack with more than 80% of their Fortune 500 corporations pitching in. Facing President Obama's ban on corporate contributions to its host committee (a point we will elaborate shortly), Charlotte lagged behind other host cities with less than one-quarter of North Carolina's Fortune 500 members contributing to its New American City fund.

Local donors are different in a number of important ways from nonlocal donors: they contribute earlier (on average, 145 days before the convention vs. 122 days for nonlocal donors, Chi-square < .001), they are less partisan (23% have contributed only to candidates of the convention party vs. 33% of nonlocal donors, Chi-Square < .001), they are more likely to be new donors (61% have never given to a federal candidate or organization, compared to 39% of nonlocal donors), and if they have been political donors, they contributed less than nonlocal donors in the previous presidential election cycle (an average of $34,893 versus $415,556).

Nevertheless, because of the "free rider" problem, raising funds for even consensual community projects—such as hospitals or youth activities—is often difficult. Supporting a political convention involves the additional hurdle of identification with a political party and its candidates. Civic-minded donors who would donate to the United Way may be reluctant to donate to the DNC. As argued by the CEO of a Raleigh marketing firm, the political climate is "so polarized that a business leader who might otherwise be interested in supporting a political convention might think twice about supporting this convention" (quoted in Funk, 2012).

Charlotte and Duke Energy provide a vivid example. Duke CEO Jim Rogers promoted the company's involvement in the 2012 DNC as good for Duke because it was good for Duke's hometown:

> I view this as really having an impact on future economic development in the long term. I view it as putting a spotlight on our headquarters city. Everybody in this community is a customer of mine, so we try to do things that at the end of the day make this a stronger community. We have a vested interest in seeing investment here, jobs created, just more customers for us. So for me to lead on this is just a natural extension of my business.[11]

Despite Rogers's assertion that the convention was good for Duke Energy, he faced protests at the company's 2011 annual meeting and a petition drive advocating his firing organized by Freedom Works, a national Tea Party–aligned conservative organization (Morrill, 2011). If local corporate leaders are not politically active donors in the first place, it is a lot to ask them to make themselves targets of unhappy shareholders or ideological activists by contributing to a party convention.

Similar pressures at times confront national corporate donors as well. Some traditional corporate donors worried about contributing to the 2016 Cleveland RNC out of concern that a polarizing nominee like Donald Trump would damage their brand or subject them to consumer protests (Martin and Haberman, 2016; Mider and Dexheimer, 2016). And because many of these corporate donors contribute to both conventions so as not to appear partisan, their decisions to reduce contributions to the 2016 RNC also impacted fundraising for the DNC (Vargas, 2016b).

Access Contributions

From the pre-Watergate days of selling ads in convention programs, access-seeking corporations have always been a primary source of convention funding.[12] The institution of public funding in the post-Watergate reforms attempted to remove the need for "special interest" contributions, but FEC decisions allowing host committees to accept contributions from nonlocal businesses have made corporations major convention funders again.

The incentive for corporations to contribute is clear. Just as cities are interested in hosting conventions because of all the influential people coming to town, there are no other opportunities for organizations to be in the presence of the cabinet, members of the House and Senate, governors, state legislatures, and county and municipal governments simultaneously. Conventions are one-stop shopping for access.

Our data show that 188 donors (8%) gave to more than one host committee. Only eleven donors gave to five or more of the six host committees. This small percentage of donors, however, provides disproportionate support to the host committees—fully 54% of the total funds. Importantly, they are an important source of early money for the host committees, providing 49% of the funds deposited one year or more prior to the conventions. Multi-convention donors are overwhelmingly corporate (78%); the other 22% included thirteen unions, seven foundations, four Native American tribes, and eighteen individuals.[13]

Host committees and the parties are happy to exchange packages of hotel rooms, receptions, credentials, and arena seats for donations. Barack Obama's use of Denver's football stadium for his acceptance speech helped Denver meet its fundraising obligations as it made more skyboxes available to entice large donors (Vaughan and Chacon, 2008). Host committees also are happy to sell "sponsorships," which allow corporations to provide gift bags, water bottles, shirts, and so on, affixed with the corporate logo, to convention attendees and volunteers. Moreover, the FEC allows corporations to provide in-kind contributions of goods and services to the host committee for free or discount rates (Garrett and Reese, 2014).

From the host city's perspective, attracting outside contributions is particularly appealing. The city uses the convention to promote itself, and collects the spending of the visitors during the convention, while nonresidents pay for much of the costs. That's a win-win! Furthermore, outside money has a bigger economic impact than simply redirecting money within the local economy (see chapter 6).

For advocates of open government and campaign finance reform, however, the open exchange of money for access at political conventions is anathema (e.g., Weissman et al., 2008; Holman et al., 2008). By giving money to host committees, donors avoid contribution limits that restrict their ability to give directly to the parties or their candidates. Moreover, the donors get to curry favor and they get an outlet for communicating their priorities that ordinary citizens do not get.

In his 2008 presidential campaign, Barack Obama showed his solidarity with these reformist concerns by banning contributions from political action committees and federal lobbyists to his campaign. On becoming the Democratic Party nominee, he extended the restrictions to fundraising by the Democratic National Committee and, after his election, to fundraising for his inaugural. There was clear precedent, then, for his decision to ban contributions from corporations and lobbyists to the 2012 host committee, and limit contributions from individuals and foundations to $100,000. Though the new restrictions already banned corporations from contributing, to make the populist point especially clear, corporations that received TARP funds during the financial crisis—and had not yet repaid it—were singled out as part of the ban. Instead, the 2012 Charlotte DNC would be the "people's convention," paid with donations from many small contributions rather than from a few corporate fat cats. Eliza Newlin Carney of *Congressional Quarterly* labeled the move "a fool's errand, a bold experiment or both" (2012).

Obama's convention fundraising restrictions were not announced publicly until the DNC announced the convention host, but the restrictions were known to the finalists as part of the contract negotiations. As explained by the chair of the DNC's site selection process, Steve Kerrigan, "No one objected. No one walked away. I was surprised and thought that they may not understand the implications. Having raised money for a convention, I knew this would really be a challenge, but they didn't seem to think it would be a problem. Or they just didn't get how much of a problem it would really be."[14] Will Miller, the chair of the Charlotte in 2012 Host Committee during the site selection process, described Charlotte officials' reaction to the president's restriction during the contract talks: "We would deal with it if we got the convention. . . . Our attitude was that if every city was asked [to abide by these restrictions], we were in as good a position [to deal with them] as anybody. We're partners, we'll do our best. At the end of the day, there will be a convention. Somebody will pay for it. They can't decide not to have a convention or decide to go somewhere else. . . . [This was the Democratic National Committee's] test to see who really wants it."[15] As it turned out, both Kerrigan and Miller were right: the limits did create a huge fundraising challenge for Charlotte's host committee and the DNC couldn't go somewhere else, so the two had to muddle through together.

Obama's ban on corporate contributions, which are traditionally the main source of private convention funds, presented a major hurdle to convention fundraising. Banning lobbyists' contributions similarly cut off a major source of access-oriented funds. But the lobbyist ban had broader implications as well since lobbyists frequently serve as bundlers for political fundraising. In other words, they use their networks of contacts to raise funds on behalf of the party or candidate and then give the contributions as a "bundle" to claim credit for the total amount (e.g., Brown et al., 1995). Bundlers assist in this way for convention fundraising in order to promote "donor events" during the convention with leading politicians as the draw. By banning lobbyists, Obama's ban also limited the amount of money that could be raised by such intermediaries.

Nevertheless, there were some loopholes in the president's restrictions. Corporations could still give in-kind contributions to the host committee, and labor unions were not prohibited from contributing. Most unions, however, did not contribute, as they were unhappy that the Democratic National Committee would select the least unionized state in the country to host the convention. The most important way that Charlotte dealt with the restrictions was by violating the spirit of them. While the host committee would meet the letter of the contract by raising money to fund the Democratic National Convention Committee's activities inside the arena, Charlotte leaders created a separate fundraising entity, called the New American City fund (a 501c6 "civic league"), to accept corporate donations to fund activities outside of the convention hall to promote the city.[16] Ironically, those "outside the hall" activities were the primary rationale for the FEC to allow host committees to raise and spend money during the conventions in the first place. New American City also paid for the host committee's overhead costs, including salaries. Duke Energy CEO Jim Rogers had already solicited commitments from corporate donors prior to the imposition of the restrictions and those contributions became the seed funds for New American City.

Philadelphia had to do a similar organizational two-step when the IRS denied its host committee's application to be a 501c3 charitable organization in 2016 (Vargas, 2016c). The host committee operated as a 501c6 business league, which allows corporations but not individuals to take tax deductions. Philadelphia then promoted its Convention and Visitors Bureau, a 501c3, as a conduit for individual tax deductible and non-profit organizational contributions to the host committee (Vargas, 2016a).

The Charlotte host committee also attempted to leverage corporate money indirectly by making itself a cartel of meeting and reception space. It asked more than 150 downtown establishments, such as bars and restaurants, to give it a "right of first refusal" contract so that it could coordinate space rentals during the convention.[17] The host committee could provide the best match of facility space to each organization—and put all space to its "highest and best uses"—rather than having space rented on a first-come, first-serve basis. The host committee had a list of criteria to determine how space would be allocated; assisting the host committee with fundraising would improve an organization's ranking on the priority list. Once the match was made, the host committee would then collect a finder's fee from the corporations, interest groups, and other organizations who want to hold gatherings during the convention (Grim, 2012). The cartel did not work well, as several key establishments did not participate.

Despite such efforts, Charlotte's fundraising targets were reduced from $36 million to $31.3 million (Dunn and Morrill, 2012), and the host committee still came up $7 million short. This amount was covered by a $10 million line of credit provided by Duke Energy as part of Charlotte's bid.[18] Cities frequently include—and the parties consistently request—a line of credit in their bids to assure that money is available early in the process, for example, to pay for construction costs, and to assure the parties that a financial backstop is present if the city's fundraising efforts fall short. Charlotte's efforts did fall short and Duke Energy provided the additional subsidy to a convention that was supposed to be free of corporate money. In other words, the ban backfired. While Charlotte did increase its funding from individual donors, it ended up being highly dependent on a single corporate donor. The lesson regarding the challenge of restricting funding sources was not lost on President Obama, who quietly dropped the ban on corporate contributions to his 2012 inaugural (Morrill, 2012), or on the Democratic National Committee, who removed the restrictions on Philadelphia's fundraising for the 2016 convention (Morrill, 2016).

The stated goal of Obama's fundraising restrictions was to make the 2012 DNC a "People's Convention." Charlotte succeeded in this regard: of the cities in our data, it had the highest proportion of individual donors (82%) and the highest percentage of funds from individuals (31%). But Charlotte's ability to mobilize local donors was constrained by a history of limited political giving (see chapter 2). Its percentage of local givers was next to the lowest (St. Paul was lowest), though it raised the third highest percentage of funds from local donors (38%). With limited local fundraising potential, Charlotte turned to a national, party-based donor network: it had the lowest percentage of new givers (20%) and the highest percentage of partisan givers (36%). So Charlotte's convention may have been funded by the "people," but they were Democratic activist people, not political neophytes or locals.

Ideological Contributions from Partisans

Since conventions are partisan events, one might expect that contributions from party donors would play an important part of funding presidential nominating conventions. We measure the "partisanship" of the donors based on the distribution of their contributions in the previous presidential election in the Center for Responsive Politics' database. While most Political Action Committees (PACs) contribute to members of both political parties in pursuit of access (e.g., Wright, 1985; Snyder, 1990), some are "party allies" and use their contributions to help elect candidates from one party (e.g., Herrnson, 2009). Likewise, many individual donors are motivated by party or ideology and consistently support like-minded candidates and organizations (Brown et al., 1995; Francia et al., 2003; Grant and Rudolph, 2002).

For descriptive purposes (our measure will differ in the statistical model later in the chapter), we classify organizations with PACs as in-party donors if 75% or more of their contributions go to the convention party. We classify PACs as "out-partisans" if 75% or more of their contributions went to the other party. Individual donors are much more party-oriented than PACs, and almost all of them would be considered "in-partisans" under the organizational threshold. So we classify individuals who gave all of their contributions to candidates or party organizations of the convention host as "in-partisans," and donors who gave all of their contributions to the other party as "out-partisans." Individuals who contributed to candidates from both parties, or PACs whose partisan skew was less than 75%, were classified as "mixed donors." For individuals who did not contribute in the previous presidential cycle, we used contributions in other cycles to assess their partisanship. Host committee donors who have made no recorded contributions to federal candidates or parties were classified as new donors.

There is a clear partisan tilt in host committee donations. "In-party" donors comprise 28% of the donors and 17% of the total funds for host committees compared to "out-partisans," who make up only 2% of the donors and 5% of the funds. Interestingly, out-party donors are more generous than in-party donors. Their average contribution is nearly $200,000 compared to $53,000 for in-party donors.[19] Clearly out-party donors are contributing for reasons other than to support the candidate or party of the convention. "Mixed donors" are less numerous than in-party donors (22% vs. 28%), but they provide a substantially higher proportion of host committee funds (48% vs. 17%). In contrast, new donors are a large share of donors (48%), but supply 29% of the funds. New donors are disproportionately local donors.

While it is not surprising that in-party donors play a larger role in funding host committees than out-party donors, it is notable that the vast majority of donors do not have strictly partisan contribution histories. That is, ironically, party conventions are largely not funded by partisan donors. Part of the reason for this, as we saw in the two last sections, is that the many convention donors are local donors who are primarily supporting the city or are access-oriented organizations. Indeed, of the "partisan" funds, 87% are from nonlocal donors. Relatedly, 91% of partisan donors are individuals, and if it is harder to raise funds from many individual donors than a few corporations, host committees will be unlikely to seek contributions from small partisan donors unless they have to.

The Dynamics of Fundraising

The ideal way to understand who funds conventions and why would be to examine the differences between donors and non-donors. However, we don't have a feasible way of gathering information on non-donors. Nor do we have access to host committees' target lists to assess which donors they strategically attempted to solicit and which donors responded (or who contributed without a request). We can, however, analyze how much donors give and when they give it to gain some insight into the dynamics of mobilizing funds for conventions.

Strategically, host committees are likely to prioritize fundraising from donors who have the highest probability of giving large amounts. These priority donors are also likely to be asked early to be "lead" donors so that their investments build momentum for and underwrite the infrastructure necessary for later, smaller donors (Box-Steffensmeier, Radcliffe, and Bartels, 2005). Host committees should prioritize prolific spenders in previous election cycles (Verba, Schlozman, and Brady, 1995). We account for both donations to candidates and parties as well as independent expenditures in measuring past political spending. More specifically, host committees should target donors who have given to other political conventions, whether the other party convention in the same year or their party's convention in other years. And they should target donors to whom they can offer some type of selective incentive in exchange for their contribution: local donors and access-oriented donors (such as businesses, donors from D.C., and donors who give to both parties). Descriptions of all variable measurements appear in appendix 3-B.

We present random fixed effects models of the total amount contributed by the donor and the timing of contributions in table 3.2. The virtue of a random fixed effects model in this situation is that it allows us to account for unmeasured variation in the behavior of the host committee and city, the donor, and the specific fundraising requirements set by the party for any

Table 3.2. Amounts and timing of contributions to host committees, panel regression (ml random effects)

	Amount		Timing	
	Coefficient	SE	Coefficient	SE
Both conventions year$_x$	160,442***	19,608	.047***	.009
Same party, different cycles	97,079***	18,707	−.016*	.008
Partisanship	−65*	36	−.0002**	.0001
Electoral spending$_{x-1}$ (nl)	5,737***	972	.002***	.0006
Local	26,576***	9,005	.061***	.005
Individual	−64,476***	11,739	−.016*	.009
Foundation	76,575***	26,276	−.096***	.018
Union	85,745**	41,449	−.107***	.026
DC	25,241	22,952	−.040***	.012
In-kind	40,385**	19,747	−.040***	.008
GOP convention	66,070*	39,959	−.024	.022
Sigma_u	46,427	15,360	.025	.008
Sigma_e	275,122	2,272	.203	.002
rho	.028	.018	.015	.010
Number =	4289		8539	
−2*log-likelihood =	119,626		2966	
Chi^2 =	406.4***		318.2***	

particular convention.[20] We present these models as descriptive rather than causal models. To analyze the amount of the contribution, we simply total all the contributions (in 2012 dollars) made by the individual or organization to the host committee for our first dependent variable. Our second dependent variable is the timing of the contribution. We standardize the timing measurement because the parties announce their host cities at different times and the cities set up their host committees at different times. It is standardized as the number of days the contribution occurred from the convention/total days the host committee raised funds prior to the convention.[21] Contributions made after the conventions have a negative value.[22]

The most desirable donor, from the perspective of a host committee, is one who gives generously and early. Table 3.2 shows three types of donors who fit this profile: donors who give to both party conventions in the same year, business donors (non-individual and non-foundation donors), and donors who spent freely in the previous presidential cycle. These types of donors are likely contributing substantial money early to use the convention for advertising purposes—to serve as advertised "sponsors" and/or to get the choice locations for hosting events. Local donors give significantly earlier than nonlocal donors, but the magnitude of the coefficient for the amount contributed is relatively small and its statistical significance depends on how the model is estimated.[23]

Donors who give to conventions of the same party in different years give significantly more, but significantly later than other donors. This suggests they are wealthy donors to whom the host committee is connected by the party network (including the presidential campaign) as the host committee expands beyond its initial lists of local and corporate donors. Foundations appear to be similar—they give a bit more, but give it late.[24] Because foundations cannot give to campaigns, it seems reasonable that they would not be obvious targets for political fundraisers and thus would be solicited later than others by the host committees.

GOP convention donors tend to give larger contributions. Confirming the descriptive findings in the previous section, out-partisan and mixed donors—people who do not consistently give to the candidates or organizations of the party hosting the convention—give significantly larger contributions (as shown by the negative sign for the partisan coefficient in the amount model) and contribute earlier than in-party donors. The fact that in-party donors contribute late also shows that host committees target access-oriented donors early in the process and mobilize partisans late as the excitement of the primary campaign and impending convention inspires partisans to get involved.

Individual donors tend to give significantly less and significantly later. In fact, as donors who give less than $250 generally are not reported to the

FEC, the findings underestimate the already low amount per donor given by individuals. Raising money "retail" from many individual donors is obviously more difficult than raising it from a few corporations, so it is not surprising that host committees actively seek out small individual donors only when their initial round of corporate solicitations does not raise the desired sums.

Washington, D.C., donors and unions also give significantly later. D.C. donors give for access, so they wait until the last minute to pay their "entry fee." Unions may follow a similar dynamic in Democratic conventions, but also may use their contributions as leverage to get the host city to deal more favorably with local unions (e.g., getting Denver to unionize a hotel, or Boston to reach an agreement with disgruntled public employee unions [Silberman, 2003]).

This analysis produces an ironic finding—the major political party convention donors are not terribly partisan. They are a motley coalition of locals supporting their city's big event and donor-class outsiders seeking access at the conventions. That latter group may not be highly partisan, but they are highly political. In this sense, the results confirm the stances of both the supporters of host committees and their critics. That is, host committees simultaneously raise local money to promote the hometown, and they collect substantial sums from corporations and traditional, high-end political donors who seek access to visiting politicians. When faced with high price tags for the convention spectacles, host committees rationally raise the money in the most efficient ways possible from those with the most resources and the most willingness to contribute.

Reform Redux

To analyze convention funding is to attempt to capture a moving target. As demonstrated by data earlier in this chapter, the role of private and federal government security financing has increased substantially, while the role of city government funding has declined over the past twenty years. Funding patterns for the 2016 conventions will shift again as Congress made significant changes to convention financing in 2014 by ending the role of funds from the presidential campaign check-off and creating a new means for the national parties to raise funds directly from wealthy donors. Changes in fundraising rules could make a substantial difference in which cities are able to bid, in how they develop fundraising strategies, and even how conventions may be conducted in the future (e.g., shortening the length or curtailing the lavishness of the conventions to minimize costs).

In 2014, Congress ended the public funding for conventions and committed its money in the presidential public funding account to pay for pediatric health research (Gabriella Miller Kids First Research Act). Conservatives had targeted convention funding for years based on objections to taxpayers funding a non-governmental activity. In an era of heightened concern about government spending and in a contest between party conventions and children's health, funding for party conventions was doomed.[25]

Soon after Congress's action, the FEC issued an advisory opinion (2014) empowering the national parties to raise convention funds more easily. The FEC allowed the national parties to establish separate accounts for convention donations and it simultaneously set a separate contribution limit for convention account donations. Since donations to party organizations were capped at $32,400 per election cycle, the FEC's decision meant that a donor could now contribute $32,400 to the Republican (or Democratic) National Committee and another $32,400 to the Republican (or Democratic) National Convention Committee. The FEC's rationale was based on the fact that donors have separate contribution limits for the national party committees, the Senate campaign committees, and the House campaign committees. The convention committees, then, for finance purposes, would be a distinct fourth federal party committee rather than a subcommittee of the national party committees.

Congress then included a rider in the 2015 budget codifying the FEC's creation of separate accounts for party conventions, and also allowing the national parties to create additional accounts for party-building funds and another for legal expenses, and tripling the contribution limits to all party committees. The maximum a single donor could give to party committees increased from $97,200 per election to $776,600 per election (or $1.56 million including both primaries and general elections), since there would now be seven party committees. After eliminating public funding for conventions in April, the parties realized the difficulty the ban would create in paying for conventions. The fact that the GOP had chosen then speaker John Boehner's home state of Ohio for its 2016 convention likely increased the salience for Congress of the convention funding changes. Rather than reinstating the use of public funds, as Democrats desired, or scaling back convention spending, Republicans sought a method of raising more funds from private donors (Confessore, 2014).

These reforms put the national parties back on center stage for raising convention funds. The new caps will allow very generous donors to give even more. Therefore, the changes will reinforce the parties' incentives to rely on a few wealthy donors to provide a disproportionate share of underwriting for the conventions. But there are caps—even if high ones—on convention contributions through parties, while there are no caps on contributions to host committees. Likewise, corporations and foundations still cannot contribute directly to the party convention accounts, but they can contribute to host committees. In short, host committees still have more flexibility in raising big money than the parties. Therefore, while the parties will have a greater role in convention funding than they have had since the passage of FECA in 1974, they are still likely to demand significant funding from host cities. Even if each party can raise the $18.2 million (in 2012 dollars) to replace the amounts that had been provided by the presidential election campaign fund, they had not been satisfied with this amount anyway and had host committees provide supplemental funding. Parties still have the incentive to push for the most lavish and well-produced events that the market of bid cities can bear. Because of these incentives, and host committees' relative advantages in fundraising, the recent reforms will alter the parties' funding role more than the cities'.

If, in the unlikely event that the parties' ability to raise their own money for the conventions takes some of the pressure from host committees, the committees may actually be in a better place to fund convention activities than they have been since FECA. Such a situation may make bidding for conventions more attractive to more cities, particularly medium-size cities with limited pools of political donors. The FEC's decision to lift the cap on out-of-town corporate contributions in 2003 allows host committees access to the easiest sources of money to raise, and cities can still offer donors the best sites for their convention-related events. Thus, cities may be raising more money from the usual suspects for promotion of the city rather than producing the party infomercial.

Nevertheless, the new fundraising regime presents at least two substantial risks for cities. One risk is that the parties now have an incentive to ask big individual donors to contribute to the party's convention account rather than allowing host committees to solicit from those individuals. Obviously, big donors can give to both the party and the host committee, but parties are likely to want to take their cuts from their top donors first. And the donors would be understandably reluctant to give twice to different organizations to support the same event. Likewise, parties have an incentive to hit up their small donor lists for convention contributions rather than allowing host committees access to them. If parties monopolize the partisan donors for themselves, host committees are likely to emphasize fundraising from corporations and local donors where they have the competitive advantage. In other words, we are likely to see a division of labor in convention fundraising.

Another risk to cities would be Congress further trimming the federal contribution by scaling back the federal security grant. Should this occur, host committees again would face pressure to come up with funds to cover the city's security costs and cities again would have to struggle with appropriating funds for security and/or serving as a backstop if their host committee failed to raise sufficient funds to cover local security costs.

In many ways, the state of convention funding is returning to its pre-Watergate roots—for better or worse. Public financing from voluntary individual contributions is gone. Parties now face considerable responsibility for raising the funds on their own. Parties will still want cities to put on the best possible show for delegates, dignitaries, and the media, so they will still encourage cities and their host committees to make generous financial commitments in their bids. And cities will still face the quandary of how and where to come up with the money: How much should come from city general funds, how much should come from tourism bureaus and hotel/restaurant taxes, and how much can be raised locally in a community-chest drive? The cities and the parties will now be more equal partners in funding conventions and, like their partnership to implement conventions, will require equal measures of planning and adaptability.

4

Unconventional Conventions

Protests, Hurricanes, and Other Logistical Nightmares

I lay awake many a night. I lay awake out of fear of hurricanes, and in anticipation of hosting this event.

—Tampa mayor Bob Buckhorn[1]

In chapter 2, we discussed the importance of the host city being a "reliable agent" for the political parties and other attendees who depend on the city to deliver on its promises during a political convention. Therefore, how well the stakeholders communicate and plan in the intergovernmental system becomes a critical dimension to the city's success. But often cities are new to this venture and in order to place a competitive bid, they may make promises that are difficult to keep. And it is easy to see why. The requirements for hosting a political convention are very different than running the day-to-day operations of a city.

In this chapter, we argue that when a city hosts a national political convention it is not like putting on a sporting event, parade, festival, or a trade association meeting. A national political convention is a more complex event than most cities have encountered. Normal routines are disrupted and typical city operations are not sufficient. City leaders have to give up some of their autonomy and standard operating procedures due to the substantial intergovernmental and inter-organizational coordination and planning that is required. Such mega-events demand working with the federal government, state government (and sometimes multiple states in the region), local governments, the DNC or RNC, private businesses and property managers, and nonprofits. Cities will find that it is much more than planning for a packed stadium of football or baseball fans. They simply cannot treat the convention like it is one of these events but just larger in scale and longer onstage. The political convention itself may not involve as many visitors (around forty thousand or less), but because of the security risk and the political nature of the event the normal routine responses to sporting events or trade shows will be ineffective.

Hosting a political convention requires an understanding of the explicit political nature of this type of intergovernmental event—conventions bring the media, elected officials, donors, campaign consultants, interest groups, lobbyists, party activists, and, in many cases, the current and past presidents of the United States to the event. Cities must anticipate that anarchists will attempt to disrupt delegates and residents and that the highly ranked political leaders are targets for assassination plots. For example, one group targeted President Gerald Ford and challenger Ronald Reagan at the RNC in 1976, and Barack Obama was targeted at the DNC in Denver in 2008 (Hosenball, 2008). This makes a political convention a "National Special Security Event" (Reese, 2013), so host cities must now also work within a new post-9/11 homeland security system, which raises the complexity and stakes of intergovernmental planning, coordination, and logistics. Cities now need to balance the significant security measures and mass demonstrations with the ordinary transportation and work needs of their residents. Most cities have limited experience with such security precautions, especially at post-9/11 levels, as well as with integrating thousands of police officers temporarily into their own department (and housing them, feeding them, and supplying their equipment).

Security is of course vital in its own right, but it is also one of many implementation activities that are critical to the city achieving a payoff from its investment in recruiting a presidential nominating convention. Much of the economic promise of a political convention is based on the public relations visibility and "branding" that media attention brings. If the city looks good on television and is well managed during the convention, its ability to attract future trade and fraternal conventions, businesses, and residents is enhanced. While the city cannot control all outcomes or the reporting of them, preparing for the worst can help the city manage or mitigate those inherent risks. There are several examples of how convention cities have had logistical problems that overshadowed the convention coverage itself and presented an undesirable image of the city and of other organizations involved. Cases like the 1968 Democratic National Convention in Chicago have even become notable historical events.

This chapter highlights some examples of past convention problems and focuses on the importance of planning, communication, coordination, and adaptability of the host city in an intergovernmental environment. It will also discuss how operations of previous political conventions have provided both academic and practical lessons that can mitigate dealing with potential problems such as protests, disruption costs, and even weather in an intergovernmental management context.

Planning and Coordination

The unique demands of a presidential nominating convention put a premium on planning and coordination across federal levels of government and between public and private organizations, allowing for the development of a general strategy decided by principals as well as nuts-and-bolts implementation by street-level bureaucrats who have face-to-face contact with the public. The city's goal is not only to learn from previous host cities and adapt the lessons to their context as they develop plans and contingency plans, but to build relationships so that when the unexpected occurs, the participants have the trust and experience to work through it effectively.

When hosting the 2012 Democratic National Convention, the city of Charlotte's planning was led by the DNC Coordination Committee. It was compromised of representatives of several city and county departments, federal security agencies, the host committee and the Democratic National Convention Committee.[2] It met twice a month in the year leading up to the convention, weekly for two months prior the convention, and every morning the week of the convention to decide and implement general strategies. Its members represented seven committees that provided a unified command structure for major implementation activities (City-Host Coordination, DNC Safety and Security, City Transportation and Operations, DNC Permitting, Parade and Event Permitting, Communications Steering, and Operations Coordination). Subcommittees had jurisdiction over specific elements of implementation. The Safety and Security Committee alone had twenty-three subcommittees.[3] Subcommittees often involved private-sector organizations that were critical to implementation. Duke Energy, for example, was critical to establishing a second power source for the arena, as well as for scheduling and credentialing key employees to be on-call during the convention to deal with electric/utility issues.[4] Such a cross-agency, public-private planning environment creates an unusual opportunity for building working relationships that facilitate communication and adaptability during the stressful days of the convention.

Security is at the core of planning and is a challenge because of its effects on all the other elements of planning, the variety of agencies involved, and the inherent limitations on information that can be shared with local residents ahead of time. Security is also the main responsibility of the city government since most of the other key logistical tasks are delegated to the host committee (see chapter 1). Host cities must now work within a new national homeland security system. According to Don Kettl, "We talk about homeland security as if we know what it means. In practice there is a surprising level of confusion, disagreement, or at the very least difference in emphasis among state and local governments. . . . At the core of the problem of homeland security is some disagreement about what homeland security is, who ought to be in charge of it, and how it ought to work" (Kettl, 2007: 322).

The Charlotte-Mecklenburg Police Department was the lead local law enforcement agency on the assignment, responsible for researching local ordinances and lobbying the North Carolina legislature for temporary state legislation allowing out-of-state law enforcement to assist during the DNC. While they knew that a secure perimeter would have to be established around the convention site, credentialing would need to occur, and a command center would have to be established, the details of such a project were unclear at the time the legislation was requested.

Within the security zone, all types of city services would need to be provided. As explained by Charlotte fire chief Jon Hannan:

> We built two fire stations in the secure zone. Then the stations grew as other city departments also needed personnel in the zone for immediate responses—solid waste, utilities. For example, if protesters made a mess or there was some type of utility problem, city leaders wanted it cleaned up immediately.[5]

A mobile hospital also was stationed in the security zone to get convention-eers back into the arena quickly and, in cases requiring emergency treatment, stabilize patients before sending them to the hospital.[6] While major facilities were constructed inside the security perimeter, the city's mass transit center, located across the street from the arena, had to be relocated outside of it and reestablished at a temporary location for the week.[7]

Outside of the security zone, a large expansion of security cameras and a new police video observation center helped security forces respond immediately to crime and security threats (Leland, 2012). The city also used specially developed software to monitor social media to identify and respond immediately to potential snafus (Bell, 2012). The software identified clusters of communications on particular city services and the location of those communications. This assisted the city in determining where traffic lights were out or where water created hazards in roadways during thunderstorms. It also helped the city identify and respond to rumors.

Moreover, the greatest challenge in security planning is not developing plan A, but developing a variety of contingency plans and retaining the capacity to adapt to unanticipated situations. Harold Medlock, the deputy chief of the Charlotte-Mecklenburg Police Department (CMPD), who was in charge of planning convention security for the 2012 DNC, observed that the biggest fear about homeland security was the "element of the unknown."[8] Despite the contingency planning, Medlock still feared that there may be complexities that they could not anticipate for a city that had no experience planning for a political convention.

While the DNC was not the largest event they had planned for, it had different challenges from other large events. One challenge was the fact that three different security arrangements had to be planned: the first for Sunday's "March on Wall Street South" protests, the second for the arena from Tuesday through Thursday, and the third for the president's planned acceptance speech in Bank of America stadium on Thursday. A second challenge was the political nature whereby any local, national, or international event could alter the course of the planning, requiring a level of immediate flexibility for adapting development and implementation of security plans. This required constructing constant alternative plans in an organization that was based on set operating procedures.[9] Last-minute changes in barricade and fence locations, for example, caused the emergency planning team to rewrite emergency routes and personnel deployment plans on convention eve.[10] Local security personnel were also not operating in a vacuum. Any change of plans meant that they had to coordinate with the host committee, the Charlotte Fire Department, the federal Secret Service, and every key business unit in the city and county (such as solid waste, utilities, transit, procurement, etc.).

Plans and changes of plans also had to be communicated to the community. As Democratic National Convention Committee president Steve Kerrigan observed, "People are hungry for information, but the worst thing to do is to give people incomplete information" (Henderson, 2012: 9A). The coordination committee established a Joint Information Center with representatives of all its committees and member organizations to disseminate information to the public and to be available to answer questions.[11] The Joint Information Center supplemented and complemented the city's normal communications mechanisms. The center established a website to be the communication hub for convention activities. It provided general information as well as the full gamut of details on road closures, health precautions for standing in summer heat during the president's expected outdoor acceptance speech, sign-ups to protest or use the parade route, fire code and capacity information for venues hosting convention events, information for vendors on obtaining contracts and permits, and so on. Users could sign up for special alerts on topics of interest to them. Importantly, the website housed the convention message board where community organizations could send their constituents to exchange information. The center also organized meetings between coordination committee members, including the city departments and the Secret Service, and employers, building managers, and others directly affected by convention planning. The meetings were particularly critical in providing information to affected organizations while it was still officially embargoed from public dissemination.

The challenges of balancing security with public access as well as planning with adaptability are most apparent in three areas: allowing peaceful demonstrations, instituting a security perimeter while mitigating the disruption costs to local businesses and residents, and adapting to extreme weather events. Managing such activities effectively can earn cities reputations for competence from attendees and residents; mismanaging them minimizes the reputational benefits a city might attain from hosting the convention.

Preparing for Protests

Just as cities seek conventions for the public relations value of them, all types of interest groups also utilize the convention as an amplifier for their views to be heard by social and traditional media (like Occupy Wall Street, Black Lives Matter, ACT UP, or One Thousand Coffins). For example, in 2000 in Los Angeles, the August Collective held their North American Anarchists conference right before the DNC took place and offered members free lodging and food to attract protesters to the convention. Right before, major riots took place at the World Trade Organization Conference in Seattle and in Washington, D.C., which hosted the International Monetary Fund troubling convention organizers. Charlotte police assisted Chicago police during the May 2012 NATO meetings and adjusted their plans in response to anarchist tactics during the protests.[12] In 2008, a group of prolife activists from American Right to Life Action put together a sign on Table Mountain outside Denver overlooking the convention that said: Destroys uNborn Children (DNC).

Conventions notoriously attract activists that are intent on capturing the spotlight from the events inside the hall and raise awareness of particular political issues such as war or the economy. Those problems are often exacerbated when the convention is held in a downtown area and requires substantial security. Outside of Washington, D.C., and New York City, most city police departments do not regularly deal with large-scale protests and thus a city's preparations and training of its forces is imperative.

The risk to a city's reputations from protesters is apparent in the exemplar that every city tries to avoid, the infamous 1968 Chicago Democratic National Convention where violence erupted when anti–Vietnam War protestors clashed with police. The demonstrations and subsequent riots occurred when a group of activists planned a protest march at the convention that August. Antiwar leaders coordinated the efforts of more than one hundred antiwar groups. Tensions were already running high throughout the country because Martin Luther King, Jr., and presidential candidate Robert F. Kennedy had been assassinated only months prior (Mailer, 2008).

Democrats were eager to move the convention out of Chicago and to Miami in order to avoid protesters and an ongoing telephone strike that would create severe logistical problems. However, Mayor Richard Daley would not let the convention go, and promised to enforce the peace. Allegedly, he threatened party leaders that he would refuse to endorse Hubert Humphrey as the presidential nominee if the convention was moved out of Chicago. Meanwhile, outside the convention violence erupted between antiwar demonstrators and police. The violence emanated from two sources: Chicago police forced protesters out of the areas where they were not supposed to be, and protesters fought police, the National Guard, Secret Service agents, and U.S. Army troops. By the time the convention ended, the Chicago police had arrested 589 people, and 219 people were injured. The riots were all over the newspapers and broadcast on television (Mailer, 2008). It would be a convention that we still talk about almost fifty years later!

To a lesser degree, the 2008 Republican convention in St. Paul also had problems managing protesters. While the city was awarded a $50 million federal security grant, largely to pay for 3,500 additional officers during the convention, protests broke out immediately (PBS, 2008). Or, as more colorfully described by a St. Paul newspaper, "Essentially, all hell broke loose" (Sundquist 2008), as demonstrators blocked intersections, broke windows, slashed tires of police vehicles, and hurled urine- and feces-laden projectiles at police. Police responded with tear gas and pepper spray. Ramsey County sheriff Bob Fletcher called it "eight hours of chaos and mayhem" (Kersten 2008, 1B). Almost three hundred people were arrested on the first day of the convention, including nineteen journalists, during an antiwar march of more than ten thousand people in downtown St. Paul. One hundred and thirty-seven were charged with felonies such as "conspiracy to commit riot" (MPR, 2008).

Several suits were filed in U.S. District Court claiming civil rights abuses by the St. Paul Police Department, the Minneapolis Police Department, and the Ramsey County Sheriff's Office (MPR, 2008).

The fact that protests and the potential for violent clashes with police will occur during political conventions is well known to cities considering bids. Once the parties announce the host city, convention organizers have about eighteen months to prepare for protests and need to start the planning process immediately. While the types of groups vary significantly, there are some common elements of convention protests. Cities can look to other examples of how protests were handled in the past, both successfully (Los Angeles, Denver, Charlotte) and unsuccessfully (Chicago, New York, and St. Paul). For example, when the DNC was held in Los Angeles, a city known for riots, the LAPD began planning right after the bid for the convention was won. They required a minimum of sixteen hours of training for police, a public demonstration area was set aside, and the police established a dialogue with protesters. At the end of the convention there were less than two hundred arrests—the majority for misdemeanors—and there were no reports of serious injuries (LAPD, 2000).

When planning for the DNC in Charlotte, city officials capitalized on knowledge from conventions of past years, especially Denver's 2008 planning processes. Denver had declared their convention an "Extraordinary Event" so they would not have to revise city ordinances for a onetime event like the DNC. The declaration allowed for the ordinance to have a specific start and end time, just the duration of the convention. Charlotte city manager Curt Walton followed suit for 2012. The key was getting all of the different local government offices, such as public works, legal, police, and permitting together, and coordinating where and how protests could take place peacefully. Convention cities need to think about balancing First Amendment rights against maintaining peace and protecting property. According to Charlotte city attorney Bob Hagemann, "Free Speech and public security are not mutually exclusive."[13] He noted that the city can legally regulate the time, place, and manner of speech. Free speech at the convention is governed by four standards: 1) Content neutrality—rules must apply to all groups regardless of the content of speech; 2) Important government interest—public safety and preserving citizens' ability to get to and from work; 3) Narrowly tailored rules—rules must be tied directly to the public interest, no all-purpose security rationale should be used; and 4) the availability of alternative method of communication—city restrictions are acceptable if demonstrators have the ability to get their messages out in other ways.

There is a long history of lawsuits against convention cities for violating First Amendment rights. In 2004 and 2008, all four cities were sued before the conventions they hosted were even under way,[14] as were Cleveland and Philadelphia in 2016. To avoid such suits, city officials need to plan carefully the times, places, and manners of demonstrations and how law enforcement officers should interact with protesters. This is often facilitated through a larger group of organizations that form a coordination committee or local core planning team. This group should develop a strategic vision that focuses on protecting the Constitutional rights of attendees and fostering a peaceful environment. The U.S. Department of Justice recommends that planning groups should work closely with conflict resolution groups and known activists to understand how to adapt their policing styles to ensure protection of activists, patrons, delegates, and VIPs (Bureau of Justice Assistance, 2013: 18).

Within this planning group, a subcommittee can be assigned the task of looking at the existing ordinances and identifying what, if any, new ordinances need to be adopted well in advance of the convention (Bureau of Justice Assistance, 2013: 18). For example, Charlotte city officials were concerned about Occupy Charlotte, a local group inspired by Occupy Wall Street, groups well known for protesting against economic inequality, governmental corruption, and corporate influence (Eskow, 2012). Occupy Charlotte deemed Charlotte the "Wall Street of the South" and built a tent city on the lawn of the old city hall building in late September 2011. While camping was prohibited in local parks, it was not banned on the lawn of old city hall, since local officials never anticipated anyone trying to camp there.[15] The incident sent a clear message that existing ordinances would be inadequate to handle the types of protests that typically accompany political conventions.

In response, the city crafted ordinances designed to avoid major conflicts with protesters while maintaining free speech. For example, the city passed an ordinance for the Enforcement of Extraordinary Events (See appendix A). The purpose of the ordinance was to allow law enforcement to identify risks and individuals intent on doing harm at a large-scale event. The ordinance prohibits specific items such as bars, chains, cables, plastic pipes, aerosol containers, spray guns, soaker devices, backpacks, coolers, rocks, bottle, bricks, and so on. No masks or scarfs can be worn to hide a person's identity. Only service animals are allowed. And it prohibits explosive items such as fireworks, smoke bombs, sparklers, and stink bombs (Charmeck.org, 2012).

Additionally, the police strategy was to contain demonstrations that moved outside of the parade routes, then "deescalate" the conflict by having the police chief personally meet with group leaders in the street and develop a rapport.[16] For example, when demonstrators blocked an intersection, police rerouted traffic around them and demonstrators moved on. The police were given the discretion to enforce the new ordinances leniently as long as demonstrators were not violent or causing larger trouble (Cooke and Alexander, 2012). As a result, only twenty-five arrests were made; fifteen of those were for obstructing traffic, and sixteen (some of which overlapped with the traffic obstructions) were "negotiated"—meaning the demonstrators wanted to be arrested.[17]

Since hosting a convention involves security of the site, a lead person should be identified from the police department who has decision-making authority, serves as the incident commander for the planning phase, reports to the planning body, and tests the operational plan prior to the event. This can be a discussion-based exercise or "tabletop exercise" aimed at identifying knowledge gaps for authorities early on in the convention planning process. The operational security plan can be tested at an earlier event, such as a Fourth of July celebration (Bureau of Justice Assistance, 2013). This will allow for the operational plans to be both tested and adjusted.

After the riots at the 2008 RNC in St. Paul, the Republican National Committee appointed a commission to investigate safety planning and implementation of the convention. The report analyzed law enforcement's public safety plan during the convention, examined the implementation of the plan, and determined how the plan was executed (RRNCPSPIRC, 2009). The commission developed several useful recommendations with regard to planning, coordinating, and adapting when dealing with protesters during the convention.

The commission's report first recommends that a vision needs to be communicated to the local citizenry prior to the convention about what a peaceful event would look like, as well as information about the potential for violence and the need for a substantial police presence. Dialogue should occur between police and protest groups about what exactly they can expect to see (such as high fencing, helicopters, and police in riot gear), and these plans should be further communicated to the public. Originally, St. Paul planned to use the "dialogue officer model" used in Europe. The dialogue officers would act as a team of police officers that had training in negotiations and would produce and distribute a brochure about the right to demonstrate and protest. While these teams were originally set to be stationed throughout downtown St. Paul during the convention, the plan was never implemented (RRNCPSPIRC, 2009: 7).

The commission also recommended that law enforcement should use the National Incident Management System (NIMS) model for event management in conjunction with the Secret Service. The NIMS framework provides for six major operations: Command and Management, Preparedness, Resource Management, Communications and Information Management, Support Technologies, and Ongoing Management and Maintenance. Initially, St. Paul did plan to use NIMS for the RNC and included it in its Civil Disturbance Plan. However, this plan was abandoned after the Secret Services said it did not use NIMS for this type of event (RRNCPSPIRC, 2009: 7).

A year prior to the 2008 RNC, St. Paul police officers attend a federal sponsored training program in Georgia titled "Managing Civil Actions in Threat Incidents." Several officers from the Minneapolis Police Department (MPD) attended the training but then objected to the use of weapon systems for crowd control. Because of these objections, the training program was cancelled and the MPD conducted their training (RRNCPSPIRC, 2009: 13). The report found that police officers need this type of training in order to stop anarchist groups, as police were not properly trained to deal with them during the riot. In addition, the committee recommended that police officers at the convention should have worn visible personal and departmental identification—including when they wear tactical gear (RRNCPSPIRC, 2009: 76–77).

At the convention in St. Paul, there were more than fifteen thousand local, national, and international journalists covering the convention. They were to be given access to the RNC's proceedings and demonstrations. However, there was a lack of clarity as to how police would identify and treat journalists during the convention. For example, there was no established protocol for arresting members of the media. This is an example of how federal recommendations were ignored because the host city believed they already knew what they were doing based on previous smaller events they had hosted. The federal government recommends that the city meet with representatives of local media prior to the convention on a regular basis and establish a working relationship (RRNCPSPIRC, 2009: 19). They also suggest that the host city should develop a system that permits journalists to obtain law enforcement–recognized credentials prior the convention in case they are detained or arrested. Community service officers should also work with public information officers to help journalists who are detained or arrested (RRNCPSPIRC, 2009: 79–80). All of these are items that cities may not have ever been exposed to and demonstrate a difference in cultures across various levels of government, especially federal-local relations.

Disruption Costs from Security

In addition to preparing for protests, cities that host conventions post-9/11 are now considered targets for terrorists and must balance economic development with increased public safety concerns (Savitch, 2003). Extra patrols, command and control centers, fencing, steel barriers, crowd control, air and water space restrictions, checkpoints, and surveillance cameras all create obstacles for local residents and workers intent on doing business as usual. These security measures are also often foreign to a host city and residents if they have not hosted a political convention since 9/11. Despite the federal security grant of $50 million to pay for additional security (see chapter 3), the grant does not mitigate the economic losses from the displacement of business activity from the security zone and adjacent areas.

The security plans required for hosting the Republican and Democratic national conventions call for closing transportation arteries and several city blocks around venues. While these measures protect dignitaries inside the security zone, they also impose significant disruption costs on employers, employees, residents, and tourists (Heberlig et al., 2016). The host city is expected to have a secure area where the convention would take place, and this involves shutting off normal access to a portion of a city's downtown area. Anyone entering the secure zone would have to be credentialed before the convention. Delivery trucks have to be inspected before being allowed in the perimeter, a measure that adds extra expense to deliveries in terms of time.

The impact of security on local residents and businesses became most apparent in the 2004 Boston DNC, the first convention to be held after the 9/11 terrorist attacks on the World Trade Center and Pentagon. The event was designated a National Special Security Event (NSSE) by the recently established Department of Homeland Security. This special designation meant that the Secret Service, not the local police force, would now be the lead agency because security measures would now be given authority to direct the local police. The planning process would now follow a top-down intergovernmental model and the security officials would be the ones to define the desired outcome, not the transportation officials or city planners. This meant that the planning and transportation officials involved in the 2004 convention would have to figure out how to achieve the desired security-orientated outcomes set forth by the Secret Service (DeBlasio, Regan, Ziker, Hassol, Austin, 2005: xv).

As Boston's Fleet Center housed one of two commuter rail lines and two of four subway lines and sat adjacent to Interstate 93, the security precautions would substantially affect the mobility of those who live and work in the downtown (U.S. Department of Transportation, 2005). All of those had to be shut down during the 2004 DNC, costing the city an estimated $36.7 million (Beacon Hill Institute, 2004). It also means that approximately thirty thousand people—any dignitaries, delegate, or members of the media who planned on attending the convention—had to be credentialed with a more rigorous screening process (DeBlasio, Regan, Ziker, Hassol, Austin, 2005). Transit riders had their bags inspected in the week prior to the convention (Rosinski, 2004). The Coast Guard increased random checks of boats and water taxis, and sections of the Charles River were off-limits without special permission (Chesto, 2004). The development of an operations plan for city officials was "slow and painstaking," because there were so many different agencies involved (DeBlasio, Regan, Ziker, Hassol, Austin, 2005: xii). Northern suburbs of Boston in particular were concerned about the gridlock and policing costs caused by the diversion of traffic off of I-93 in their communities (Caywood, 2004). It required federal, state, and local governments to collaborate on how to keep the city secure during the convention.

The operation plan required transportation planners to figure out how to reduce road traffic in the area by 50% in order to prevent complete gridlock. The plan designated forty miles of roads to be closed or restricted for four days including Interstate 93 nightly during the convention (Straub, 2004). Massachusetts Bay Transportation Authority (MBTA) and private transit providers also had to adapt their services around the secured perimeter. This meant five commuter rail lines were stopped north of Boston and two subway lines were "expressed" through the area without stopping (DeBlasio, Regan, Ziker, Hassol, Austin, 2005: xiii). While Boston communicated extensively with the public to warn them of the transportation disruptions and alternative options, it is telling that part of the strategy included "frighten[ing] people with tales of nightmare traffic jams so many commuters leave town on vacation or call in sick during the Democrats' summer parley" (Meyer, 2004). As Mayor Menino admitted, "What we're doing is ringing the alarm bell and saying the sky is falling" (quoted in Meyer, 2004). Headlines in the hometown paper stating, "Commuter Hell Begins in Just a Week" (Szaniszlo, 2004), are undoubtedly not what city leaders anticipated when they recruited the DNC.

As Boston demonstrated clearly, the security required at a political convention now disrupts normal operations of the city and causes major headaches for the people that own businesses or live or work within the convention's security area. This of course can be mitigated by good communication with the public and employers. With appropriate planning, many businesses may be able to use remote work locations or allow employees to work at home during the convention to relieve the stress on local transportation and the loss of productivity to the employers. Effective communication may include meeting frequently with property owners and managers in and around the security zones to providing them with information to pass on to their businesses and residents. This means working with the school district to assist with rerouting buses around the parade routes and with surrounding towns whose hotels would be hosting delegates, media personnel, and affinity groups. This means cities need to understand the importance of having integrated databases for successfully communicating road closures, disruptions in public services, how to make deliveries within the security perimeter, and the relocation of public transit with citizens. Cities also should use different forms of social media to get information out to the public in a proactive way.[18]

Philadelphia was selected to be the host city for the 2016 Democratic National Convention primarily because the city did not need as large a perimeter around its convention facilities as the other cities that bid, and most hotels were within a fifteen-minute walk. A Democratic official familiar with the decision said the choice was "a close call among the three" and came down almost entirely to logistics. A factor that hurt both Brooklyn's and Columbus's bids was the huge security perimeter of a modern convention, which requires surrounding blocks to be fenced off well ahead of the convention (Cheney and Allen, 2015).

As demonstrated in the examples above, planning and communication for transportation logistics is critical in the bidding process and throughout the duration of the convention. This need is heightened by the extra security that needs to be provided in the post-9/11 era. Transportation is often one of the major issues that will impact the perception of how well the city has hosted the convention for both its residents and visitors. The Report on Managing Large-Scale Security Events recommends extensive collaboration with the stakeholder, developing an operational plan, having the ability to be flexible, using police officers and signage to notify citizens and visitors to alert them of transportation changes, and separating traffic command into smaller activities. They also note the importance of special transportation for VIPs/delegates. This may often involve including a plan to transport the president to and from the convention site. A best practice for cities hosting a convention would be to work with city traffic engineers to design road closures (Bureau of Justice Assistance, 2013).

Weather

Republicans ended their national convention in 2012 a day early because of the threat of Hurricane Isaac, potentially a category 2 storm that wound up remaining a tropical storm. This was the second consecutive time the RNC's schedule was adjusted due to weather. The first was in St. Paul in 2008 because Hurricane Gustav was heading toward New Orleans after it hit Florida. At the start of the convention on the first day, events were canceled to avoid the appearance of insensitivity.

Unlike protests, which are a given with a political convention, weather is less predictable and more of an "unknown." Conventions are often held during the hurricane season (August), when it can be unusually warm and stormy. Outdoor venues such as stadiums may make convention events rather unpleasant for visitors. And for security reasons, most umbrellas are banned (Wilmath, 2012).

While weather is a factor taken into consideration, it typically takes a backseat to the importance of timing because the chance of such an event would be highly unusual. In fact, the odds of a hurricane hitting the Tampa Bay area between August 27 and 30, when the 2012 Republican National Convention took place, was less than 1%, according to the National Weather Service (Wilmath, 2012). Yet it came close.

Planning for extreme heat, floods, or hurricanes during these events has also largely been ignored in the planning and communication literature, but is essential to convention planning. Even in the Bureau of Justice Event Planner there is not a mention of preparing for specific weather conditions. They include "weather hazard" in the pre-event planning matrix and a section on conducting a hazard vulnerability assessment, which could include severe weather like a tornado, hurricane, or flood. They recommend assigning a frequency distribution for each potential hazard but do not go into detail about planning.

In the case of Tampa, delegates and protesters headed to Tampa Bay despite the warnings about Tropical Storm Isaac. State and local officials started monitoring Isaac's development closely and began to plan for the case of the RNC canceling the event or Tampa's evacuation. Back in May, Florida state emergency officials conducted a tabletop exercise called "Hurricane Gispert," named after retired Hillsborough County emergency manager Larry Gispert, as their annual disaster drill. They planned for it to hit in the middle of the convention with fifty thousand visitors, fifty-six hundred delegates, and up to fifteen thousand journalists in the storm's path (Wilmath, 2012). But local officials noted after the exercise that the decisions to evacuate Tampa would have to be made during the event by the mayor of Tampa, even though ultimately it would be up to the Republican Party and convention organizers to determine whether the convention itself would be canceled. There was a real possibility that if a hurricane were forecast, the mayor of Tampa would be put on the "hot seat" if he evacuated and the storm veered off at the last minute. But the mayor said it was a risk he was willing to take (Wilmath, 2012). "If you think about it, a storm on the scarier side would make the decision easier on convention planners and the city," said Daniel Noah, a forecaster from the National Weather Service. "In that case they would probably just cancel the whole thing" (Wilmath, 2012).

Unfortunately for Tampa, they got a more ambiguous forecast. The RNC was uncertain about canceling the convention, or even part of the convention, until the day before it would kickoff. Two days prior to the convention, officials from the RNC, the state, federal, and local government, and the National Hurricane Center met with the governor of Florida (Rick Scott) and discussed what issues would be involved if high wind, heavy rain, flooding, power outages, and bridge closings occurred in Tampa during the convention. At that meeting, they decided that the convention would not be disrupted by Tropical Storm Isaac. Festivities would continue as planned.

However, the next day, one day prior to the start of the start of the convention, at a briefing at the Broward County Emergency Operations Center, there was a projection that Tropical Storm Isaac was expected to become a category 2 hurricane, with a potential to strike the Keys and the Florida Panhandle. The RNC decided to respond by revising its schedule holding the convention only briefly on Monday morning, but then recessing until Tuesday in hopes that the storm would have passed by the area by then. The governor also canceled his appearance at the convention. This decision shortened the convention from four days to three. Fortunately, the storm did little physical damage during the convention. However, it certainly sidelined attention from presidential candidate Mitt Romney (Kurtz, 2012). At the end of the convention, one could say Tampa narrowly avoided a huge disaster—one that would have damaged its image considerably, ruined months of planning, and wasted millions of dollars.

Lessons Learned: Intergovernmental Management Considerations

With eighty-eight thousand-plus governments and private and nonprofit actors, the U.S. federal system is riddled with complexity, interdependence, and bargaining (Wright, 1974; O'Toole, 1988). The responsibilities vary significantly across different policy areas. Lines of authority can be distinct, blurred, and even misunderstood depending on the nature of the policy (Wright, 1974; O'Toole, 1988). For this reason, scholars such as Agranoff and McGuire (2003) have developed different management models of intergovernmental networks in order to understand these dynamics. Viewing the participants involved in convention planning, coordination, and communication as an intergovernmental management network is potentially useful to both scholars and practitioners.

When cities engage in hosting a convention, they are used to utilizing a jurisdiction-based model for planning events. According to Agranoff and McGuire (2003), a jurisdiction-based model of management is most apparent in a highly complex administrative context. An example of this type of management would be a city hosting a political convention receiving input from the other major stakeholders such as political parties, interest groups, businesses, and other governments in formulating their plan. The host city also receives funding in the form of a grant from the federal government to defray security costs. Because the city is accustomed to this model, they assume that have considerable autonomy in controlling the planning process as they do with most of their operations involving large events. But hosting other large conventions or major events is typically different from hosting the Republican or Democratic National Convention because of the increased risk of terrorism, riots, and heavy national and international media exposure. Cities also are not used to the federal government's involvement beyond giving monetary assistance in the form of grants-in-aid, especially when it comes to directing local police and firefighters.

However, because of the new national focus on homeland security post-9/11, the old way of following the jurisdictional intergovernmental model needs to be altered to one that allows for a top-down federal approach in the area of security with the flexibility to allow for local government input and culture. This new type of intergovernmental model essentially needs to call for a balance of local autonomy and customs in some areas but must give way to federal autonomy in others important to national security. Top-down intergovernmental relations and jurisdictional and management models have not really been developed to accommodate this give and take. Instead, when there is federal involvement, the top-down model has persisted throughout time in intergovernmental relations. Vertical relationships work well with traditional bureaucratic models that value efficiency and effectiveness (chain of command, specialization, span of control), but they commonly clash with the political and legal values of responsiveness, representation, due process, and accountability in the intergovernmental system. Typically, when they encounter top-down models of federalism from the federal governments, subnational governments are essentially "coerced" into implementing those particular policies but do not necessarily embrace them. An example is categorical grants that stipulate very strict criteria on how money is spent. Subnational actors act simply as "monitors," which strains implementation of the policies (Agranoff and McGuire, 2003).

A significant weakness of the top-down model is that it is very rational and assumes perfect information and cooperation in the implementation process.

But it does not take into consideration state and local officials' organizational cultures and norms (Agranoff and McGuire, 2003). For example, in the case of the 2008 protests in St. Paul, the local police believed the type of training the federal government wanted did not fit their local way of doing things nor what residents were used to in terms of riot gear and tall, barbed-wire fences. They did not complete the recommended training by federal officials nor did they follow through on the recommendations of meeting with the protesters and educating citizens prior to the event. This proved to be a very costly mistake for the city and resulted in injuries and the death of a reporter.

Implementation from the top-town model is also highly dependent on Congress and the presidency to set the policy direction and not the state or local governments. It does not account well for jurisdictional differences, and this cookie-cutter approach may not work everywhere (Agranoff and McGuire, 2003). Its strength lies in that national control can be advantageous when state and local resources and knowledge are overwhelmed and dealing with extraordinary events like political conventions. .

Conclusions: Preparing for the "Unknown"

Hosting a convention is a risky proposition, given that it takes area cities and residents to be both well informed and flexible in working with a complex network of actors, and willing to give up some autonomy over everyday operations to the federal security agencies. Cities must know to the best of their ability what resources they have at their disposal to coordinate how they would respond to the "unknown." Most importantly, these cases illustrate that the "unknown" is actually pretty well known, but lack of knowledge of the actual probability of the event and the details that could help them prevent or mitigate it nevertheless causes considerable anxiety for government officials as in the case of Tampa's Mayor Buckhorn in the introductory quote. Potential disasters such as hurricanes, violent protests, and death threats can create tremendous stress prior to and during the convention and there is a large investment at stake. But as this chapter has demonstrated, city officials hosting conventions can plan for these events in a systematic way by learning from past convention planning and understanding the dynamics of intergovernmental relations. It is also likely that a lasting effect of hosting a political convention is an opportunity to improve the working relationships and trust between cities, counties, states, the federal government, businesses, nonprofits, and citizens. It is an opportunity to learn in a system of government where cities act as "laboratories of democracy" when hosting extraordinary events.

Successful hosts will pass on policies about dealing with ordinances, communicating with the public, and securing venues during the events. Less successful hosts will signal what can and will possibly go wrong.

An example of these intergovernmental laboratories at work was when Charlotte hosted the DNC in 2012. Recall, Deputy Police Chief Medlock from Charlotte (who was in charge of security planning for the police department during the 2012 Democratic National Convention) sought advice from immediate past hosts such as the cities of Denver, St. Paul, and Boston. He said their overall message to Charlotte was simple: remain flexible. Flexibility means that plans can be altered or modified in necessary situations, making the potential for the unknown less troublesome.[19] Or as Charlotte fire chief Jon Hannan put it: "Planning is key, but also knowing how and when to deviate from the plan."[20] And Charlotte did indeed have three "unknowns" occur during the 2012 Democratic National Convention. Thanks in part to these other cities, Charlotte was ready.

The first unknown was the moving of Labor Day's Carolina Fest from Charlotte Motor Speedway in the neighboring county to downtown Charlotte. This event would have occurred completely outside the city of Charlotte's jurisdiction, so the Charlotte police were initially not too involved with planning for security and safety of the delegates and other attendees.

A second unknown that occurred in Charlotte during the convention was the venue change for the president's hotel. Originally, President Obama was supposed to stay very close to uptown Charlotte. But only two weeks prior to the convention, Democratic National Committee officials informed the Charlotte-Mecklenburg Police Department that the president would now be staying in the southern edge of the city at a new venue. The CMPD had to quickly reconfigure their safety and transit plans to ensure the president's safety as well as to ensure minimal impact on local residents.

Finally, the third unknown arose when the DNCC abruptly decided to move the president's acceptance speech from Bank of America Stadium (with a capacity of seventy-five thousand) to Time Warner Cable Arena (with a capacity of twenty thousand) two days before the speech. The consensus among Charlotte city leaders was that this decision actually made implementation easier for them: they merely continued to implement the plans from the first two days of the convention and did not have to switch to their alternate plans for the stadium.

It is also worth noting that the detailed cross-agency and cross-organizational planning fosters improved working relationships across government. City workers come out of their "niches" and build relationships of trust across months of collaboration. Out of this experience comes the basis for ideas of how to engage in cross-training, pooling resources, and providing integrated responses to cross-agency problems.[21] Moreover, supervisors find new talent, as workers who did not have managerial experience are put into conditions of long hours and stress and do exceptionally well.[22]

As this chapter demonstrates, city planning, communication, coordination, and implementation matter when hosting a convention. And it is not just for the safety, security, and enjoyment of attendees and residents during the convention. As our evidence shows in the next chapter, successful implementation during a high-profile event affects the way residents evaluate the competence of their local government.

5

The Political Benefits of
Political Conventions

You don't win a state just by having a convention there; it's how you
use that convention to your benefit. You really have to talk to the people
of the community, engage them, make them feel like they're part of it.

—2012 National Democratic Convention
Committee chairman Steve Kerrigan[1]

In a gathering of the politicians, by the politicians, for the purpose of selecting
a politician for the most visible and powerful political office in the nation,
Kerrigan's quote seems self-evident. Yet more often than not, the political
benefits the national parties and local politicians seek are those that do not
come directly from engaging local residents in convention activities. As our
evidence in this chapter shows, they may have missed opportunities.

Conventions offer the national parties a unique opportunity to mobilize
and persuade local voters. Local media coverage of the upcoming event is
intense for months. Many residents presumably are interested in finding out
what all the fuss is about. Yet for most of the twentieth century, the party's
political benefit from conventions was derived from its ability to leverage
television coverage to present an appealing image of the party and its candidates to viewers nationwide. The short-term measure of a convention's success
was the magnitude of the candidate's bump in national public opinion polls
following the event. Even before television, the political party's goal for the

convention was to win election by unifying and mobilizing the party and conducting a party business meeting in which its platform is ratified. In either era, these primary goals could be achieved without engaging the residents of the convention city. Certainly the party could conduct activities to mobilize or persuade local residents, but the extra effort required to do so could detract from the higher priority activities inside the hall. And if many urban centers are "political monopolies" (Trounstine, 2008), there would be little incentive for the "out-party" to do anything other than targeted engagement. The main goal with respect to locals was to avoid antagonizing them with disruptions and inconveniences. So the party's focus typically has been on party business inside the hall, while it delegated outside activities to the city government.

Intuitively, local politicians would want to earn the gratitude of the party by helping to deliver their city for the nominee, but that presumes local politicians share the party of the convention. Many mayors do not (as in six of the fourteen cases between 1992 and 2016). In a polarized political environment, "out-party" politicians "get no credit for doing anything other than protesting."[2] Traditionally, local politicians' foremost concern has been making their cities look good to visitors and minimizing disruptions to residents—not helping the party mobilize local votes. Their political benefits come largely from solidifying their support from the growth coalition that benefits economically from the city's convention bid. Bringing more residents toward the convention would aggravate the security and traffic situations, and probably the tempers of the residents that the city was trying to engage. Furthermore, since existing fundraising demands are a challenge (see chapter 3), city leaders would not be anxious to find additional funds to pay for the activities, and host committees are restricted from "political" spending to receive charitable status and accept tax-deductible contributions. Whatever political benefit city leaders could claim from the convention—such as receiving credit for national recognition of winning the bid or their competence in executing the convention without embarrassing the city—could be gained with getting residents involved.

In this chapter, we rely extensively on a survey of residents of Mecklenburg County, North Carolina, following the 2012 DNC in Charlotte, to analyze the effects of hosting a convention on local residents. Our evidence shows that the effect of a convention on voter turnout is minimal, but conventions can affect vote choice and the specific ways residents participate in the presidential campaign. The evidence shows that the effects largely occur through the informational influences of the convention rather than opportunities for direct participation in convention activities. We also show that the residents' evaluation of the convention affects their ratings of city government, providing an important opportunity for local officials to buttress their image. The convention ratings bump, we find, is larger among "out-partisans" who otherwise have an incentive to be more skeptical about the performance of the city's leaders. Finally, we show that conventions affect mayoral career choices. Mayors of host cities are more likely than other mayors to seek higher office. Their accomplishment and their experience raising funds for the convention convince them that they can run a successful campaign. The political limits of a convention are apparent in the fact that host city mayors are not more likely to win when they seek higher office. Conventions are accomplishments that are hard to translate to the lives of voters, especially those who live outside the city.

Conventions as Campaign Tactics

Conventions matter as campaign events, beyond their role in selecting the candidate and mobilizing party activists, because they are a focusing event for the public. The conventions and the presidential debates are one of the few times when a high proportion of the politically interested public pays attention to the actual events of the campaign (Erickson and Wlezien, 2012). From the beginning of presidential nominating conventions in the 1830s, the parties' choices to hold the conventions as public meetings showed their recognition that they could be used as rallies to influence the general public (David et al., 1960: 29). How the parties have used conventions tactically to engage the public, and which publics they attempt to engage, however, have varied over time as the favored techniques of campaigning have evolved.

For the first century of conventions, they were public extravaganzas (see especially Bryce, 1959; Hayes, 2012; Ostrogorski, 1902). Delegations representing city clubs or entire states would arrive en masse in the host city. They would be met by local representatives and paraded through the streets to their hotels. Locals avidly attended the conventions, watched from the galleries, and participated with cheers, jeers, and tossing flowers. Demand for tickets, as today, was consistently higher than the seats available. Evenings were filled with speeches, parades, and band concerts in public squares and outside the hotels of party leaders. In other words, conventions incorporated the standard campaign techniques of the era (McGerr, 1986). Sometimes, dueling spectacles occurred as both parties, or more often, different factions of the same party held simultaneous rallies. The candidates did not appear at the conventions during this era. But once a nominee was chosen, the rallies promoted the nominees as well as the party's principles. In this era, the parties used their conventions to engage the residents of the host city as part of their efforts to hone their campaign messages and techniques.

Early on, the parties took advantage of changes in communication technologies to use conventions to convey campaign messaging across the country. With the invention of the telegraph, news from the conventions was quickly disseminated. In localities across the country, residents—no doubt dominated by members of local political clubs—congregated at the telegraph offices to await the news from the convention (Hayes, 2012: 86). Unlike later communications technologies, reporting by telegraph and newspaper did not require the parties to choreograph their conventions to entertain a mass audience. The audience at this time was made up of only the delegates and the locals who participated in the festivities.

This changed to an extent with the advent of radio. Voters could now hear the activities of the convention. Franklin Roosevelt, who had been the first candidate to travel to a convention to accept the nomination in 1932, became the first candidate to address the convention—and the country via radio—in 1936. In 1944, Roosevelt gave his acceptance speech by radio without attending the convention, highlighting his obligations as a wartime president (David et al., 1960: 279–81).

The arrival of television changed campaigning entirely and conventions with it. The messages of campaigning focused on what could be effectively communicated through the medium. Other campaigning activities that complemented television, particularly fundraising, received more emphasis. Grassroots campaigning, which required lots of time and volunteer effort yet reached fewer people, was deemphasized.

Conventions immediately became television-centric. In 1948, the networks wanted both conventions in Philadelphia, so that they would only have to pay once to set up (Reinsch, 1988). The parties accommodated because they could get the conventions broadcast from Boston to Washington, D.C., from there. In 1952, Chicago was chosen because the central time zone would allow for an effective national broadcast. Party leaders, as we saw in chapter 1, adapted the content, timing, operations, and physical layout of convention activities to take advantage of the medium's ability to broadcast their message instantaneously. They emphasized the choreographed spectacle inside the hall that could be packaged for viewers nationwide. Traditional elements of conventions that engaged local residents lapsed into history. Parades were anachronisms. Speeches in the public square were unnecessary when anyone could watch speeches from the convention podium at home. In the television era, locals and delegates often had less information about what was happening at the convention than viewers at home (Reisch, 1988: 74). Local residents became problems to be managed (how to get them out of security zones, how to get them to work, how to get demonstrators off of television) rather than an integral part of the campaign. There were three basic options for dealing with the local residents: 1) shutting down the city's downtown during the convention to keep them out of the way; 2) maximizing "business as usual" for residents but aggravating them with interruptions and inconveniences; or 3) holding the convention in an out-of-the-way arena where it was hard to engage anyone.[3] Any "campaign effects" on local residents would be the result of more intense local media coverage than physical interaction between residents and the convention attendees (Atkinson et al., 2014).

Grassroots mobilization as a campaign tactic, though never rivaling the dominance of media campaigning, made resurgence in the late 1990s. When the Republicans gained majority status in Congress and the access-oriented fundraising capacity that goes with it, labor unions led the Democratic coalition in emphasizing a grassroots strategy where they had a competitive advantage (Asher et al., 2001; Francia, 2006). Democratic successes in the 1996 and 1998 congressional elections led the GOP to develop their own grassroots strategy: the seventy-two-hour task force. Scholars also were reaching the conclusion that person-to-person contacts were more effective methods of getting voters to the polls than television (e.g., Rosenstone and Hansen, 1993; Green and Gerber, 2008). The expansion of Internet and mobile technologies made it increasingly easy to form networks of like-minded individuals during campaigns.

The new emphasis on grassroots mobilization eventually made its way to convention planning. The 2008 Denver DNC showcased how a convention could be used as a public engagement and political mobilization opportunity for the benefit of both the party and the city. Most prominently, the Obama campaign filled Invesco Field—the Denver Broncos football stadium—for an open-air acceptance speech and campaign rally. Following the lesson of Olympic cities (MacAloon, 2006), Denver created a "public good" for residents—a festival atmosphere including music, arts, and events for children. Local residents could have fun participating in activities surrounding the convention. In the view of a delegate to multiple party conventions, "Denver set a new standard on how to use a convention as a showcase for a city. They integrated the convention into the life of the city and showed how their residents could benefit from the convention too."[4]

From the DNCC's perspective, the festival activities were not about engaging the public out of pure civic goodwill, but about getting participants registered to vote, getting their contact information, getting their friends' and relatives' contact information, and following up with them with pro-Obama information. At Obama's Invesco Field acceptance speech, the DNCC had voter registration, phone banks, and group texting. The DNCC used the stadium video board as a map of the United States and encouraged people to call or text someone in another state. When the person did it, they would see the location light up on the map. They were then asked to text the information to the Democratic National Committee.[5] In an era where campaign gold is an email address, a cell phone number, and information to micro-target, such an event produces the mother lode.

Party officials argued such activities could create a "convention effect" on participation, as the convention would generate ripple effects of activities through the personal networks of people involved in convention activities. Bruce Clark, Charlotte mayor Anthony Foxx's 2011 campaign manager, voiced the political logic of public festivals accompanying the 2012 DNC: "The [Carolina Fest street festival] and the stadium [President Obama's planned Bank of America stadium acceptance speech] are mobilizers for the southern strategy. The participants in these events will mainly be from three states [North and South Carolina and Virginia] and will provide contact information for mobilization in critical swing states. One hundred thousand people are expected at [Carolina Fest]. If you can get half of them to talk to a friend or neighbor, you have a huge impact."[6]

Charlotte's 2012 DNC built on the perceived successes of Denver, declaring itself "The People's Convention." It banned corporate contributions and funded the convention with small individual donations (see chapter 3), had a Labor Day street festival (Carolina Fest) on the traditional first day of the convention, and reprising Obama's Invesco Field speech, planned to hold the president's acceptance speech at Bank of America stadium (home of the NFL's Carolina Panthers). Though the stadium event was canceled at the last minute due to threatening weather, organizers had used the desire to get tickets to leverage volunteer participation and had already captured the contact information of credential holders' acquaintances (Funk and Morrill, 2012a; Funk and Morrill, 2012b).[7] Similarly, Philadelphia hosted a multi-venue "PoliticalFest" at the 2016 DNC to engage local residents (Vadala, 2016), suggesting the convention-oriented jubilees and campaign-mobilization events are being institutionalized for the Democrats.

Does direct engagement with the local public produce political benefits for the party through a mobilization effect? Certainly parties have an incentive to seek a marginal advantage in any way they can get it. Nevertheless, even if thousands of local residents participated in the convention events directly, they would still constitute a small proportion of the population of a metropolitan area. Or do the parties gain political benefits locally from an information effect due to the saturation coverage of the local media (Atkinson et al., 2014)?

The Local Convention Benefits for the Party

To explore the political benefits for the party, we first take a "macro" approach and examine the differences in turnout between host counties and non-host counties. We then turn to our post-election survey of Mecklenburg County residents to assess whether individual-level behavior was affected by the convention—and if so, whether it was driven by consumption of convention-related information from the media or by the respondent's direct engagement with convention activities.

County-level Turnout

Akinson et al. (2014) find that conventions have minimal effects on turnout (see also Berry and Bickers, 2012; Powell, 2004), but until 2008, parties and campaigns had not emphasized using them for this purpose. Moreover, Aktinson and colleagues analyzed media effects across an entire metropolitan statistical area (MSA), which could affect voting decisions, but would be less relevant for turnout since most of the counties in the MSA would not have been subject to any direct contact with convention activities. We use Atkinson and team's data to assess the differences in turnout between convention counties and other counties in the same election year, as well as to compare changes in turnout in the convention host county in the years before and after the convention.

The data show that convention host counties have a turnout increase that is 2.8% higher than the national average in the convention year. In the presidential election cycle preceding the city's hosting of a convention, turnout increased on average by 1.5%, so the 2.8% convention boost was almost twice the city's previous increase. But host counties also boosted turnout by 6.9% in the election cycle after hosting the conventions. The fact that the host cities had even larger increases following the conventions suggests that the changes in turnout were not due entirely to the convention.

In fact, despite the mobilization-oriented activities during the Denver and Charlotte DNCs, the turnout in their convention years was both less than the increases in turnout in the preceding elections (Denver 10.3% in 2004 vs. 4.6% in 2008; Charlotte 6.3% in 2008 vs. 1.5% in 2012). And Tampa had an equally impressive increase in turnout as Charlotte (1.6%) despite the fact that the GOP did not create public engagement opportunities and the fact that Hurricane Isaac removed much of the local population around the time of the 2012 convention (see chapter 4). So, event though the Democrats made more intentional efforts to mobilize local residents in 2008 and

2012, the evidence at the county level suggests they had a limited impact on turnout. In fairness, however, it is probably a bit much to ask that activities months before the votes are cast and that involve a relatively small proportion of city residents would have a large and discernible impact unless there was follow-up by the party and the convention inspired residents to follow the campaign more closely.

Individual Engagement

We attempt to assess Charlotteans' engagement with the convention and the convention's effects on their attitudes and participation in the 2012 election. We surveyed 964 residents of Mecklenburg County immediately following the 2012 presidential election (November and December, 2012). The Social and Behavioral Research Lab of Winthrop University conducted the survey, with funding provided by Duke Energy. The survey was conducted two months after the DNC to capture the effects, if any, the convention had on residents' participation and vote choices in the 2012 election. Details on the survey methodology are presented in appendix 5-A.[8]

We asked respondents about several types of electoral participation in the 2008 and 2012 elections. Survey data on election participation is always somewhat suspect as respondents overreport their activities due to social desirability effects. We take this into account for 2012 by asking respondents about the same activities in 2008. Asking people to recall their activities four years hence is obviously subject to respondents' recall problems. We asked about their 2008 activities early in the survey and their 2012 activities late in the survey to reduce the chances that their responses to one election would contaminate their responses to the other.

In both years, we asked respondents about whether they volunteered for a presidential campaign, whether they attempted to persuade anyone to vote for a particular presidential candidate, and whether they voted in the presidential contest. We used a more rigorous screen to assess turnout in 2012, which may partially explain the drop in turnout from 2008 to 2012.[9] Finally, for those who reported voting, we asked about their presidential vote choice, randomizing the order of Obama and McCain (2008)/Romney (2012). Table 5.1 presents the changes in the rates of participation between the 2008 and 2012 elections.

Rates of volunteerism (15% and 14%) and persuasion (43% and 46%) remained remarkably similar in aggregate.[10] There is little evidence, however, of a convention effect since the rate of volunteerism among Democrats declined more than it did among Republicans. Independents actually claimed a bit

Table 5.1. Campaign participation by Charlotte survey respondents, 2008 vs. 2012

Activity	All	Democrats	Republicans	Independents
Volunteer	−1.1	−3.9	−2.9	+1.3
Persuade	+3.4	−2.3	+9.9	+1.4
Turnout	−6.4	−3.6	−9.4	−6.2
Obama vote	+9.1	+13.4	+0.0	+7.1

Data source: Authors' calculations with data from the 2012 Post-Election Survey, Mecklenburg County, North Carolina.

more campaign volunteerism in 2012 than in 2008. Likewise, the percentage of persuaders increased slightly, but the increase came from a 10% increase among Republicans. Democratic persuasion efforts actually declined slightly. Only on turnout is there potential evidence of a convention effect on participation. Self-reported Democratic turnout declined, but less than the decline among independents and Republicans.[11]

The survey shows a big boost for Obama in respondents' vote choice from 2008 to 2012. The size of the increase in the Obama vote from 2008 to 2012 is surprising given that Obama's vote share declined slightly in Mecklenburg County in those two cycles. These results may be due to a question order effect. The series of questions about the Democratic National Convention may have primed some respondents to lean more Democratic in their partisan responses. Multivariate models may be able to control for this by including the respondent's self-identified party affiliation and ideology, both of which were asked soon after the 2012 election questions.

The lower rates of participation in 2012 compared to 2008, particularly among Democrats, shows that the DNC activities did not generate an increase in participation. Yet the context of the 2012 election was markedly different than 2008. It featured a president seeking reelection with a slow-growing economy. The excitement of the historic nature of the 2008 Obama campaign had worn off. Turnout was down nationwide, so perhaps the convention's effect kept participation from falling even more dramatically. Indeed, although 47.8% of American National Election Study respondents reported participating in at least one campaign activity in 2012 compared to 41.6% in 2008, Democratic participation fell from 54.4% to 48.7%.

Therefore, we turn to the question of the means by which a convention could affect residents' political action. A convention could affect local political participation through two mechanisms: 1) by providing local residents with information that allows them to participate in the election more easily and effectively; and 2) by mobilizing them directly through providing them additional opportunities to participate and having agents recruit them to participate in the election.[12]

The survey shows that local residents were not equally engaged by the convention. There is a predictable partisan skew. Participation in DNC by volunteering or attending Carolina Fest was highly partisan: 63% of participants were Democrats, 35% were independents (and 43% of independent participants classified themselves as "leaning Democratic"), and only 2% were Republicans (who classified themselves as "weak" Republicans).[13] Consuming news about the DNC was also highly partisan: 33% of strong Republicans did not follow any part of the DNC on any news source (3.5% followed the DNC daily in multiple sources); 32% of strong Democrats followed the convention daily in multiple news sources (Chi-square = 194.0, p < .001). The key question, then, is whether participating in the convention or consuming convention news mobilized Democrats and independents to do anything that they would not have done anyway.

To assess this question, we delve further into our survey to analyze respondents' actions during the 2012 presidential campaign. Each of the dependent variables—volunteering, persuading, and turnout—are dichotomous variables so we use logit as the estimation procedure. We control for other variables that are likely to affect participation: the respondents' engagement in the same activity in the 2008 presidential election (volunteering, persuading, or voting, respectively); their levels of political efficacy, education, and interest in politics; and whether they are a minority, a new voter, a Democrat or Republican (independents are the excluded category). We enter party affiliation as separate dummy variables because if the DNC is having a mobilizing effect, it should affect Democrats more than Republicans or independents. Measures of all the variables are available in appendix 5-B. We estimate the magnitude of the changes in probability of the dependent variable based on a one standard deviation shift around the mean in the independent variable, while the other variables are held at their means.

A related wrinkle is that one of the key mechanisms of convention planners for mobilizing the Obama vote was inviting the public to attend his acceptance speech at Bank of America stadium. On the Wednesday of convention week, the DNCC canceled Thursday's Bank of America events due to threatening weather and moved the acceptance speech inside Time Warner Arena, where the preceding days' activities had been held. This left sixty thousand ticketholders unable to attend. The question is whether residents' disappointment over not being able to attend the grand finale of the convention affected Obama's supporters. We asked respondents whether they had tickets to Obama's acceptance speech and whether they thought it was the "right decision" to move the speech indoors (for exact wording of the questions, see the DNC measures section of appendix 5-B). Of the ticketholders, a clear majority (59%) approved of the move indoors, but that leaves another 41% who were irked by the decision. Did their dissatisfaction with the DNC reneging on their tickets affect their behavior in the campaign? Our results appear in table 5.2 on page 118.

The evidence shows convention effects on participation in the 2012 campaign, mainly through the informational effects of intently following news coverage of the DNC. Convention media consumption and actual engagement with the convention (volunteering or attending Carolina Fest) are both significantly related to volunteering in the 2012 campaign. Charlotteans who followed the news of the DNC frequently during the week were 7% more likely to volunteer during the election, while those who participated during the DNC were 11% more likely to volunteer. Not all partisans were equally affected by the convention, however. When we run the models separately by party, the informational effect is significant only for independents, increasing their likelihood of volunteering by 8%. Participating in convention activities also increased independents' probability of volunteering during the campaign by 8%. Participation during the DNC had an even larger mobilization effect on Democrats, increasing the probability of their campaign volunteering by 26%. Campaign volunteerism is the only act on which participation during the DNC had an effect.

A standard deviation change in following convention news coverage increased the probability that the respondent attempted to persuade another person by 8%, though the marginal level of significance (p < .10) suggestions some caution. Active convention watching had a particularly large effect on Democrats' persuasion (a 14% increase), suggesting that the DNC provided information to Democrats that made them comfortable speaking with acquaintances. Participation in convention activities did not affect the likelihood of persuasion.

Disappointed ticketholders generally participated at lower rates than others, but it is only significantly related to lower turnout, where they were 5% less likely to vote. Regardless of the extent of the impact, the word to the wise for future convention planners is to avoid reneging on commitments to participants. Similar to our findings earlier in the chapter, convention watching and participation did not have overall impacts on turnout. Presumably those interested enough in politics to participate in convention activities and follow it conscientiously in the news are already likely voters. The evidence does

Table 5.2. Effects of 2012 DNC news and participation on 2012 campaign engagement

| | Volunteer | | Persuade | | Turnout | | Follow campaign | |
| | Logit | | Logit | | Logit | | Ordered logit | |
	B	SE	B	SE	B	SE	B	SE
Convention news	.21**	.08	.08*	.05	.08	.06	.55***	.11
Convention participation	2.10***	.31	.37	.36	.04	.40	-.42	.39
Mad at ticket loss	.24	.59	-.17	.59	-.97**	.47	.94	.62
Efficacy	.25*	.15	.01	.11	.45***	.12	.19	.18
Education	.02	.09	-.04	.07	.14*	.08	.02	.10
Political interest	.50**	.21	.34**	.13	.48***	.12	.59**	.20
New voter	-.25	.51	1.11**	.36	.25	.36	1.20	.78
Minority	.20	.26	-.20	.21	-.40*	.23	.19	.31
Democrat	-.16	.28	.22	.22	.55**	.24	.47	.32
Republican	-.18	.23	.84**	.25	.28	.26	.73	.33
2008 participation	1.82***	.26	2.88***	.19	1.84***	.26	NA	
Constant	-.98	.96	-1.55**	.75	1.58**	.80	Cut1 -4.31	1.12
							Cut2 -2.65	.98
							Cut3 .45	.99
Adj. R² =	.21		.36		.19		.11	
-2*Log Likelihood =	1034		1608		1362		588	
% predicted correctly =	88.7		80.9		83.8			
N =	868		864		877		862	

Note: *** = p < .01; ** = p < .05; * = p < .10

indicate, however, that media usage increased turnout for Independents (7.0%) and Republicans (6.8%). Given that few Charlotte Republicans avidly watched the DNC and that we controlled for 2008 turnout and general interest in politics, we interpret these results to mean that the DNC heightened the interest in the campaign for the few independents and Republicans who followed it closely, enough to encourage them to show up at the polls two months later.

Indeed, the results of table 5.2 show that consuming news about the DNC significantly increased the respondents' interest in the 2012 presidential campaign. The effect for Democrats was roughly twice the impact on independents and Republicans (.45 verses .27 and .22, respectively) and the effect was significant for all partisans. Though we have controlled for interest in politics in general, we should be cautious about causality in this case. Following the DNC closely and following the 2012 campaign closely are driven by the same general interest in the campaign. Without asking the respondents before and after the convention, it is impossible to tell whether watching the convention "caused" the respondent to become more attentive to the rest of the campaign. Nevertheless, the result is consistent with the other participatory acts, which show that consuming convention news boosted 2012 campaign activities.

Vote Choice

We also examine the convention effect on the respondents' vote for President Obama's reelection. We used a binary dependent variable (vote for Obama or not) so we estimate the equation using logit. We use the same convention news-utilization and convention-participation measures as our independent variables of interest, but use different control variables than we did in the engagement models. The control variables are: ideology, strength of party identification, new voter, minority, female voter, religious commitment, and voting for Obama in 2008. Measurements are detailed in the political demographics section of appendix 5-B.

Table 5.3 on page 120 provides support for an informational effect of the convention. DNC news connoisseurs were significantly more likely to cast votes for President Obama. Consuming more pro-Democratic information even months prior to the election tipped some votes toward the party's candidate. Participating in convention activities had no effect on vote choices. The magnitude of the convention effects (.15 change in probability), however, pale in comparison to traditional explanations of voting behavior. Party identification, ideology, racial minority status, and voting for Obama in 2008 all had substantially larger effects on 2012 vote choice than consumption of DNC news. Nevertheless, it is noteworthy that consuming convention news

Table 5.3. Vote for Obama 2012 (Logit)

	Coefficient	SE	Probability
Convention news	.20**	.09	.15
Convention participation	−.90	.59	−.09
Mad at ticket loss	−.57	1.02	−.05
New voter	.99	.84	.15
Ideology (liberal)	.56***	.18	.28
Party ID (Dem)	.79***	.11	.72
Minority	1.69***	.45	.29
Female	−.25	.35	−.05
Religious attendance	−.10	.09	−.08
Obama voter 2008	2.23***	.37	.45
Constant	−7.49	.92	

Adj. R² = .73	−2*Log Likelihood = 664
N = 672	% predicted correctly = 92.4

had an effect at all given the expected importance of the traditional explanations of vote choice as control variables.

When we run the voting equation separately by party (not shown), we find a small but statistically significant informational effect for Democrats, but none for independents or Republicans. Presumably their convention media consumption reminded them why they were Democrats and gave them the added boost to support the president. At the same time, participation in convention activities actually significantly decreased Democrats' probability of voting for Obama (by .01). This result should be taken with some caution as only three of forty-six Democratic convention participants (7%) voted against Obama. We can speculate that they were turned off by logistics problems such as crowds and parking (Penland, 2012), or the cacophony of democracy in protests and counter-protests (Hibbing and Theis-Morse, 2002). It is consistent with Atkinson et al.'s finding (2014) that Republicans proximate to the RNC site are less likely to support the GOP nominee.

From the parties' perspective, our results offer mostly positive news: conventions can affect the political behavior of local residents. Our evidence shows effects on volunteering, persuasions for in-party Democrats, interest in the 2012 campaign, and voting for the party's candidate. Our results show that the convention effects on residents mostly occur through consumption of convention news. In this sense, the effects of the convention are similar for locals as they are for the rest of the country, who have little other choice than to follow the convention in media coverage.

The effect of actual participation in convention activities is limited to boosting volunteering for 2012 campaign activities. As volunteering is one of the rarest types of political engagement—only donating money is typically less frequent—having convention activities that recruit campaign volunteers is an achievement. Each additional volunteer may participate in more than one campaign activity. Moreover, producing more volunteers may have a ripple effect for the campaign as the volunteers may recruit other volunteers, register more voters, and transport more voters to the polls. For the party, the public engagement activities of the convention are "worth it" if the benefit of the additional volunteers and votes generated are greater than the cost of executing the events. Since the host committees are executing and paying for the public engagement events, the answer is almost assuredly "yes."

The Benefits of Conventions for City Politicians

Local Government Evaluations

If the parties benefit from the conventions by having cities host them, pay for them, and help them mobilize action and votes from local residents, what's in it for *local* politicians? Our main argument is that cities attempt to raise or maintain their national and international profile or "brand" by hosting a convention for the purpose of attracting businesses and residents. And if the convention succeeds in drawing businesses, the resultant economic growth benefits local officials if they effectively handle the attendant increases of demands for public services. These are long-term effects, however, and elected officials are usually thought to be more worried about the next election than about historical evaluations of their stewardship. Moreover, changes in perceptions of the city's brand most directly benefit the city among nonresidents.

The short-term potential of hosting a convention for local politicians is twofold. First, competing with other cities and "winning" a convention is an accomplishment to advertise to voters. Many constituencies will be especially pleased with the promises of an economic windfall brought by the convention. Second, conventions provide local officials an opportunity to demonstrate their competence (or expose their lack of it) in a salient environment. As Charlotte-Mecklenburg deputy police chief Harold Medlock commented, "[CarolinaFest] was a great decision because it allowed Charlotteans to feel more included in the event and its success eased the public's impression that the DNC would be nightmare."[14] Few citizens may notice or reward effectiveness or efficiency in building inspections or upgrading sewage treatment facilities, but they will notice if the convention paralyzes city traffic or if police and protesters fight pitched battles in the streets. And with the international media in town for the week, local residents aren't the only ones who will know! City officials confront a critical challenge of providing security and special services to impress the visiting dignitaries while maintaining the delivery of basic services to residents during mega-events.

A substantial literature documents the importance of local government performance in citizens' evaluations of local government. Simply put, the better the local government is at delivering services, the better ratings residents give their government and the more likely high-profile officials (e.g., the mayor) are to be reelected (Arceneaux and Stein, 2006; Howell and Perry, 2004; Radin, 2006; van Ryzin, 2006, 2007, and 2011). So it would be easy to hypothesize that successful performance during a convention would boost citizens' evaluations while poor performance would decrease their evaluations.

Our survey, however, is of one city at one point in time. So we cannot evaluate whether citizens' evaluations changed from before to after a convention, nor can we compare the consequences of "good" city performance to "bad" city performance. What we *can* do is compare the evaluations of residents who are likely to give the city higher ratings for its performance—residents who share the partisanship of the political party governing the city—with residents who are likely to be more skeptical because of their status as partisan outsiders. We argue that salient performance during a mega-event is likely to have the greatest effect on the evaluations of partisan outsiders.

In the case of the Charlotte 2012 DNC, Democrats are more likely to give higher ratings to city government because Democrats controlled the mayoralty and the majority of the city council and they tend to be more favorable toward government generally. Essentially, we argue that residents engage in "motivated reasoning"—they evaluate government performance in ways that are biased toward their own partisan goals (Kunda, 1990; Taber and Lodge, 2006). Under ordinary circumstances (i.e., without a salient event), Democrats are likely to credit their team with greater success in part because doing so reaffirms their wisdom in being Democrats. Republicans and independents have more incentive to find reasons to criticize the party in power because their self-identity is not at stake and because Republicans in particular need a rationale to replace the party in power. So if a city's hosting of the convention is a "success," it is more likely to have a positive impact on the evaluations of Republicans and independents than it is on Democrats' evaluations. Democratic partisanship and a positive evaluation of the convention should independently boost evaluations of city government, but we also expect an interactive effect in which out-partisans who view the convention as a success should also rate the effectiveness of local government more positively.

In our survey, we asked respondents to evaluate several aspects of city government: approval of the mayor; approval of the city council; perceptions that Charlotte city government is competent, responsive, and effective; satisfaction with living in Charlotte; and attachment to the region. The specific question wording is in the city evaluation section of appendix 5-B.[15] We combined these questions into a single variable using factor analysis, which reduces the information in the seven responses to a single underlying common dimension (alpha = .82).[16] The factor score of the local government evaluation questions will be our dependent variable.

The respondents' evaluations of the city generally should be affected by their assessment of the salient event of hosting the DNC. Our survey question inquired: "Overall, how would you describe Charlotte's performance as a host for the Democratic National Convention?" The response options ranged from very successful to very unsuccessful on a 5-point scale. The responses were skewed in the positive direction (skewness = 2.20): 64% responded that the city was very successful; 94% responded that the city was very or somewhat successful. To lessen the skew and aid interpretation of the interaction with partisanship, we collapsed the responses to a dichotomous variable (very successful = 1; others = 0).[17]

Our survey shows clear partisan differences in evaluations of the city and its officials. It also shows that the extent of partisanship differences varies across evaluative dimensions. The mean evaluations for each party are presented in table 5.4. The response options for most of the evaluation questions were a 5-point scale, with 5 indicating a high evaluation and 1 a low evaluation.[18] We ordered the evaluations from the largest to the smallest partisan gap.

Table 5.4. Partisanship and 2012 City of Charlotte evaluations

	Democrats	Independents	Republicans	Difference
Mayor	3.1	2.8	2.5	.06*
Convention success	4.6	4.4	4.1	.05*
Competence	4.0	3.6	3.5	.05*
Responsive	3.8	3.5	3.3	.05*
City council	2.6	2.4	2.3	.03*
Satisfied	4.4	4.3	4.2	.02*
Effective	3.2	3.1	3.0	.02*
Attachment	4.0	3.8	4.0	.00

Note: Values are the means for each party. A difference of means tests assesses statistical significance * = p < .05.

Data source: Post-2012 Election Survey of Residents of Mecklenburg County, North Carolina.

Not surprisingly, table 5.4 shows that the ratings of the mayor (a partisan office) had the largest partisan gap. The city's success as a host for the DNC was rated highly by all partisan groups, but also had a large partisan gap. Democrats gave significantly higher ratings of the convention's success than Republicans.[19] Ratings of the city government's competence and responsiveness also had partisan gaps nearly as large as the mayor's. Ratings of the city council, satisfaction with the region, and the city's effectiveness in spending money exhibited significant, though smaller, partisan gaps. Though the city council has a majority of Democrats, it is likely that many citizens don't pay close attention to its activities, thus muting the ratings overall as well as the partisan gap (the city council received the lowest mean evaluations). Only attachment to the region exhibited no differences between Democrats and Republicans, though independents offered slightly lower assessments.

To show that these partisan differences are not just the result of other attitudes toward local government or demographic differences, we estimate an equation using several other control variables such as respondents' ideology, efficacy, length of residency, race, and gender. Our dependent variable is the factor score of the local government evaluation questions.[20] Table 5.5 presents the results.

Table 5.5. City evaluations (factor score), ordinary least square regression

	Coefficient	SE	Beta
Partisanship	.178***	.023	.40
Convention success	1.55***	.121	.75
Party* success	−.130***	.036	−.39
Ideology	.070***	.027	.08
Interest	.040	.034	.03
Local efficacy	.124***	.031	.11
Education	.017	.020	.02
Length of residency (nl)	−.046*	.023	−.05
Female	−.090*	.052	−.05
Minority	.201***	.061	.10
Constant	−1.24***	.194	

N =   790
Model F =   69.74 (p < .01)
R^2 =   .46

Note: *** = $p < .01$; ** = $p < .05$; * = $p < .10$

Our key theoretical variables perform as predicted: in-party identity and positive assessments of the DNC both significantly increase evaluations of local government. That is, strong Democrats are significantly more likely to rate local government more positively than strong Republicans. The respondents' assessment of the city's DNC performance also substantively affects their overall city evaluations. Respondents who believed the city was a "very successful" host of the DNC gave the city higher evaluations generally.

Critically for our theory of motivated reasoning, the interaction between partisanship and DNC performance is negative and statistically significant. The negative coefficient shows that higher DNC ratings increase government evaluations of out-partisans (strong Republicans).[21] In other words, out-partisans are willing to rate local government highly if they see a successful example of effective performance; in this case, successfully hosting a political convention. These respondents may be skeptical, but they are not blind or obstinate and are willing to give credit when they see evidence to warrant it.[22]

Higher feelings of efficacy toward local government, ideological liberalism, and racial minority status are also significantly associated with higher evaluations of local government. Longer-term residents and women offered lower evaluations of city government (at a marginal level of statistical significance).

The opportunities for local government officials to demonstrate their effectiveness in a way that would make a salient impression on a large number of citizens is relatively limited—and some of those salient opportunities such as natural disasters and crises are clearly undesirable (Arceneaux and Stein, 2006; Atkeson and Maestas, 2012). Similarly, while not everything that happens during a convention can be controlled by local officials, likely problems can be anticipated and planned for (chapter 4), thus mitigating the political uncertainty. A visible demonstration of competence and higher performance evaluations would conceivably lead citizens to give local officials a bit more leeway in making discretionary policy decisions (e.g., Fenno, 1978) and make them more supportive of their reelection efforts. So regardless of the long-term status and economic consequences for the city, higher evaluations of city performance from residents give local officials an incentive to recruit conventions and execute them effectively.

Mayoral Careers

Improving evaluations of local governments is nice, but the bottom line for most politicians is their electoral prospects. Recruiting a presidential nominating convention for one's city would seem to be an ideal credit-claiming opportunity (Mayhew, 1974) to boost those prospects. Though most mayors are consistently active in trying to recruit businesses to their city and attract large business and fraternal conventions (e.g., Eisenger, 2000; Judd, 2003), competing successfully to host the event is an important civic validation of the city and the effectiveness of its entrepreneurial efforts. Local residents presumably should be impressed by the tourism dollars brought to the city as well as the media attention. Mayors certainly have every reason to expect that citizens will reward their involvement in mega-events, and will incorporate this expectation into their decisions regarding how to continue their political careers.

In seeking to understand the relationship between conventions and advancement, we focus on mayors. Though mayors often do not originate the idea of recruiting the convention, they are usually the lead promoter, lead fundraiser, and public face of the convention to local residents, as we detailed in chapters 2 and 3. Moreover, like other executives, they have greater ability than legislators to control the agenda and focus on issues that voters favor, and to claim sole credit for accomplishments (Burden, 2002: 88–89). Likewise, the party of the executive is usually held responsible for the performance of government (e.g., Cover, 1986; Gomez and Wilson, 2001; Peffley, Feldman, and Sigelman, 1987). As such, their ability to claim credit for recruiting the convention and its successful implementation should play a prominent role in their career decisions.

All mega-events demand effective coordination among multiple levels of government, effective communication among stakeholders and local residents, and the simultaneous delivery of routine services to residents while catering to the special needs of visitors and dignitaries. However, not all mega-events are likely to have equal effects on mayors' career decisions. Presidential nominating conventions are a special breed of mega-event because of their explicitly political orientation. Mayors spend considerable time and effort lobbying party officials to win the bid. Furthermore, once the host city is selected, mayors spend significant time persuading major donors to contribute to the host committee. Having contacts with a large number of nonlocal mega-donors is rare for most local politicians and thus can help convince mayors that they can generate the financial support needed to seek higher office. "In-party" mayors (58% of host mayors since 1992) are especially likely to make contacts with and receive encouragement from the variety of party officials, activists, campaign consultants, and donors who attend the convention. And from the beginning of the convention recruitment process through the convention itself, mayors receive intensive media coverage. All of these features of the convention-hosting process are likely to encourage mayors to believe that they have the resources and skills to run competitively for higher office. Thus, we hypothesize that those mayors who host political conventions are more likely to seek higher office than mayors who host other types of mega-events.[23]

In fact, this appears to be the case. Of the sixteen mayors of host cities in our data set (including cohost cities of Minneapolis/St. Paul and Tampa/St. Petersburg), eight (50%) sought another office compared to only 10.3% of non-host mayors (Chi-square = p < .01). In contrast, mayors who host other mega-events seek other offices at the same rate as other mayors (11.1% v. 11.2%). And only 6.7% of mayors from bid cities that were not selected sought other offices. While bidding may be an indication of ambition, the fact that unsuccessful bid mayors are unlikely to seek another office suggests that the lack of credit-claiming opportunity, the lack of interactions with activists and donors, and the relative deficit of media attention inhibit their ability to run.

In assessing the effect of political conventions on mayoral ambition, we also should consider the possibility that other accomplishments would have a similar effect. Encouraging economic development and fighting crime also are core responsibilities of local government and outcomes for which mayors are likely to be subject to some level of electoral accountability (Arnold and Carnes, 2012; McNitt, 2010). At the very least, a mayor will be a bit more reluctant to seek another office if he or she does not have positive accomplishments to tout in these areas or can anticipate attack ads from opponents on these issues.

We also control for several other variables that would affect mayors' career choices. These include the opportunity structure (Schlesinger, 1966), including whether the mayor is term-limited, whether there are open seats available for other offices, and the overlap between the mayor's current constituency and the statewide electorate. Likewise, we account for the mayor's age and tenure. Details on all measures appear in appendix 5-C.

To analyze mayoral careers, we return to the list of cities we analyzed in chapter 2 as large enough to be eligible to host a convention. They were the cities that had a population greater than the smallest city to be invited to host a convention or to bid for one—namely, Salt Lake City. To assure we are comparing the careers of mayors of similarly sized cities, we use the 104 cities that were larger than Salt Lake City for the entire twenty-year time frame. Each city meeting the population threshold is a case in each convention cycle between 1992 and 2012. We gathered information on mayors' careers, ages, and tenures with NewsBank searches. Many mayors appear multiple times in the data set as they serve across multiple convention cycles. The analysis employs robust standard errors clustered by city to adjust for the fact that these observations are not independent—cities are cases in each election cycle from 1992 to 2012.

We employ multinomial logit to analyze the career choices made by city mayors in each election cycle (Kiewiet and Zeng, 1993). Multinomial logit is appropriate because the three choice options—retire, seek reelection, or seek another office—are unordered. Multinomial logit allows us to compare the effects of each independent variable relative to each choice option. In this case, we analyze the choices of retirement and seeking another office compared to the choice of seeking reelection. Table 5.6 presents the results. For each independent variable that attains statistical significance, we calculate the variable's substantive effect on the career choice. Specifically, for continuous variables, we calculate the effect of a two standard deviation change—one standard deviation above and one standard deviation below the mean. For discrete variables, we calculate the effect of a change from the minimum to the maximum value.

Table 5.6 provides evidence that political conventions spur mayoral ambition to seek other offices. With appropriate caution for the marginal level of significance due to the low number of cases (and therefore high standards errors), convention-hosting mayors are marginally more likely to seek other

Table 5.6. Multinomial logit regression of mayoral career choice, 1992–2012

	Sought Other Office			Retired		
	Coeff.	SE	Probability	Coeff.	SE	Probability
Accomplishments						
Population growth	.004**	.002	.04	.004*	.003	.07
Income growth	−.15	.11	−.06	.02	.08	
Violent crime	−39.44*	30.40	−.03	−26.17**	14.10	−.04
Convention host	.94*	.61	.17	−.94*	.59	−.19
Convention bid	−.71*	.46	−.04	−.82**	.42	−.14
Mega-events	−.50	.46		−.11	.35	
Opportunity structure						
Term-limited	3.05***	.68	.09	3.48***	.55	.52
Open seats	.60***	.21	.06	.34	.16	
Population ratio	.0005**	.0003	.04	−.0002	.0003	
Age	−.03**	.02	−.09	.05***	.01	.22
Tenure	.07**	.03	.05	.03*	.02	.04

N = 561
Model Wald X^2 = 140.75 (p < .01)
McFadden's Pseudo R^2 = .15

Note: ***p < .01; **p < .05; *p < .10, one-tailed test.

offices than other mayors. In the process of implementing the convention, they develop networks and a sense of accomplishment that persuade them that they can do big things. The political and donor contacts in particular help convince them that higher office is achievable. Thus, they are more likely to seek other offices.

Unlike hosting a political convention, bidding for a convention or hosting another mega-event does not spur mayors' ambitions. Mayors of unsuccessful bid cities, in fact, are less likely to seek another office (or to retire) than the average mayor. This evidence helps assure us that seeking conventions is not an indicator of ambition in the same way that seeking office is. These results show that conventions seem to act as a stimulus for mayors' political careers: they are more likely either to use the experience to advance their careers, or to use it as a rationale to continue their investment in the city through reelection.

Table 5.6 also shows that mayors seek to take advantage of other accomplishments as well. Mayors of cities experiencing higher levels of population growth and mayors of cities with larger declines in violent crime are more likely to seek other offices. Interestingly, increasing income growth does not spur mayors to seek other offices. Perhaps the good economic times in the city give them greater incentive to stay.

The opportunity structure variables are all significantly related to office seeking. Mayors who are term-limited, who have more open seat opportunities, who have large constituencies relative to the state population, who are younger, and who have longer tenures as mayor are all significantly more likely to seek other offices. The probability scores indicate that term limits and age have a moderate effect, while open seats, tenure, and the city-to-state population ratio have small effects on mayors' decisions to seek other offices. Retirements are significantly more likely when the mayor is term-limited and when the mayor is older and has a longer tenure.

But Do They Win?

The evidence in table 5.6 shows that host mayors are more likely to seek other offices. When they run for office, do their accomplishments make them more attractive to voters? First, we examine the effect of conventions on winning reelection. Only one mayor (5.9%) who hosted a political convention was defeated in seeking reelection (David Dinkins of New York). In comparison, 11.7% of non-hosting mayors were denied reelection (Chi-square = p < .46). Other mayoral accomplishments do not significantly affect mayors' chances of reelection either, with one critical exception: increases in violent crime. When the rate of violent crime has increased, 16.4% of mayors lose reelection compared to 8.9% of mayors who presided over a decrease in violent crime (Chi-square = p < .03).

When seeking another office, mayors must convince a new constituency of their qualifications and accomplishments. Our data suggest that doing so presents a significant challenge to big-city mayors. Slightly less than half (45.7%) who seek to advance actually win. Mayors of host cities fare even more poorly than the average, with only 37.5% emerging victorious (p < .59). Hosting other mega-events, presiding over economic growth, or presiding over decreases in crime did not significantly improve a mayor's ability to win higher office either.

Surprisingly, few of the accomplishments are related to a mayor's chances of reelection or their chances of winning other offices. Part of the story is surely that mayors tend to be defeated for idiosyncratic reasons (Oliver, 2012). But why would accomplishments entice mayors to run for office, yet fail to help them attain those offices? Accomplishments likely induce mayors to run because they give the mayor a message on which to campaign. It is an element of the campaign they can control. Many other elements that affect the outcome of the campaign cannot be controlled by the mayor—including their opponent's experience and accomplishments, the national economy and political environment, and voters' willingness to weight criteria other than partisanship and name recognition.

Moreover, to the extent that a big-city mayor's accomplishments are seen by voters as unique to a big-city environment, voters outside the city may not see those accomplishments as predictors that the mayor will understand and assist with their problems. Since voters outside of big cities view urban candidates with skepticism (and often as an outright threat), uniquely urban experiences such as mega-events are unlikely to be a strong selling point without a broader message of how the mayor's experience will help to improve governance and the quality of life. The people with whom the mayor speaks are likely to tell them how great the convention was, leading them to overestimate the value of the convention to residents and non-city voters. Having a record of short-term accomplishments increases the probability that the mayor will decide that the time to run is now, but it is apparently not sufficient to outweigh all the other elements of the choice that voters consider.

Conclusion

Winning elections is the ultimate political goal. For the party, conventions do not guarantee that its presidential candidate will win the host state. Nor can mayors who are associated with a convention glide into their next office. But the evidence in this chapter suggests that conventions have other, narrower benefits both for parties and for local politicians. Evidence from our survey shows that conventions can boost volunteerism, efforts to persuade other voters, interest in the campaign, and voting for the party's candidate among local residents. The effects were particularly pronounced among Democrats, exactly the people on whom a DNC should have mobilizing effects. These effects occur through media utilization because that is the means by which most residents—particularly the less politically active—are likely to engage with the convention. Our results show that direct participation in convention activities generally did not significantly affect political action during the 2012 DNC, though the one activity in which it did—volunteerism—is valuable because it is one of the hardest actions for the party to generate. The fact that the city pays for the public engagement events means that any marginal political support that can come from the event is a benefit to the party. Thus, parties have every incentive to urge their city partners to sponsor public engagement events on their behalves. The IRS's denial of charitable status for Philadelphia's 2016 host committee (see chapter 3), because they thought the committee would pay for political activities, shows some risk to cities in becoming mobilization agents for the parties.

The city benefits from the public's engagement in convention events by providing a public good to residents. This allows them to share in the city's moment in the limelight, while still demonstrating its ability simultaneously to provide city services. Our analyses show that the salient event gives residents the opportunity to evaluate the performance of local government and, if they see that the city can effectively execute a high-profile event, reward city officials accordingly. The city particularly benefits when partisan outsiders extrapolate from their positive assessment of the mega-event to the city government's performance. Our findings also suggest that mayors sense that residents credit them for their success in recruiting and implementing the convention because they are significantly more likely to seek to advance after hosting a convention.

Opportunities are often what we make of them. To the extent that parties have attempted to maximize city spending inside the convention hall and have seen conventions only as infomercials for television audiences, and to the extent that host cities have emphasized keeping residents away from security zones, the parties and the cities have missed opportunities to engage with residents in ways that would be mutually beneficial politically. Parties' increased emphasis on grassroots campaigning, the increased priority on selecting host cities in competitive states (chapter 2), and the newly opened opportunities for large donor contributions for conventions through the parties (chapter 3) increase the likelihood that parties and cities will take advantage of opportunities to generate political benefits from local residents in future conventions.

6

Conventions as Economic Development

Do They Matter?

Dollar bills have no politics. Green is green.

—Gaston County (NC) Commission chairman Donnie Loftis[1]

The previous chapters highlight the differing aspects associated with the public decision to bid, win, and host a major political convention. In this chapter, we turn our attention to the most commonly cited reasons for *why* cities might want to pursue and host such a mega-event: economic impact and/or development, as well as national and international media attention. And while these are the most often cited reasons for wanting to host, they are both quite challenging to establish empirically. As a result, citizens are often overwhelmed with large numbers backed up with fuzzy math mixed with wishful thinking.

Political conventions are similar to other mega-events like the NFL Super Bowl, the Olympics, or the World Cup. They bring in tens of thousands of out-of-town visitors for several days. While there, visitors need places to stay, food to eat, entertainment, and souvenirs. In short, they will spend money in the local economy. That money employs people and circulates in the local economy to some degree. The churning of capital is the fuel of any local economy and, as noted in previous chapters, the local economy is often the primary concern of local officials and the growth coalition.

Pursuing national conventions is part of a larger pattern of contemporary economic growth goals that typically include three stages. In the broadest sense, these stages begin with the involvement of public sector financing of some aspect of a growth strategy. Today, these efforts finance various tourism attractions, such as convention centers, cultural or entertainment centers, or sports venues of some sort. Once the commitment to the investment is made, the second stage of trying to realize the benefits from the investment is to ensure that middle- and upper-class consumers come to the investment site. A sports stadium needs sports fans; a convention center needs conventions. In the final stage, the circulation of dollars will ultimately support employment, draw new workers, and drive up residential property and commercial values in the areas near the investment site (Eisinger, 1988; Logan and Moloch, 1987; Judd and Swanstrom, 2012; Rosentraub, 2010).

Given the size and scope of a major national political convention, growth interests find the political convention an appealing prize to seek, based on their perceptions of conventions as having significant impacts on the local economy. But are the impacts real? Are they significant? Do they lead to long-term changes? As noted in chapter 4, conventions are not cost-free. Are the expected benefits worth those costs?

This chapter provides an overview of the possible economic payoffs that might be attributable to hosting a national political convention. We will highlight the role of the growth coalition and its role in local economic development policy. We will also provide an overview of how we got to a point where convention chasing is part of the growth policy du jour. The chapter includes a primer on what exactly analysts mean by "economic impact" and "economic development," as well as how to measure impact and the common criticisms of those measures. And finally, we explore the question of why cities might pursue a convention if the impact is small through an examination of several "legacy projects" that continue in host cities after the convention has ended and the visitors have left town.

Growth Regimes and Economic Development

In previous chapters, we introduced the concept of the growth coalition (also referred to in the literature as growth regimes or growth machines), a concept common in the urban politics and policy literature. The core of the concept is the recognition of several pro-growth interests within cities (usually the major central cities of metropolitan areas). These interests represent primarily businesses, especially real estate. But these interests also include unions (a growing economy employs more workers), local media (more watchers and readers), utilities (more services to deliver and charge for), and even universities (a bigger population means more students and the need for larger campuses, which leads to increased land speculation around those campuses) (Logan and Molotch, 1987; Stone, 1989).

The interests of the coalition are, simply put, growth. This is a goal that often divides political elites at the local level from the citizens. But the growth is a means to an end, and the end is profit (or rents, to borrow from the economists). Intensifying economic activity in a specific geographic space often attracts other demands on nearby space. Those demands drive up property values. The owners of those properties (namely, members of the growth coalition) benefit from the economic activity that drives up the value of the property assets that they own. That increased value can then be used as collateral or to leverage additional growth in the community.

Economic conservatives will argue that this model of positive economic growth at the local level will not be limited to wealthier citizens. Rather, the increased circulation of capital in the local economy will mean more and better paying jobs, thus creating a trickle-down effect initiated by the growth. Additional income, consumption spending, and higher property values will yield greater tax revenues for the city at lower tax rates, allowing the city to invest in better infrastructure and services that fuel even more economic development opportunities.

Detractors will argue that the increased property values will disproportionately accrue to the wealthy and members of the growth coalition. Furthermore, they will argue that the increased property values will lead to higher nominal taxes for residents and will force lower-income residents to relocate to lower land value areas, thereby gentrifying neighborhoods near to the economic activity. Thus, the critics argue, this kind of growth policy exacerbates the economic segregation prevalent in most American cities.

More often than not, interests in the growth coalition win when the two groups come into conflict over growth opportunities. One of the primary reasons for their tendency to win is the ability to coalesce around a growth-oriented issue as a strong, single-issue interest group and pool their resources in a manner that can combat any opposition, which is usually splintered and relatively poorly funded. Another advantage the coalition has is that many times the local government (or individuals within the local government, such as the mayor) is a *de facto* member of the coalition. This may be because the individuals are elected to office from those institutional interests central to the coalition (for instance, former part-time Charlotte mayor Pat McCrory who retained his position at Duke Power while in office), or because members of the coalition are often significant campaign contributors and thus have better access to decision makers than other citizens. Regardless of why they are successful, they are effective. And therefore, these coalitions are often behind the efforts of many communities that seek to attract mega-events like a national political convention.

Local Economic Growth Policy

Growth coalitions are nothing new. In fact, some scholars suggest that the colonies were founded by growth regimes that paid homage to the crown through charters (Burns, 1994; Eysberg, 1989; Warner, 1968). The colonies were centers for capital formation through the extraction of resources. As cities evolved, they became independent centers of manufacturing where natural resources could be converted into products and shipped to markets. But for cities to assume this role, they had to have adequate infrastructure to support this kind of development. That primarily meant that they needed transportation (initially rivers or coastlines, later railroads, and more recently highways and airports), but they also needed clean water, sanitation, and public safety. These were not easily created privately, so they evolved stronger local governments with the power of taxation to provide the necessary infrastructure and public services that would be needed to grow cities as centers for capital formation (Judd and Swanstrom, 2012).

This basic pattern served as the fundamental blueprint for local economic development policy at least through World War II. Cities were designed to support manufacturing needs through infrastructure and public services. By the 1980s, this manufacturing focus had ebbed. During that time, the suburbanization of the nation had mushroomed and manufacturing centers dispersed, along with wealthier residents, to suburbs with lower land prices and greater amenities, or offshore to other nations with cheaper labor and weaker environmental regulations. The American economy shifted away from a reliance on manufacturing to a service-based economy.

As a result, the type of economic development policies shifted at the local level as well. As production-centered manufacturing dried up or moved away, cities increasingly competed with each other to lure the remaining manufacturers from one location to another, or to encourage existing manufacturers to expand on site, with promises to help acquire needed property even if it required the use of eminent domain.

But with the rise of the service economy, the nature of the role of central cities evolved to support different kinds of businesses, particularly in the finance, insurance, and real estate sectors (FIRE). Instead of "smokestack chasing" like in the earlier years, cities and their growth coalitions adapted to a new kind of strategy focused on consumption opportunities. The primary target of this new kind of growth policy became tourism.

This brings us to today. For the past couple of decades, cities have invested billions of dollars in building convention centers, football and baseball stadia, basketball and hockey arenas, countless museums, and numerous cultural or entertainment districts. As Sanders notes, the massive investment in convention space in the 1990s and early 2000s has increased competition due to the number of cities building ever-larger convention facilities (2005). The number of sites available exceeds the convention industry's needs and has diluted the concentration of where conventions are held. For instance, as Judd and Swanstrom note, the most successful city in America for attracting conventions is Orlando, Florida (2012). However, even though it is the most successful, Orlando still only manages to capture less than 5% of all conventions annually. No one city dominates this field given the proliferation of convention centers and available square footage.

But there is an often-overlooked aspect to this current focus on tourism and convention-centered economic development policy. Unlike the efforts of the "smokestack chasing" days when local governments might provide a tax incentive or land deal to lure a manufacturer to relocate, the convention game requires a different approach. Someone has to build the convention building (or stadium or arena, etc.). Since the 1980s, these facilities have required significant, if not complete, subsidization by public funds. Most often, this has been accomplished through general obligation bonds, backed by tax revenues. As such, these commitments of public capital required input and approval by the public, often through a referendum (Sanders, 2014).[2]

In order to win public support for these investments of public capital, the growth coalition played an important and coordinating role in messaging and building the necessary public support for the investment. Often, proponents couched these campaigns in terms of job growth and community economic development. And more often than not, these referenda succeeded. In those communities that did not have a coherent growth coalition that could coordinate and resource a focused message campaign, there was a higher likelihood of defeat (Burbank, Andranovich, and Heying, 2001).

Over the past fifteen years, a new strategy has gained popularity that avoids the "hassle" of a public vote on such referenda. Today, many cities (as well as many states) have established independent special districts or business improvement districts whose sole purpose is financing such convention, sports, and entertainment facilities. This end-around has allowed growth coalition interests to sidestep the need for campaigns to secure the financing as these special purpose districts do not require public votes for the use of public financing obligations (Sanders, 2014). Ironically, even as public financing mechanisms relying on public expenditures have become less democratic, there is evidence to suggest that establishing tourism as a basis for economic health is a sound basis for building trust in local government (Nunkoo, 2015).

Returning to the earlier point that there has been an enormous proliferation of convention centers and square footage in recent years from which the convention industry can choose, many of these publicly funded convention centers go underutilized, including such places as Phoenix, Albuquerque, or smaller communities like Council Bluffs, Iowa. When they are underutilized by convention events, financing, operations, and maintenance costs are not covered by revenues generated by the venue. And in such situations, costs must be covered by more public dollars. And yet, even while these patterns are fully known by the industry and cities alike, the competition for and investment in tourism continues unabated, much like the intercity and interstate competition for economic development more broadly. Today, more is spent in subsidies and incentives to engage in this competition for an increasingly diminishing return on that investment.

Measuring Economic Impact

Communities pursue strategies to bolster the economic health of their community and protect against urban decline. Growth regimes help spread the word about the value of new opportunities that will bring economic activity to the community and is therefore in line with the growth strategy. Every four years, dozens of growth coalitions mobilize to encourage their city to bid for one of the national political conventions as a mega-event capable of achieving two primary goals: 1) significant economic impact, and 2) national and international media exposure.

To help bolster their claims, boosters of the bid often tout the purported impacts of previous conventions on other host cities. Such estimates are often done as projections prior to the event (*ex ante* impacts) or after the event has occurred (*ex post* impacts). As table 6.1 illustrates, for example, Denver conducted a post-convention economic impact analysis and estimated the impact of the 2008 DNC at $153.9 million (City and County of Denver, 2008). The 2008 RNC in St. Paul had an estimated impact of $168.9 million (Minneapolis Saint Paul 2008 Host Committee, 2008). The 2004 RNC in New York City had a $255 million impact. But leaders were not as quick

Table 6.1. *Ex ante* and *ex post* convention economic impact estimates (nominal $millions)

Location of event	Year	Ex Ante— low Estimate	Ex Ante— high Estimate	Ex Post Estimate
Chicago (DNC)	1996	45.0	122.0	360.0
San Diego (RNC)	1996	300.0	300.0	No study
Los Angeles (DNC)	2000	n.a.	137.0	No study
Philadelphia (RNC)	2000	300.0	300.0	345.0
Boston (DNC)	2004	154.0	154.0	14.8
New York (RNC)	2004	n.a.	n.a.	255.0
Denver (DNC)	2008	n.a.	n.a.	266.1
St. Paul (RNC)	2008	n.a.	n.a.	168.9
Charlotte (DNC)	2012	128.7	250.0	163.0
Tampa Bay (RNC)	2012	150.0	153.6	404.4
Philadelphia (DNC)	2016	170.0	250.0	TBD
Cleveland (RNC)	2016	400.0	400.0	TBD

to point out the less successful 2004 DNC in Boston, which only had a reported $14.8 million impact (Beacon Hill Institute, 2004).

While citizens might expect something as analytical-sounding as "economic impact analysis" to yield *an* answer, such estimates actually vary for a number of reasons. As table 6.1 illustrates, the claims prior to conventions can vary substantially, but even the estimates after the event appear to fluctuate wildly, from a low impact of the 2004 Boston DNC of $14.8 million to a significantly higher impact of the 2012 Tampa Bay RNC of $404.4 million (particularly odd given that the convention was shorted by one day due to severe weather). What explains such wide-ranging estimates for fairly similarly scaled events? There are several reasons.

First, these are relatively rare economic events. Therefore, each one tends to be somewhat idiosyncratic in terms of specific external factors that can influence the extent of economic impact. For instance, much of the relatively small impact of the 2004 Boston DNC has been blamed on the higher costs of security for that convention (Beacon Hill Institute, 2004). This was the first DNC held after 9/11 and the security apparatus was not as strong as it was in New York for the RNC that same year.

Second, the projections estimated for the size of the economic impact of a convention (or sports event or university, etc.) are often motivated by proponents (or opponents) of the event/investment. Regarding political conventions, most of the analyses undertaken to date (both *ex ante* and *ex post*) have been conducted under contract with proponents of the convention who are often members of the growth coalition. As such, there may be political motivations that create an upward pressure on the estimates (Burbank, Andranovich, and Heying, 2001).

Third, there is a range of assumptions that go into an economic impact analysis and many times these assumptions are more generous than they perhaps should be. As a result of this tendency, many economists conclude that the estimates tend to exaggerate event impacts on host city economies (Noll and Zimbalist, 1997; Mills and Rosentraub, 2013). Some scholars have even gone so far as to note that economic impact studies have become propaganda devices for those who can afford to generate one that will yield the results they want to see. And if one study doesn't project the "correct" magnitude of impact, just hire another consultant to do another study that will (Crompton, 2006; Rosentraub and Swindell, 2009).

In order to explore the question of how to measure economic impact, one must first understand the differences among several commonly misused terms: economic impact, economic development, and economic growth. These three terms are often used in public discussions surrounding competition for mega-events or attracting a business to an area. They are often used interchangeably. However, while related, these terms actually refer to different concepts.

Many urban scholars and economist have noted that *economic development* is one of local government's core functions (Judd and Swanstrom, 2012; Logan and Molotch, 1987; Sharp, 1990). But there is debate even among scholars as to what exactly constitutes economic development. For instance, economists focus their definitions on aspects of well-being (a.k.a. welfare), using various measures of income and wealth as proxies for such well-being (Malpezzi, 2003). Musgrave and Musgrave (1989), writing from the public finance perspective, note that economic development ". . . should be broadly defined to include all expenditures of a productivity-increasing nature" as a means of achieving the goal of capital formation (p. 781). Therefore, *economic development* efforts are not aimed at specific businesses but instead focus on environmental attributes (Rosentraub and Swindell, 2009). Such attributes include: the jurisdiction's situation within the regional economy, market access, the diversity of the jurisdiction's economic base, factor costs for local businesses, the local business climate, and amenity levels in the community (Malizia and Feser, 1999). Economic development focuses on structural change (e.g., new water or transportation infrastructure) and is a goal of economic growth. We differentiate economic development from *economic growth* in that growth ". . . is a process of simple [quantitative] increase, implying more of the same, while economic development is a process of [qualitative] structural change, implying something different if not something more" (Flammang, 1979: 50). Political interests should talk about their economic goals in terms of economic growth. So why is the talk always about "economic impact"?

Simply put, economic impact is a bigger number than economic growth, and therefore has added political value in public discussions. Impact is nothing more than the sum of all direct, indirect, and induced spending related to an activity or event (e.g., a political convention). To argue that impact is the same as growth would mean that all the economic activity associated with an event would be completely new money that would not otherwise have been spent in the local economy but for the event.

An economic impact analysis tries to capture all the economic effects derived from the presence of a new project or event (Rosentraub and Swindell, 2009). This includes "direct spending effects" having to do with economic transactions or the exchange of money (e.g., renting a convention center for the RNC). But that is only one element, and perhaps the easiest to measure. The more challenging aspects of an economic impact analysis are the calculations of "indirect" and "induced" spending effects. An indirect effect is a measure of how a dollar spent directly gets re-spent as it circulates through the local economy. For instance, when the RNC pays to rent the convention center, the convention center uses a portion of the proceeds to pay management staff salaries. One staffer may take a fraction of her paycheck to pay for lunch next door one day. The amount she pays for her lunch will contribute a small fraction to the paycheck of the waiter that serves her lunch.

While some of the original money brought into town and spent renting the convention center (the direct spending) will circulate in the local economy (the indirect spending), most of that direct spending will "leak out" of the local economy quite rapidly. To return to our convention staffer, most of her paycheck is spent on rent. If she lives outside the city, most of her paycheck leaks out that way. But even a large portion of the direct spending by the RNC will immediately leak out of the local economy unless the convention center (or hotel, restaurant, shopping center, or souvenir shop, etc.) is owned locally, otherwise the money will flow to the financing agent.

Finally, economic impact analyses also try to capture estimates of "induced" spending. This is spending that is not directly or indirectly related to the actual spending at the event. Rather, this would be spending that occurs due to the presence of the event. For instance, perhaps our convention center staffer has a brother. He hears that the RNC is planning to come to Tampa Bay and he buys a storefront to sell retail merchandise because he expects the RNC will trigger more commercial traffic for his new store during and after the convention. His investment in the new store is "induced" by the coming of the convention. We see similar examples of induced spending by restaurants and hotels when new stadia and arenas are announced. Economists try to estimate the indirect and induced spending associated with an event or project through an array of multipliers that gauge the number of times a dollar gets spent in the local economy due to the event, adjusted for the different sectors that make up the local economy.

The economic impact study of the 2012 DNC in Charlotte highlights the different elements of such a report. As part of the process of evaluating the city's overall investment in bringing the DNC to Charlotte, city leaders wanted to determine if the city saw a net positive economic impact. The City of Charlotte joined with the Charlotte Regional Partnership, the Charlotte Center City Partners, and the Charlotte Chamber of Commerce to hire a consulting firm (Tourism Economics) to undertake an economic impact analysis of the 2012 DNC. The report concluded that Charlotte netted an economic impact of $163.6 million (see table 6.2). The report included an array of assumptions (see below) with their methodology explaining how they addressed the issues that commonly arise with such impact estimates. Even when tightening the study's assumptions considerably, the estimated impacts are still $117 million. While less than the more optimistic $163.6 million, both estimates are rather modest in the context of Charlotte's multibillion-dollar local economy. Regardless, when placed in the framework of a cost-benefit analysis, the impact suggests that the economic benefits considerably outweighed the city's costs without even including an estimate of the value of any successful "branding" effects associated with national and international exposure.

Thus, economic impact is the sum of all the direct spending associated with the event itself (e.g., renting the arena), the indirect and induced spending that happens because of the event (e.g., hotel room bookings that

Table 6.2. Total economic impact

	FTE jobs	Labor Income ($ mil)	Value added ($ mil)	Business sales output ($ mil)
Direct	853	30.3	47.5	91.0
Indirect	257	14.1	21.5	34.5
Induced	317	14.2	25.0	38.1
Total impact	1,427	58.5	94.0	163.6

Source: Tourism Economics (2013).

would not have happened but for the presence of the event), and the circulation of that spent money as it changes hands before leaking out of the local economy. Given the nature of calculating such impacts, there are many common mistakes that can occur in which the bottom line becomes inflated.

One of the most common mistakes, for instance, is in calculating the circulation of the money spent. This is calculated using those economic multipliers that represent how many times a dollar will be spent in the local economy before it gets spent outside the local economy. How many times the dollar is spent and re-spent inside the local economy determines the size of the multiplier used in calculating the economic impacts associated with the convention (Crompton, 2006).

Larger multipliers yield larger overall impacts. Furthermore, dollars spent in different sectors of the local economy leak out of the local economy at different rates and thus have varying multipliers. So to capture an accurate assessment of the economic impact of a project or event, analysts must know the sectors into which the original money is going, and know the appropriate multipliers to apply to each of those amounts in each sector. In other words, there is not only one multiplier; there is one for each sector of the local economy. Spending associated with conventions and entertainment typically falls predominately in sectors of the economy associated with the hospitality industry. These sectors have smaller multipliers than, say, the manufacturing sector's multiplier. Thus, accidental or purposeful errors in choosing multipliers can have a significant effect on the size of the bottom line impact estimate.

Another important aspect is only to count *additional* spending in these calculations (Hudson, 2001). One of the best aspects of the DNC coming to Charlotte in 2012, for instance, was the convention's date—the week of Labor Day. This is a traditionally slow week with limited convention activity and low hotel booking rates. Therefore, much of the convention activity represents economic activity that would not have happened had Charlotte not won the bid to host. But there still would have been *some* level of economic activity in the absence of the convention, and that amount of "normal" activity must be reduced from the estimates of the convention's economic impact in order to isolate better the *new* spending associated with the event (Crompton, 2006). This suggests that much of the spending was new to the local economy given the historical pattern of prior years when that particular week was a slow convention week.

Finally, the calculation of economic impacts should be sensitive to substitution effects (Rosentraub and Swindell, 2009). Staying with the Charlotte example, Charlotteans normally go about their work in the absence of conventions. The question to consider is whether the presence of *this* convention caused people to shift their spending patterns in the local economy. To have an actual economic impact, the event must induce *new* spending by bringing in new people to the local economy to spend money that they might otherwise have spent outside the local economy, as well as money spent *in addition to* what locals would have normally spent in the absence of the convention. Only this new spending should be included in the calculation since the remainder of the "normal" spending is simply substituting with the convention's presence. Analysts must also remove lost economic activity (e.g., for those that may leave town because of the expected congestion caused by the convention, taking their normal spending outside the local economy). As economist Victor Matheson noted in an interview for *Outside the Beltway*, "Cities are good at adding and multiplying. . . . They're not good at subtraction" (Mataconis, 2012). For these reasons, the calculation of reasonable economic impact estimates are fraught with possible errors that can easily inflate their size.

Deriving accurate estimates can be particularly challenging since there are economic and political reasons to inflate projections. Furthermore, the total impact of a convention is not felt evenly across the local economy. Some sectors do extremely well (e.g., hotels and security). For example, during the 2012 DNC, 98% of uptown Charlotte hotels were occupied with an average daily room rate of $311, and 92% of the rooms in the Charlotte region were occupied with an average daily rate of $220. In comparison, during the same week in September 2011, 57% of Charlotte hotel rooms were occupied at less than half the room rates (Tourism Economics, 2013). Juxtaposed, other businesses may have been hurt as their normal work clientele stayed home.

Do Conventions Matter, Economically Speaking?

Relying on a cacophony of economic impact studies that range considerably in their estimates due to wide-ranging assumptions, one might be inclined to answer this question "yes." However, economic impact studies are not the only way to do such analyses. Some rely on analytic approaches they argue overcome the difficulties of *ex ante* and traditional economic impact analyses. For instance, Coates and Depken (2006), Baade, Baumann, and Matheson (2008), Rosentraub and Swindell (2009), as well as Mills et al. (2014), have advocated the use of taxable sales data to detect changes over time or over geography that might be attributable to a mega-event like a convention or major sporting event. This is one example of an *ex post* analysis.

Baade, Baumann, and Matheson (2010) argue for *ex post* approaches to better capture the effects of mega-events on an economy. As they note, *ex post* analytic approaches tend to use regression analysis to capture the effect on a dependent variable (some measure of economic performance, such as real per capita income or the unemployment rate) that can be explained by changes in the economy attributable to the mega-event. As with any such regression approach, a major challenge is "to isolate the effect of the mega-event on the performance variable in the presence of a myriad of other causal changes" (p. 82).

These *ex post* approaches paint a significantly different picture of the effects of mega-events for local governments. Coates and Depken's analysis found that the 1992 RNC in Houston *reduced* taxable sales by $19 million (2006). It was also associated with a decline of almost $1.4 million in tax revenues for the city. Baade, Baumann, and Matheson's analysis of the 2002 Salt Lake City Olympic Winter Games found that while the effects varied by sector, the net effect of hosting the games was a loss to the local economy (2010). Similarly, their analysis of political conventions found no changes (positive or negative) in employment, personal income, or personal income per capita for host cities (2009).

Our data allows us to examine several aspects of the impacts of conventions relative to those in comparative cities (chapter 2). Using data from the Census Bureau, we can compare population growth and income growth from 1990 to 2014. We use data from various editions of the Census Bureau's economic census of employment in hospitality industries (hotels, restaurants, museums, etc.) to compare changes in tourism employment as a proportion of the city's total employment. Using data from the Federal Aviation Administration, we can compare changes in the number of passenger boardings from 2000 to 2014. And from the FBI's Uniform Crime Statistics, we can compare changes in the rates of violent and property crimes (adjusted for population) to assess whether the amount of equipment and training corresponding to hosting a convention affects the detection of crime. We present the mean differences between host and non-host cities in table 6.3.[3]

Table 6.3. Comparison of mean economic and crime statistics for host and Non-host cities, 1990–2014

	Population growth	Income growth	Air passengers	Tourism employment	Violent crime	Property crime
Host cities (n = 14)	19,793**	0.57**	17,613,986**	.10	.011	.041
Non-host cities	13,940	0.32	6,277,077	−.11	.009	.056

** Difference of means p < .05

A difference of means test shows that a statistically meaningful difference exists between host and non-host cities in their rates of population growth, income growth, and number of airline passenger boardings. There is no difference in the cities' rates of violent or property crimes.[4] Further analysis shows, however, that these simple differences are misleading because host cities already had higher rates of growth than other cities prior to the convention. For example, though host cities exhibit a higher rate of income growth than non-host cities, their rates of income growth were larger on average in the election cycle prior to their hosting a convention. The conventions, in other words, may not be the stimulus that causes host cities to increase their rates of economic or population growth or airline boardings. Once we add controls for previous rates of growth (and, in the case of airline boardings, city population size), there is no evidence of significant differences between host cities and other cities. In other words, we find no evidence that hosting a presidential nominating convention significantly affects a city's key economic and crime statistics.

Coming back to the question as to whether or not conventions matter, from an economic perspective, does the question itself matter? Regardless of whether the economic impacts are overly optimistically positive or even slightly negative as suggested by some of the *ex post* studies, cities and their public officials are the ones pursuing the bids and agreeing to host these events. As representatives of the citizens (including the business community), public choice theory suggests that communities should be allowed to make decisions based on what their citizens want as long as the negative externalities and costs do not spill over onto citizens in other jurisdictions who will not benefit (Tiebout, 1956). Economist Allen Sanderson was quoted as saying in a *Wall Street Journal* interview: "If Charlotte or Tampa or London or Rio wants to argue that they're going to throw a huge party and, with their eyes wide open, they are willing to blow some fraction of their disposable income to do it, fine by me" (Bialik, 2012).

Survey data seem to back this public opinion position fairly clearly. The Beacon Hill Institute at Suffolk University conducted a poll of Boston residents in the days just prior to the 2004 DNC. Economic impact estimates were already predicting very small if not negative effects on the local economy as security costs had skyrocketed leading up to the convention that year. So while 44% of their respondents believed the city would lose money on the convention and only 39% believed the city would come out ahead, over half of the respondents (55%) said they would recommend to other cities that hosting the convention is a good idea. John Barrett, who directed the survey research, concluded: "There seems to be a paradox at play, while a majority of residents would recommend that other cities host a convention, they also acknowledge that the event is likely to lose money for the local economy" (Beacon Hill Institute, 2004). Similarly, data from our survey of Charlotte residents after the 2012 DNC also found high marks for the event and that it was a good investment for the community. In chapter 7, we take this one step further and quantify the value of this intangible benefit residents feel about having hosted the DNC.

If Not Economic Impact, Then What?

Media Exposure

At the outset of this chapter, we noted that public officials and members of the growth coalition tend to highlight two major arguments in support of pursuing a mega-event like a political convention. First, they focus on economic impact. Claims of the economic importance of mega-events continued in the lead-up to the 2016 Cleveland and Philadelphia political conventions. Meryl Levitz, who leads Visit Philadelphia (an institutional member of the city's growth coalition) was quoted in a CBS news interview saying, ". . . jobs created by the [2016 DNC] convention will remain after the delegates leave and expand going forward" (Hunter, 2015).

But in more recent years, the economic argument has lost some of its appeal as many citizens are coming to understand better the relatively small (if any) economic payoff provided by hosting a mega-event. In place of the economic arguments, proponents now like to herald the importance of the mega-event as an opportunity to shine a national or international spotlight on the host city. As Julie Cocker Graham, executive vice president of the Philadelphia Convention and Visitors Bureau (another member of the growth coalition) noted in an interview: "First and foremost, landing the DNC for us is huge, huge visibility for the city. It puts us on an international and national stage in terms of visitors and convention attendees coming to Philadelphia, and it really does prove what we've always known—that we are a city that offers the complete package" (Oot, 2015). Bob Morgan, the president and CEO of the Charlotte Chamber of Commerce, said in an interview after the 2012 DNC that the convention might not transform a city's economy, but he was able to treat the 2012 convention "like a debut" for national and international audiences (Oot, 2015). And in another interview, Morgan noted: "The [Economic Impact] study will tell us about the net economic benefits: dollars spent versus dollars displaced. I'm less interested in that. . . . What I'm concerned about is that Charlotte showed well, that the journalists and others who were here had a generally positive experience. . . ."[5]

But if measuring the economic impacts of hosting a mega-event like a political convention can be considered challenging, trying to capture these less tangible benefits that may accrue to host cities may be even more so. Dan Murray, executive director of Charlotte's host committee, was quoted in an interview saying: "Before the convention, we had people who had asked where in South Carolina Charlotte was, when we were in North Carolina. So that was a big plus for us. Since then, there is a sense that people get more of what Charlotte is about" (Oot, 2015). "Offering the complete package," "getting what we are about," and other similarly vague references to benefits derived from being on the national and international stage for four days during a political convention make quantifying such claims rather difficult for social scientists, but a boon to the growth coalitions across the nation.

Data on Internet searches provide one means of assessing the impact of media exposure for the host city. Google trends[6] data show that searches for the host city[7] spike during political conventions. For seven of the eight host cities since Google trends records started in 2004, the convention month on average is the second-highest month of searches for the host cities.[8] Philadelphia is the exception, as its searches have declined steadily since September of 2005.[9] Moreover, comparing the host city to the other cities that bid for the party conventions in 2012 shows meaningful gains in searches for the host. In the year before and the year after the 2012 Republican National Convention, Tampa's searches averaged 16 points less than Phoenix and 34 points more than Salt Lake City. During the month of the convention, Tampa gained 11 points on Phoenix and an additional 7 points on Salt Lake. Charlotte's gains in Internet searches were less dramatic but still notable: 3 points on St. Louis and 4 points on Minneapolis. The evidence shows that the host cities are able to capture some increase in public attention by piggybacking on the parties' big media events.

Embedded within claims that all exposure is good exposure are multiple examples of city images taking a beating due to events beyond their control during conventions. Chicago's 1968 convention is probably the most famous. But, says Don Davis who served as financial director for Chicago's 1996 convention committee, hosting in the DNC in 1996 yielded immeasurable benefits. "It put 1968 behind us. It showcased the city as one of the most livable cities, if not the most livable city, in the United States" (Stewart, 1998).

Chicago's unfortunate experience is not unique. Unrest during the 1972 conventions in Miami, police clashes in Los Angeles in 2000, significant cost overruns in Boston in 2004, police clashing with protesters in St. Paul in 2008, and bad weather in Tampa Bay along with barely populated streets in 2012 have all limited the possible "fuzzy, feel good" buzz that cities might experience from this kind of media exposure. So just because a community scores a mega-event does not automatically mean that the city will be indelibly imprinted on the mental maps of others around the world for all the right reasons.

Legacy Projects

Spending during a political convention is a short-term benefit at best and is limited to particular sectors of the local economy. Big contracts often go to out-of-town vendors. And local residents are frequently inconvenienced by the additional traffic and security issues, particularly in the post-9/11 era. While economic impact and media exposure are the primary benefits touted by the growth coalition pursuing mega-events, recent years have seen an increase by local officials to promise new programs or projects that will continue after the event is over. Increasingly, local officials and growth coalition representatives try to "sweeten the pot" with convention "legacies" to demonstrate some broader benefit to the community. The Olympics and World Cup tournaments frequently leave substantial legacies of physical infrastructure and redevelopment in the host city. Indeed, local politicians try to purposefully use the Olympics to these ends (Preuss, 2004). Because parties choose host cities with infrastructure already in place (chapter 2), the physical legacies of presidential nominating conventions are much more modest. Tampa Bay, for example, trumpeted road resurfacing, hotel renovations, technology upgrades in convention facilities, beautification projects, and police securing a variety of new equipment as the legacies of the 2012 RNC (Tampa Bay Host Committee, 2012). In many cities, these types of projects would have happened anyway, but the convention advanced their deadline.

Some city leaders have developed more intentional strategies to use legacy projects to build public support for the conventions. Legacy projects are also valued as means to create events and themes for the media to cover in the lead-up to the convention to assist the city's branding efforts.[10] Part of the rationale for Boston's bid for the 2004 DNC was to show racial integration and replace images of divisions from the 1970s busing controversies. In its bid, Boston touted its infrastructure for outreach to the disadvantaged and the city committed to developing an inclusive directory of local vendors who would be advantaged in winning convention contracts (Roche, 2004). The directory's legacy was its use of convention "spoils" to "integrate the entrepreneurial class" (Jones, 2003). The directory also became a legacy in future RFPs to bid for DNCs.

Denver burnished its environmental image by hosting the first "green convention." It hired a "Director of Greening" for the convention with private funds. It set a goal of a carbon-neutral convention and developed multifaceted programs to minimize emissions and promote environmental consciousness during the 2008 DNC. It introduced bicycle sharing, reusable water bottles, and refill stations; promoted locally grown organic foods at events and restaurants; designated "green" businesses in the host committee vendor directory; held six "green business" training workshops; and celebrated the daylong Green Frontier Fest that attracted about eight thousand people (Denver 2008 Host Committee, 2008). Thereafter, the DNC added green requirements to their RPFs for the 2012 and 2016 conventions.

The Charlotte host committee used one hundred interviews and four focus groups with community leaders and impromptu conversations with ordinary citizens to select four legacies. The conversations produced a set of broad guides: 1) Take something that already exists in plans and make it happen using the convention as a catalyst; 2) Highlight activities that are already being done but getting little attention; and 3) Use the convention volunteer list to get people involved in community service projects before the convention. Two of the resulting legacy projects were from previous DNCs—sustainability (Denver) and economic inclusion (Boston)—and the other two aligned with priorities of Charlotte political leaders: youth employment/civic education (Mayor Anthony Foxx), and healthy children and families (president of the Charlotte in 2012 Host Committee, Dan Murrey).[11]

Because legacy spending was not in the formal contract with the DNC, community organizations would own such projects after the convention. Therefore, the Charlotte host committee prioritized projects that had already been planned and used the convention as the catalyst to implement them.[12] For example, Project Lift was a public/private partnership to assist high poverty schools in West Charlotte. The DNC provided a spotlight to attract volunteers and donors to build playgrounds and community gardens, and provide internships. The sustainability legacy could be used to boost the city's ongoing energy-efficiency programs and its priority of recruiting energy companies. The city set up refillable water stations during the convention, bought "big belly" trash/recycling compacters to reduce the volume of waste and the number of pick-ups, set up a bike sharing program, and promoted its Envision Charlotte program to reduce uptown energy use 20% by 2016.[13]

The economic inclusion agenda incorporated a requirement in the contract with the DNC that required the host committee to establish a searchable website to promote minority vendors during the convention. Nearly five thousand businesses participated in the directory, 78% of them local (C. Smith, 2013). As part of its economic inclusion legacy program, the host committee pledged one-third of its spending to minority-owned businesses (including women, veterans, the disabled, and LGBTQ). The host committee claimed to exceed these goals with 47% of contracts going to these businesses (C. Smith, 2013).

One of the key challenges to making legacy projects more than a photo-op is to find an organizational sponsor once the host committee disbands after the convention. Community members criticized Boston's host committee for not making its directory publicly accessible after the convention (Roche, 2004). The Denver Host Committee's donation of its surplus to their sustainability project and the engagement of multiple preexisting community organizations in the project gave it the potential for longer-term impacts (Denver Host Committee, 2008).

Corporate Recruiting

The final intangible benefit tied to hosting a political convention involves the myriad opportunities for recruiting possible business transfers. City leaders are constantly attempting to entice corporations to relocate. The vast majority of cities have existing public relations and branding campaigns, often institutionalized in a nonprofit or quasi-public convention and visitors' bureau (though these go by many various names). Recruiting a convention is integrated into these ongoing public relations campaigns and provides the opportunity for additional exposure for the city. Similarly, political conventions may be used as the drawing cards for site visits for potential business recruits, in the same way that cities typically use major sporting events and artistic performances.[14] Since the National Democratic Institute brings hundreds of foreign political and business leaders to town during the convention, the Charlotte Chamber of Commerce led them on site tours in the energy, education, and health care sectors on the day before the convention in the hopes of encouraging foreign investment in the city.[15]

When the DNC selected Charlotte to host the 2012 convention, the chamber sent a letter to all Fortune 500 CEOs saying "we're here to help" if you plan to have representatives at the convention. Shortly before the convention, it sent another letter to them from Charlotte's Fortune 500 CEOs touting Charlotte and inviting representatives from the other Fortune 500 companies to meet with them during the DNC.[16] During the convention, Duke Energy hosted a forum on American competitiveness for business leaders at which a "[p]anel of economists and business leaders lauded Charlotte as a model of economic efficiency in today's modern global economy" (Mayhew, 2012).

Most of the Charlotte chamber's recruitment efforts, however, were more targeted. The chamber developed a list of thirty-two companies in energy, finance, and health care based on the following attributes: inadequate air service, limited presence in the Southeast, those who might have difficulty recruiting a properly skilled workforce in their current location, and companies with new leaders who may be open to making a signature change.[17] They were sent Kindle Fire tablets with a preloaded promotional video.

While relocation of a company headquarters would draw headlines, the more likely economic impact comes from the cumulative effect of more ordinary business decisions: the students who were impressed and decide to move to Charlotte after graduation, portfolio managers who might buy assets in the city, or corporations that might open a Charlotte office (Dunn, 2012b). Quantifying these long-term and more diffuse benefits as part of a rigorous analysis of the costs and benefits of evaluating the hosting decision simply are not possible beyond the vague and ephemeral claims often made by local officials and growth coalition advocates. As noted by Charlotte Chamber of Commerce president and CEO Bob Morgan: "You can't say that they watched the convention and now they're interested in Charlotte. It's not that simple. It's about creating a positive impression of Charlotte that will pay positive dividends for a long, long time to come."[18]

Conclusion

Political conventions remain among the most powerful staples of mega-events in the United States. Even though the role they have played historically in electing presidents has changed, there is no denying the excitement and activity generated by the spectacle surrounding the nominating convention. As such, there is no reason to suspect cities will lose interest in trying to lure such mega-events to their community to capture whatever economic and less tangible benefits might spin off from such investments of public capital. And citizens of a given jurisdiction are well within their rights to perhaps want to have a community celebration around such events, since it is their collective public capital spent on it.

However, what we have tried to provide in this chapter is a comprehensive overview of the factors involved in this decision from an economic perspective. Growth coalitions are members of the community, but their resources might carry additional weight with the public officials who make the spending decisions on bids and hosting. Or, to paraphrase Orwell, some members of the host communities may be more equal than others. As such, the information in this chapter provides officials and citizens alike with a broader perspective on which to make that decision about whether or not throwing that party is a good use of public capital.

Even the most optimistic studies concluding millions of dollars of economic impact suggest that such events are but small drops in the lake that is a local regional economy. The difference is that these small drops, like sports, bring more excitement and media coverage than investments in a new high school or sewer sanitation line, both of which provide higher rates of return on the dollars spent than a mega-event. This pizzazz factor can skew clear economic thinking on allocating scarce public resources in ways that have the biggest bang for the buck, as well as the fairest distribution of benefits for citizens across the community.

7

Generating Support for Mega-Events

The Democratic National Convention chose *us*. And *you* should too!

—Charlotte Regional Visitors Association buttons

Most Americans only experience a presidential nominating convention through watching a few hours of prime-time speeches during parts of two weeks in the summer before a presidential election. And for most of those viewers, their reaction to the convention will depend largely on two things: 1) their interest in politics, and 2) whether they are a fan of the party whose convention they are viewing. The less interested and less partisan may watch to get more information on the presidential candidates and to hear what a few famous politicians or other notable public figures will say. The more interested and more partisan will tune in to root for their team and get their talking points for arguing with their wrong-headed family members and coworkers.

For the people who are physically present for the convention, the following reactions partially, though inadequately, capture their experiences:

For the journalist, trying to describe a political convention to the uninitiated: "Think church because it's a congregation of like-minded believers. Think bazaar because of all the vendors hawking trinkets. And think carnival with the cacophony of shouts and colors. . . . [It's] crack for political junkies."[1]

For the resident of a host city, "Now every time you turn on the TV anywhere, they're talking about [my hometown]. That's as cool as it can be."[2]

For participants, a convention offers the opportunity of delegation breakfasts attended by up-and-coming national politicians, a day of caucus meetings to learn more about the issues on which you are passionate, forums with elite thinkers and media personalities, chance meetings with the stalwarts of the party ("Hey, there's Senator Dole!") or celebrities ("Hey, there's George Clooney!"), and receptions at which to network with activists and officials who have great ideas for your hometown. If you are so fortunate as to get a ticket inside the hall, it is a chance to observe history. For a delegate, the convention includes the honor of selecting your party's nominee to be president of the United States and ratifying the platform for which your party stands. For political geeks, the presidential nominating convention is the Super Bowl, the World Series, and a royal wedding all rolled into one!

For city leaders, the value of the convention or any mega-event lies in the potential for a short-term economic boost from attracting outside spending as well as long-term public relations and reputational benefits of being seen as an attractive place to visit and reside. Mega-event strategies are generally thought to be driven by a city's economic and political elite (e.g., Andranovich et al. 2001; Burbank et al. 2001; Eisinger, 1988; Logan and Moloch, 1987; Judd and Swanstrom, 2012; Rosentraub, 2010). There rarely is a grassroots movement to demand the city prioritize investments in tourism infrastructure or to do more to attract large events even if residents use some of the same amenities as conventioneers. Thus, the level of public buy-in for a mega-event development strategy is unclear. And while city residents are likely to be less invested in the city's public relations efforts than city elites, they pay for the convention in disruptions and inconveniences if not out-of-pocket, and certainly have no small amount of civic pride at stake. So if city leaders seek to prioritize mega-event-based development strategies, residents must at least remain tolerant or quiescent about the costs and inconveniences. And cities that are considering such a strategy would be assisted by knowing how the public reacts to its implementation.

To evaluate public support for mega-event strategies, we rely on our post-2012 election survey of Mecklenburg County residents and their perception of the Charlotte DNC. As we will show, whether residents approve depends on whether they think previous events have been successful and yielded economic benefits. So before we analyze survey results of mega-event strategies, we analyze how and why they evaluate the success of mega-events.

To conclude the chapter, we return to the lessons of what makes a successful convention and their implications for future convention planners.

Residents' Evaluations of the Convention

By almost all accounts, the 2012 DNC went smoothly. Fears of being over-run by protesters proved overblown. There were only twenty-five arrests, sixteen of which were "negotiated" (that is, protesters who wanted to be arrested).[3] Fears of traffic gridlock were largely unrealized—in part because uptown offices told their employees to work from home during the week. As a *Charlotte Observer* editorial (2012) put it: ". . . [I]t's a good thing when the big traffic story is a dancing cop. . . ." Significant sections of uptown Charlotte were shut down for the security zone around Time Warner Arena, but media representatives coming from the Republican National Convention praised Charlotte for not seeming like an "armed camp" (Ordonez, 2012). Survey respondents even gave protesters a generally positive rating for their behavior (a mean of 3.8 out of 5); less surprisingly, the police received high levels of approval for their work (4.5 out of 5).

We use three different sets of questions to measure residents' perception of the convention's success. The actual questions are listed in appendix 7-A in the section on DNC measures. The first question simply asked how success-ful Charlotte was as host. Respondents rated Charlotte's performance during the DNC as quite successful, on average almost midway between very and somewhat successful, as illustrated in table 7.1. The second and third measures tap the themes of economic development and the creation of a national repu-tation brand for Charlotte that were promoted by city leaders. Respondents

Table 7.1. Evaluating the success of the DNC by party identification

	Success as host 5–1 scale	Economic impact 9–1 scale	Reputation +2.6 to –3.5
All respondents	4.44	7.09	.11
Democrats	4.67	7.86	.50
Independents/others	4.40	6.88	.10
Republicans	4.09	6.14	–.54

Note: Cells indicate the mean scale rating.

Data source: 2012 Post-Election Survey, Mecklenburg County, North Carolina.

estimated the perceived economic impact of the three-day convention to be moderately positive (seven out of nine). We also asked respondents to rate various organizations based on their contribution to Charlotte's national reputation. Respondents rated the DNC as contributing slightly more to the city's national reputation than their average rating of the contributions of other prominent Charlotte organizations, even more important than the NFL Carolina Panthers.

The organizations and their ratings are listed in table 7.2. Cultural facilities, Bank of America, and Duke Energy clustered close together with the highest rankings, with the DNC close behind; sports teams rated somewhat lower. The reputation score used in table 7.2 and in the analysis below subtracts the respondent's average rating for all organizations from the respondent's rating of the DNC's prominence in Charlotte's national reputation. Larger positive values indicate how much more the DNC was important to Charlotte's reputation than the average organization; larger negative values show how much less important to Charlotte's reputation was the DNC than other organizations according to the respondents.

The average evaluations of the 2012 DNC obscure meaningful partisan differences, despite the fact that the survey asked convention evaluation questions before questions about partisanship and ideology to avoid priming a partisan effect. In rating Charlotte's success as host, respondents differ by party but not dramatically. On average, all partisan groups rate the city between a 5 (very successful) and a 4 (somewhat successful) as a host. A lack of major incidents during the convention and positive media coverage buoyed all partisans' evaluations of the city's success as the convention host. Democrats are nearer to a rating of 5 while Republicans are closer to a 4, and independents rate the city at the survey average.

Table 7.2. Mean rating of organizations' contribution to Charlotte's national reputation (5 = very important, −1 = very unimportant)

Arts, museums, etc.	4.35
Bank of America	4.33
Duke Energy	4.30
Democratic National Convention	4.21
Panthers (NFL)	4.07
NASCAR	3.97
Bobcats (NBA)	3.48

Data source: 2012 Post-Election Survey, Mecklenburg County, North Carolina.

The partisan differences are more apparent in evaluations of the convention's economic impact and contribution to the city's national reputation. Democrats rated the convention's economic impact to be a full point more robust than independents' ratings (roughly, a somewhat large economic impact [D] versus a moderately large economic impact [I]) and Republicans rated the convention's economic impact to be about three-quarters of a point less than independents (roughly, a small, positive impact). Even more dramatic were the partisan differences in the respondents' assessments of the DNC to Charlotte's national reputation. Democrats rated the DNC's contribution as half a point more positively than their average for other prominent Charlotte organizations; independents rated the DNC as essentially the same as other organizations; and Republicans thought other organizations contributed more to Charlotte's national reputation than did the DNC by half a point. In short, respondents were largely in agreement that Charlotte succeeded as a host for the 2012 DNC, but differed on the extent to which the city succeeded and what that might mean for the city in terms of the economic impact and how outsiders would now view Charlotte.

Perhaps not surprisingly, respondents appear to make their evaluations of a political convention through a partisan lens. But we are also interested in the ways in which residents' engagement with the convention affects their evaluations. Charlotte, for example, created opportunities for residents to participate in convention activities by throwing a Labor Day street festival and inviting people to attend President Obama's acceptance speech in Bank of America stadium (an invitation that was cancelled due to weather; see chapters 4 and 5). Moreover, host cities spend considerable effort to mitigate the disruption of a national security event (chapter 4). Nevertheless, residents who live and work near the security zone faced greater costs and inconvenience than others. And there are some residents who work in industries that stand to benefit financially from the convention (tourism, media, and entertainment). How did residents' direct experiences with the convention, or indirect engagement through media usage, affect their evaluations?

We hypothesize that residents' evaluations of the convention would be driven by three types of variables: their political attitudes, their engagement with the convention, and the extent to which they were impacted as a resident by the convention. As documented above, Democrats and liberals should evaluate the convention more positively to credit "their team" with generating positive benefits for the community. Women and minorities are likely to follow suit, though less strongly. We have mixed expectations for political interest. Highly interested residents are likely to highly rate the city's success as a host because they are more likely to observe that events went smoothly and that local news coverage was positive. Politically interested residents are less likely to credit a short-term event with creating a significant long-term economic or reputational impact to the convention, as they have not noticed a boost for previous convention cities.

Those who participated in convention activities or followed the convention closely in the news are likely to give higher evaluations. Further, residents who obtained tickets to Obama's acceptance speech and disapproved of the decision to move the speech inside will give consistently negative appraisals of the convention's impact. Residents who left the city to avoid the convention would have been exposed to less direct information than their neighbors, but their decision to leave town suggests negative expectations, so their ratings are likely to be negative. Residents whose routines would be changed by the convention, particularly center-city residents and those who claim a work disruption, are likely to rate it more negatively. Those who work in industries that stood to gain from the convention are more likely to rate it positively. Long-term residents, as we saw in chapter 5, give the city government lower ratings. Presuming that part of their dissatisfaction is with how the city has handled growth, they probably also would be less approving of an event that highlighted "big city status" and forced the city government to balance serving long-term residents with out-of-town celebrities.

We use the three assessments of the convention as our dependent variables: the respondents' rating of the city as a successful host, their assessment of the economic impact of the convention, and their assessment of the DNC's contribution to Charlotte's national reputation relative to other well-known Charlotte organizations. We estimate each of the models using Ordinary Least Squares regression.

Table 7.3 shows that party identification and ideology consistently correlate with evaluations of the convention and had some of the largest effects on the evaluations according to the beta values. Not surprisingly, Democrats and liberals not only believe the convention was a success but also believe it brought substantial economic and reputational gains to the city. Most of the other political affinity variables show some differences across the three evaluations. Minorities, for example, did not differ from whites in evaluating the convention's success but were more likely to credit the convention with a positive economic and reputational boost for the city. And residents with high levels of political interest were significantly more likely to rate the convention as a success, but less likely to believe that the convention contributed to Charlotte's national reputation. As people who have paid attention to previous conventions, they appear to realize that the attention to the host city is fleeting.

Table 7.3. Evaluations of the 2012 DNC by Mecklenburg County residents

	Successful host			Economic impact			City's reputation		
	b	SE	Beta	b	SE	Beta	b	SE	Beta
Political affinity									
PID (Democrat)	.09***	.02	.20	.17***	.04	.20	.11***	.02	.24
Ideology (liberal)	.12***	.03	.15	.15**	.06	.09	.15**	.04	.17
Political interest	.08*	.04	.06	.01	.08	.00	-.09*	.05	-.06
Female	.01	.07	.01	-.05	.12	-.01	-.04	.07	-.02
Minority	-.09	.08	-.05	.38***	.14	.10	.17**	.08	.08
Engagement with the convention									
Convention news	.004	.02	.01	.01	.04	.01	.03	.02	.06
Participated	-.18	.11	-.05	.37*	.21	.06	.07	.11	.02
Mad at ticket loss	-.31*	.16	-.07	-2.26***	.29	-.27	-.32*	.17	-.07
Left city	-.02	.14	-.00	-.06	.26	-.01	.06	.05	.01
Impacted as a resident									
Work disrupted	-.04	.04	-.04	-.24***	.06	-.12	-.07**	.04	-.07
Related industry	-.10	.09	-.04	-.34**	.17	-.06	.15*	.09	.05
Center city	-.06	.16	-.01	-.30	.28	-.03	.01	.16	.00
Length of residence (nl)	-.04	.03	-.05	-.09*	.05	-.05	.01	.03	.01
Constant	4.13***	.22		7.00***	.39		-.99***	.22	
N =	832			826			805		
X^2 =	8.02 (p < .01)			20.52 (p < .01)			17.03 (p < .01)		
Adjusted R^2 =	.113			.235			.203		

Residents whose tickets to Obama's acceptance speech were cancelled due to the weather threat and who disapproved of moving the speech indoors gave the convention low ratings on each question. Not surprisingly, if they thought the main event was mishandled, they would not expect positive benefits for the city. Indeed, having tickets revoked produced the largest beta coefficient in the model of economic evaluations. In chapter 5, we found minimal effects of the cancellation on the ticketholders' political behavior in 2012, but their view of the collective benefits of the convention for the city was clearly damaged.

Participating in the convention had a significant effect on a respondent's assessment of the economic impact. Participants, particularly in the street festival, were able to see thousands of people uptown, and this experience led them to increase their assessment that all those people would leave some money in the local economy. Interestingly, however, their engagement did not increase their assessments that the city was a successful host or that the city's reputation would be enhanced. Perhaps the cacophony of the crowds, the thunderstorms, and the protesters were a turnoff. Indeed, when the evaluations are estimated separately by party, independents who participated rated the convention's success significantly lower than those who did not participate (Republican participants rated the convention's success significantly higher than other Republicans). Independents would more likely be turned off by the conflict inherent in protests around political conventions (Keith et al., 1992; Hibbing and Theiss-Morse, 2002). Intently following news about the convention consistently did not affect respondents' evaluations of the convention's impacts. This contrasts with the increase in participation and attention to the 2012 campaign that was documented in chapter 5.

Residents on whom the convention imposed costs reveal their displeasure in the economic and reputational impact estimates. Residents whose work was disrupted estimated significantly lower economic benefits and reputational benefits for the city, and the beta coefficient indicates a moderately large impact of the variable. Long-term residents gauged the economic benefits to be significantly lower. Interestingly, residents who worked in industries that were most directly affected by the convention gave mixed evaluations. They rated the economic impacts as significantly lower than other residents. Perhaps their expectations were that the convention would be an economic bonanza and they found that its impacts were more limited or concentrated than their dream scenarios. At the same time, they believed that the convention had a higher positive impact on the city's national reputation. We interpret their response to mean that they recognized that the convention was a major, impactful event, even if they didn't strike economic gold in the way they hoped.

The Value of Mega-Events

As noted in chapter 6, there are significant problems with traditional economic impact analyses applied to political conventions and other mega-events that may be part of a city's growth strategy. While we concede the point that even optimistic economic impacts associated with conventions are small relative to a local economy, we found from the Boston and Charlotte resident surveys that citizens can still want these events. If citizens do want such events and it is not motivated by economic development concerns, then what benefits do they perceive they are getting for spending limited public capital on hosting such events? Chapter 6 suggests that the perceived benefits are less tangible and center on the national reputation that hosting brings to a city.

Measuring intangible or psychological benefits such as these is possible using a contingent valuation methodology (CVM). This approach emerged over the past forty years from efforts to quantify the intangible benefits associated with environmental public goods (e.g., Mitchell and Carson, 1989; Yoo and Chae, 2001). Following a blue-ribbon commission by the National Oceanic and Atmospheric Administration (NOAA) in the early 1990s, CVM became accepted as a viable methodology for measuring these intangible benefits in government studies (Arrow et al., 1993). Since then, CVM has been applied to a wide range of other intangible impacts that spill over from public goods. More recently, the approach has been used to measure the intangible benefits, including civic pride, spilling over from public investments in sports facilities (Johnson, Mondello, and Whitehead, 2007; Rosentraub and Brennan, 2011; Söderberg, 2014; Swindell, Rosentraub, and Tsvetkova, 2008).

The goal of the CVM is to have target respondents place a reasoned value on the non-monetary or psychological values tied to some event or investment beyond simply the economic impact. In other words, the CVM attempts to monetize this externality and does so in the context of a hypothetical market setting. At the core of this approach for our purposes related to political conventions, we want to measure the extent to which citizens are willing to pay for the benefits they perceive are associated with these kinds of mega-events. Approving of an event or strategy is nice, but being willing to put resources behind it (even if only rhetorically) is a stronger commitment.

We framed the question in two different ways and offered values on two different scales to provide a more robust measure of the respondents' support for mega-events.[4] Specifically, the questions read as follows:

1. We would like to see if people can put a dollar value on any civic pride they may feel when their region hosts a large event.

In other words, we are interested in understanding the value citizens place on large events like the presidential convention as an amenity that generates civic pride.

Do you think that hosting large events in this region is worth $4 per month to you? [If yes,] Worth $8 per month? [If no,] Worth $2 per month?

2. Recently, there has been talk of the Charlotte region pursuing large events such as a future Republican National Convention, the Super Bowl, or the Olympics. Would your household be willing to pay $40 per year to fund city efforts to pursue and host events like these? [If yes,] $80 per year? [If no,] $20 per year? [If no,] What amount per year would you be willing to pay to attract and host these events?

In table 7.4, we present the percent of respondents who were willing to contribute particular amounts to finance mega-events. Despite the different framing and dollar amounts in the questions, the aggregate proportion of respondents is similar in each spending category. Two-thirds of the respondents were willing to contribute something (of course, whether they would if it weren't a hypothetical question is another matter), and one-half would be willing to contribute the middle dollar amount requested or higher. In the last column of table 7.4, we combined the responses to the two questions[5] to create a single scale (0–8) to measure a respondent's overall willingness to support mega-events financially. Respondents who were willing to contribute the maximum amount in both questions have the maximum value (8), while respondents who were not willing to contribute anything in either question

Table 7.4. Willingness to contribute

	Worth per month?	Willing to pay per year?		Combined	
$8	27.8%	$80	21.4%	8 (max)	11.3%
$4	26.1%	$40	32.4%	5–7	31.5%
$2	12.3%	$20	11.5%	1–4	33.4%
		< $20	5.1%		
0	33.8%	0	29.5%	0	23.9%

N = 938

Data source: 2012 Post-Election Survey, Mecklenburg County, North Carolina.

receive a 0. This process moves a number of respondents out of the most extreme categories and into middle points on the scale.

Our survey focused only on a sample of households from Mecklenburg County. Based on the U.S. Bureau of the Census American Community Survey's July estimates, the estimated number of households in the county in 2012 was 366,689.[6] The breakdown of the analysis is in table 7.5. Combined with the survey results, this provides a conservative estimate of the value for the civic pride and intangible benefits for the population of the county residents at $17,348,424.[7]

Using a similar approach applied to the next set of questions and using the lowest value in each category, we can also conservatively estimate citizens' willingness to pay for these intangible benefits (differentiated from the value they ascribe to those benefits). Table 7.6 on page 166 illustrates the components of the calculation, again applied against the number of households in Mecklenburg County. This calculation conservatively suggests that residents would be willing to pay $12,652,129; fully $4,696,295 less than the value residents place on these intangible benefits (a positive consumer surplus).

Next, we use the combined ordinal rankings of the value and the willingness to pay categories in table 7.4 to analyze who is willing to pay more to support a mega-events strategy.[8] We hypothesize that a respondent's willingness to pay will be based on a number of variables. First, respondents who have more trust in the competence of local government will be more

Table 7.5. Annual value of the intangible benefits of hosting mega-events

Value of intangible benefits	% of respondents at this level	Projected number of Mecklenburg households	Total projected value
$0–$2 / month ($0–$24 / year)	30.1	110,533	$0
$2–$4 / month ($24–$48 / year)	9.33	34,213	$821,112
$4–$8 / month ($48–$96 / year)	27.2	99,567	$4,779,216
$8+ / month ($96 / year)	33.4	122,376	$11,748,096
Total	100.0	366,689	$17,348,424

Data source: Authors' calculation based on data in the 2012 Post-Election Survey, Mecklenburg County, North Carolina.

Table 7.6. Willingness to pay for the intangible benefits of hosting mega-events

Value of intangible benefits	% of respondents at this level	Projected number of Mecklenburg households	Total projected value
$0 / year	28.8	105,671	$0
$0–$20 / year	4.6	18,33	$18,335
$20–$40 / year	11.2	41,070	$821,400
$40–$80 / year	31.6	115,877	$4,636,080
$80+ / year	20.9	76,640	$6,131,200
Total	100.0	366,689	$11,606,015

Data source: Authors' calculation based on data in the 2012 Post-Election Survey, Mecklenburg County, North Carolina.

willing to support its mega-events strategy. We use the factor score of the seven local government evaluation questions (chapter 5) as our measure of a respondent's attitudes toward the city government. We also include the respondent's level of efficacy toward local government because citizens who think they can influence city government should be more willing to provide resources.

Second, support for mega-events should follow political ideology. Liberals and Democrats should be more willing to give money for public purposes than conservatives and Republicans. We include dummy variables for Democrats and Republicans in the model and exclude independents as the baseline category.[9]

Third, those who believe these events produce an economic benefit either to the city collectively or to themselves selectively should be more willing to offer financial support. Specifically, those who perceived the DNC as having a larger economic benefit for the city or who believe that the DNC boosted Charlotte's reputation should be more willing to invest additional funds to attract similar events. We do not hypothesize that merely believing the city was a successful host of the DNC will have an effect on the respondents' willingness to fund future events. Rather, the economic value of the event is the critical issue in spurring people to make a personal financial commitment. Those who work in industries that would benefit from mega-events and those who live uptown where the mega-events should be staged will be more supportive. Long-term residents are likely to be more skeptical.

And finally, the magnitude of the contribution should depend on the contributor's social status. Respondents with higher levels of income should be willing to contribute more merely because they have more discretionary income. Providing forty dollars can be a large or small commitment depending on the respondent's resources, and higher income respondents have greater flexibility to agree to that level of support. Respondents with higher levels of education are likely to be more aware of the city's need for high-profile events to compete with other cities and should be more supportive. Women and men emphasize different aspects of economic development policy, with men preferring traditional programs based on infrastructure and incentives while women prefer "people-based" strategies such as investing in education and work-force training (Read and Leland, forthcoming). Moreover, many mega-events are sports-related (the Super Bowl and the Olympics were specifically mentioned in the second question), which may be more appealing to male respondents. Minorities may be more supportive of major events that would bring economic benefits and opportunities to the city.

Table 7.7 presents the results. The respondents' evaluation of local government has the largest effect on their willingness to invest in a mega-event

Table 7.7. Public support for mega-events, OLS

	B	SE	Beta
Support for local government			
Evaluation of city government	.62***	.14	.22
Local efficacy	.14	.16	.04
Political ideology			
Democrats	−.1.01***	.33	−.17
Republicans	−.1.10***	.37	−.16
Ideology (liberal)	.36***	.13	.15
Economic impact			
Success as DNC host	.02	.15	.01
DNC economic impact	.22**	.08	.14
DNC reputational impact	.32**	.15	.11
Related industry	1.04***	.36	.13
Center-city resident	1.06	.67	.07
Length of residence (nl)	−.01	.01	−.04
Social status			
Income	.13**	.05	.11
Education	.03	.11	.02
Male	.25	.27	.04
Minority	.53*	.33	.09
Constant	2.03*	1.15	

N = 379
X^2 = 66.75 (p < .01)
Adj. R^2 = .27

***p < .01; **p < .05; *p < .10 two-tailed test

strategy. If residents trust their leaders, they will be more willing to buy into the leaders' economic development proposals. Furthermore, trust is based on demonstrated results. As predicted, the DNC increased respondents' hypothetical contributions if they believed it had large economic and reputational benefits for the city. Crediting the city as a successful host by itself was insufficient to produce a greater willingness to invest in mega-events. Substantively, belief in the DNC's economic and reputational effects had similar impacts, according to the beta scores, as ideology and income. Residents are willing to invest in a mega-events strategy when they believe it has already paid dividends. Respondents who work in related industries also were willing to invest significantly more money in a mega-events strategy.

Politically, table 7.7 reveals some expected and some unexpected results. Those who have higher evaluations of city government are significantly more willing to spend on mega-events, as are liberals. Republicans are willing to part with significantly less money than independents. Surprisingly, Democrats also are less willing to contribute to mega-events than independents. We can speculate that, despite being the "pro-government" party, Democrats may prefer economic development strategies based on human infrastructure rather than mega-events strategies that subsidize sports team owners and the tourism industry (e.g., Hatcher et al., 2011), while independents see mega-events spending as an appropriate economic development tool. Finally, the higher the respondent's income, the more he or she is willing to spend on mega-events.[10] Minority respondents are also willing to spend more on mega-events at marginal levels of statistical significance.

These results are important in demonstrating that cities can build support from residents in a mega-event-oriented development strategy. The effects of the DNC economic impact and reputation variables demonstrate that residents are willing to invest more in such a strategy when they perceive that past mega-events have delivered on their economic promise. The evidence also shows that merely hosting a successful event is insufficient. Residents must be convinced that there is an economic benefit from the event if they are to double down on the strategy. Furthermore, respondents who have higher levels of trust in local government are more willing to invest in a mega-events strategy. Residents are less willing to devote their resources to promising ventures if they believe those funds are at risk of being squandered by a wasteful or incompetent government.

Lessons for Scholars

For such a seminal event—for the political parties, for the candidates for the most powerful office on the planet, for political geeks—we know little about the politics of conventions. In part, that is because the politics are no longer about selecting the nominees, which are the politics on which scholars and media pundits focus. The politics of the contemporary convention are outside of the convention hall in the process of the selection of the city, the fundraising to put on the show, the implementation of the event, the engagement of local residents, and the calculation of the economic benefits. The critical player in the new politics of conventions is the city. The city is the partner of the national party in the convention production, and they need each other to benefit from the convention.

The city, we have argued, matters for the national parties because the parties can control the message of the convention *when* they have selected a competent host city as the reliable agent. The national party is dependent on the host city as its problem fixer, which keeps the delegates and dignitaries happy and demonstrators out of the way; this allows the party to signal its competence and focus the media on its preferred message about its nominee and agenda. The city likewise captures the international media spotlight and the word-of-month endorsements from community leaders from across the country in recruiting and hosting a convention. Winning a convention, as the Charlotte Regional Visitors Authority button attests, demonstrates the credibility of a city's assets and entrepreneurialism in a competitive environment and signals its *bona fides* to potential businesses, residents, and meeting planners.

For both partners to benefit, however, the convention needs to be "successful." The *party* succeeds if it maintains its unity inside the convention hall and its nominee is able to present an appealing message to the viewing audience. The party's message is most likely to get through when the city is able to keep the attendees happy, the weather is good, and demonstrators are out of the way. The *city* succeeds when the convention coverage helps it magnify its image to the country and the world.

While focusing on the role of the political convention in the selection of the party nominee may be obvious, it is not the only aspect of convention activities in which politics occur and where power is allocated. Conventions dedicate substantial sums of money and prestige, and this makes the competition to recruit and implement them intense. Cities vary in their capacity to host mega-events such as political conventions, as well as in their interest to do so. Furthermore, their capacities and motivations change over time as cities invest in various infrastructure projects, gain (or lose) consistent streams of tourists, and the cost/benefit ratios of hosting conventions change based on the security environment and economic constraints on cities. Cities' local political funding capacities vary, and thus the amounts and timing of their convention fundraising operations will differ. Host cities must adapt their fundraising activities to external constraints and opportunities presented by federal campaign finance law, the parties, and even decisions by the parties' candidates. Cities vary in their willingness to forgo their usual decision-making and implementation processes to learn from other host cities and to defer to the security expertise of federal agencies.

Conventions can produce modest "campaign effects" by boosting volunteerism, persuasion, campaign interest, and voting in favor of the party's nominee. Such effects will most likely be apparent *when* the national party and local government make intentional efforts to engage local residents to produce those effects. Parties and cities have not regularly made public engagement a priority. If parties change their goals and tactics for engaging local residents, the resultant campaign effects are likely to change correspondingly. Likewise, as parties prioritize mobilizing votes from local residents, they are likely to put more weight on selecting host cities where such efforts could make a difference in the electoral college. Our evidence suggests that parties have put more emphasis on a host state's competitiveness recently as they have implemented more activities to take tactical advantage of their locational choice.

Mega-events can affect how local residents evaluate local government. Few events are as salient and intensively covered by the local media, or give residents the ability and incentive to view their city government in operation. Not only does our evidence show that residents' perceptions of performance during the event affect their evaluations of city government and its leaders, but that performance has a particularly strong effect on residents who are political "outsiders" to the city's partisan regime and who do not have an incentive, for partisan reasons, to rate it highly. How citizens evaluate government is dependent upon their political predispositions, but most are willing to recognize and attribute constructive performance, including those with the least political incentive to do so.

Furthermore, such evaluations have a long-term benefit in building citizen support for attracting mega-events as part of a city's economic development strategy. Residents who had more positive evaluations of city government and those who viewed past mega-events as having positive economic impacts on the city were more supportive of investing in hosting additional mega-events.

Lessons for Public Administration Scholars

Cities that host a convention successfully in the eyes of the public help legitimize local government administrative activity and even increase their capacity by providing additional resources for communities in the future, especially in the area of homeland security. This is important for at least three reasons. First, an enhanced reputation of a city's level of professionalism and expertise fosters voluntary compliance with administrative directives and decisions when the public has confidence in their local government, and governments more broadly. Administrative legitimacy, the population's belief that public administrators have a right to make and implement public policy and exercise discretion and authority, is a critical lynchpin in our system of representative democracy because public administrators (who are typically unelected) still engage in policymaking.

Second, from an efficiency and effectiveness standpoint, hosting a complex mega-event demonstrates technical competence on the part of local governments in the traditional public management sense and fosters good relationships with citizens as "customers" under the New Public Management framework. If citizens are satisfied with how their city handled hosting the convention, this serves as a form of evaluating how well a city provides critical infrastructure and services as a part of a local government's performance. Hosting a successful convention in the public's eyes also improves public trust (which has remained at record lows since Watergate and Vietnam in the 1970s) by demonstrating accountability and responsiveness to citizens. Trust is established when local government demonstrates that it can handle a big political event with international coverage in a professional manner without being subject to corruption.

Finally, public administrators can also benefit when citizens are more educated about how and why services are provided (Rosenbloom, Kravchuk, and Clerkin, 2009: 461). Hosting a mega-event like a political convention reminds citizens of the valuable services they receive daily by the extensive media coverage. For example, they may not have realized how police, fire, and other emergency personnel coordinate to keep their city safe until they see an event like this in action. They also may not realize all of the public facilities the city has to offer.

Lessons for Urban Scholars

How power is distributed locally in a federal system like the United States is very different than at the national or international level. Studying conventions as mega-events also allows urban scholars to better understand regime theory and in particular metropolitan growth coalitions. These interests are made up of businesses (especially real estate), unions, local media, utilities, universities, and, simply put, anyone who wants to see a city's population expand (Logan and Molotch, 1987; Stone, 1989). It also helps scholars understand the economic development strategies of cities, regions, and states. In the absence of a national industrial policy, cities constantly compete with one another over residents and businesses. Tourism is viewed as the latest economic development strategy many cities undertake. Who bids for political conventions and who wins the bid is telling of who is pursuing and who is successful at this strategy and allows scholars to assess the outcomes.

Our results consistently show the importance of attention to context. Cities (and parties) operate in environments that are changing. Sometimes this change is a slow evolution, such as competitive cities adapting to one another's activities. Other times, the change is more rapid, such as in a security or economic calamity or a substantial change in federal law. And sometimes the changes are due to the strategic actions of the cities and parties themselves. The parties, for example, have dialed back their fundraising demands as fewer large cities have bid since 9/11, just as cities have shifted the costs of conventions onto the federal government and nonlocal private donors. Our research designs, then, as well as our confidence in the generalizability of our results, must be sensitive to the fact that the incentives for the behaviors we are studying are usually in flux. Incorporating contextual variation into our research designs and our interpretation of our results will produce more confidence that we are producing viable long-term understandings of political phenomena.

Best Practices for City Leaders

Though this book primarily analyzes how and why the participants in political conventions behave the way they do, and is not a how-to manual for "doing" political conventions, our reading, interviews, and evidence suggest useful advice to share with city officials who are considering bidding for political conventions. These observations can help officials create the conditions under which a convention is more likely to be regarded as successful.

Bids

There are several key considerations in whether cities should bid for a presidential nominating convention, attributes that are fundamental to whether they can host a convention successfully. In particular, these include having the right infrastructure and involving the right people in developing the bid.

Invest in infrastructure or chasing conventions is the wrong game to play. The key asset, of course, is the arena. Parties clearly prefer them to convention centers. The tradeoff for cities is that conventions centers are the better option for all other types of organizational conferences. A steady stream of sporting events and major concerts is necessary for arenas to be viable. A center-city arena will facilitate synergy between the convention and city residents and simplify transportation for more delegates, but may create more disruption costs for residents and workers and create a more complicated security operation. Nevertheless, the party and security officials can plan effectively whether the arena is downtown or in a massive suburban parking lot.

The other key piece of infrastructure is the airport. Hub airports are a plus to make it easier for many delegates to arrive on single flights with multiple daily options. But it is more critical that the airport has the capacity to handle the large numbers of attendees who descend on the airport the day after the convention. The airport is the first and last experience of the city that convention attendees have, so it has a disproportionate impact on how they evaluate the city.[11] Having entertainment available helps ease travel frustrations and creates positive impressions of the city. Other types of public transportation may help the city's impression as a modern, accessible city, but delegates are transported by charter buses (usually rented because the city's buses must continue their normal routes), so this investment also is likely more relevant for residents and other types of tourism. The city can also facilitate clusters of hotels—particularly high-end, full-service hotels—that serve as transportation hubs for delegate buses. Having a large percentage of hotels within walking distance of the arena and entertainment district (for all the sponsored receptions) is certainly a plus for the parties and for the delegates' convention experience. Finally, having park space near the arena for public festivals accompanying the convention and/or for demonstrations is necessary.

Hosting a mega-event is a short-term "gig" lasting only three to four days, so even if the disruptions to ordinary commerce are low and no crises besmirch the city's image, the direct economic effects are a drop in the bucket of a city's annual economy. This event needs to be part of an overall economic and image-development strategy for long-term economic growth for the city. And though the event itself is short-term, the planning is not. Local leaders need to:

- integrate players from finance, hospitality, and security and emergency response early in the planning process;

- identify the decision makers and lobby them aggressively;

- be prepared to make multiple bids, learn from what you hear, and revise your bids for subsequent cycles.

The mayor may not originate the idea of recruiting a convention, but he or she is the visible champion of the bid. The mayor is best positioned to bring together key players from across the community, represent the city before party committees, raise funds, and communicate with local stakeholders and residents. If the mayor is not enthusiastic about submitting a bid, reconsider. If you expect turnover in the mayor's office (especially a situation with a lame duck mayor due to circumstances such as term limits), reconsider. The mayor's leadership and presence must be consistent in the process.

Planning and Organization

Even if your city is used to handling large conventions and has hosted national security events in the past, don't assume that these experiences are sufficient preparation (especially if they occurred prior to 9/11 and the establishment of the Department of Homeland Security). The safety demands of a political convention, and the demonstrators and potential threats they attract, are on a different order of magnitude. Security takes priority over how the city and its residents and businesses operate. There will be major changes for any that live or work inside the perimeter.

That said, having some experience with large conventions and high-security events is certainly a plus. Security planning is easier when police have interacted with federal security agencies for other events. Likewise, such experiences are important in convincing the parties that your city can protect national and international dignitaries for a week.

Hosting a political convention also means being in the national spotlight prior to, during, and after the event. Coverage starts once the bid has been awarded. This translates into the fact that the convention will be impacted by factors beyond the city's control and subject to the political mood of the nation. Incidents just prior to the convention, such as a terrorist threat or attack, an unpopular war, political scandal, a pandemic, riots or an assassination of an important political leader in another city, or a natural disaster, can impact the tone and preparation of the convention. It can also attract surprise visitors and a media focus on aspects of the city that are not expected. Planning needs to start as early as possible, and should ostensibly begin even when the city submits its bid. Implementation of the event also requires not just plans (and back-up plans), but people who are used to working with one another across many government agencies, levels of government, and private organizations. The sooner these networks form, the better.

Consult early with cities that have hosted conventions and utilize the natural "laboratories of democracy" present in our federal system. Learn what works and what does not work from them. Adopt successful strategies and make early adjustments for past mistakes and for local characteristics. This is where post-convention reports become invaluable for planning.

Review your public safety, protest, and parade ordinances early. Consult broadly to balance First Amendment and public safety concerns. Create specific ordinances just to deal with the unusual nature of this type of event that will not normally be used. Train your police to deal with larger and potentially more violent demonstrations than they typically face. It is critical to engage in a dialogue with protesters and citizens ahead of time about what they can expect, such as police in riot gear, the use of tear gas on an out-of-control crowd, or security fencing. Take advantage of the expertise of federal security agencies; in the end, they will make many of the critical decisions regarding security matters. If local protests in your city are usually peaceful, do not assume this is the case with the types of protests conventions attract. Remember, these events are designed to attract intentional media attention and social media–savvy protesters can make even minor incidents appear bad for local law enforcement. Security is critical for the city's ability to achieve its public relations goals during the convention. Regardless of whether everything else goes perfectly, security breakdowns or battles between police and protesters will dominate news coverage and people's evaluations of the city's competence.

If the arena is the critical asset for hosting a presidential nominating convention, renovations are a critical element of planning. The parties require access to the arena one month before and one month after the convention. This requires coordination with sports teams and other organizations that regularly use the arena, so that they do not need that location or have alternative locations for the two-month period. Of course, the city must also facilitate the permits and inspections (often across multiple agencies) for arena and hotel renovations.

Communication is critical. Many organizations must coordinate. The public needs to know how they will be affected and what to do when their normal routines are disrupted during the convention. Social media and your web presence must be proactive and not reactive so that normal service-delivery issues can still be addressed by local government personnel.

Financing

Changes in federal law allowing the parties to raise funds directly from large donors should mean that cities will have less responsibility for paying for inside-the-hall convention activities. Despite their new fundraising capacity, the parties are still likely to push cities to raise and spend as much money as possible. But it will also mean that national access–oriented and large party donors that cities traditionally relied upon will be more likely to give to the party committees than to the host committees. In the first few cycles of the new national party convention fundraising committees, there will be uncertainty about what activities the parties will pay for and what cities will pay for. Parties should make clear in their RFPs what they expect to see in the city's bids regarding the cities' purchasing obligations, and cities should be clear in their bids what they are willing to pay for. That said, cities must always be prepared for unplanned expenses and have reserve funds to deal with contingencies.

Cities will have to rely on local donors and/or convince the national donors that there is a reason for them to support the city's convention activities in addition to contributing to the national party's convention fund. Regardless, fundraising will remain a tremendous challenge for cities. The parties rightly require a fundraising plan as part of the bid. Cities that are tempted to exaggerate their fundraising capacity in the bid should reconsider a bid because they are setting themselves up for months of frustration (and bad press) trying to meet an unrealistic commitment.

If Congress withdraws the post-9/11 security grant, it is likely that many cities will conclude that hosting a convention is no longer worth it. Even with the grants, the number of bids has declined since 9/11. It seems unlikely that many cities will want to raise an additional $50 million or take even a fraction of that from the city budget. Parties may have to pick up some or all of the security budget under these circumstances to entice cities to bid.

Public Engagement

Engaging local residents during the convention is unlikely to tip the electoral outcome of the host state. But like most campaign activities, it has a marginal effect, and in competitive states any marginal benefit should be taken advantage of. The value of public engagement activities is higher for the city government than the party. Public engagement events create a public good for the local residents who otherwise just experience interruptions to their routines. Moreover, open events give the public the ability to see local government in action—and for the local media to cover local government in action—in a way that affects public attitudes toward the competence and effectiveness of local government.

Economic Impacts

Don't oversell the impacts. A regional economy will not notice the presence (or absence) of a political convention. Furthermore, convention spending is concentrated in a few areas: renovating the arena, security, catering, hotels, and transportation. And many of those services (especially security forces and transportation) will be provided largely by out-of-town contractors. If all local residents expect a financial windfall, they will be disappointed.

Legacies

Since the economic benefits of a convention are relatively small and uneven across the local economy, organize a specific legacy project or set of projects that can provide a collective benefit to the community. Envision them during the bid process. What do you want the city to be the day after the convention? How can you tell your residents that the city will be better because of this event? Clearly identifying such projects is an important element in building community support for accepting the inevitable disruptions the convention will cause. Include the project(s) into planning and budgeting. The host committee will expire, and any project is unsustainable without continuous organizational and financial support. Projects that already have organic support in the community are therefore more likely to survive and benefit from the boost of attention and resources delivered by the convention. Finally, legacy projects need not only a fundraising stream but also an organizational home if they are going to be sustainable.

Mega-events are splash, but winning and executing them is about nuts and bolts. The cities that win political conventions have both invested in the infrastructure and demonstrated to the parties that they will be competent and effective hosts. Just as hotel rooms, arenas, airports, and fundraising capacity matter, so does the ability of the local governments, business leaders, and civic organizations to demonstrate that they are united in support of a common good. Likewise, planning does not make for exciting headlines, but it helps police forces that don't typically face these types of demonstrations deal with very large and potentially violent protests. Having city agencies and private organizations working together throughout the bid and planning processes builds their skills and trust, which will be critical to effective coordination during the convention. Competent execution is rewarded when residents observe that the city has pulled off an event that has garnered positive media attention. Thus, not only are there potential image benefits for the city in winning a mega-event and capturing media attention during the event, but the city can reap rewards from existing residents for a job well done.

Appendices

Appendix 1

Interviews and Presentations

Wayne Broome, Charlotte Emergency Management. Interview by David Edwards, November 13, 2012.

Gillian Burgess, daughter of Charlotte City Councilwoman Susan Burgess. Interview by Eric Heberlig, June 18, 2013.

Bruce Clark, PPL and 2011 Campaign Manager for Mayor Foxx. POLS 3010, June 6, 2012.

Dockery Clark, Chief of Staff, Charlotte in 2012 Host Committee. POLS 3010, May 24, 2012.

Warren Cooksey, Treasurer, Carolinas 2000. Interview by Eric Heberlig, January 28, 2013.

Pat Cotham, Mecklenburg County Commissioner, Democratic National Committee member, POLS 3010, May 23, 2012.

Courtney Counts, Volunteer Director, Charlotte in 2012 Host Committee. POLS 3010, May 22, 2012.

Jeff Dulin, Deputy Chief, Charlotte Fire Department. Interview by Bo Fitzgerald. November 8, 2012.

Marc Friedland, Secretary, Mecklenburg County Democrats. POLS 3010, June 7, 2012.

Bob Hagemann, City Attorney. POLS 3010, June 4, 2012 and Southeastern Conference of Public Administrators, September 26, 2013.

Robyn Hamilton, Senior Advisor, Charlotte in 2012 Host Committee. Gerald Fox MPA Conference, November 2, 2012.

Jon Hannan, Chief, Charlotte Fire Department. Southeastern Conference of Public Administrators, September 26, 2013.

Robin Hayes, Chair, North Carolina Republican Party. POLS 3010, June 6, 2012.

Mary Hopper, University City Partners. Interview by Eric Heberlig, June 5, 2013.

Carol Jennings, Assistant to the City Manager. Southeastern Conference of Public Administrators, September 26, 2013.

Clark Jennings, Director of Operations, Democratic National Convention Committee. The Washington Center convention seminars, August 27, 2012.

Ken Jones, CEO, Tampa Host Committee. Interview by Eric Heberlig, November 17, 2014.

Steve Kerrigan, Chair, 2012 DNC Technical Advisory Group and Director, 2012 Democratic National Convention Committee. Interview by Eric Heberlig, April 23, 2013.

Ricky Kirshner, Executive Producer, DNC 2012. The Washington Center convention seminars, August 28, 2012.

Larry Kopf, Chief Operations Planning Officer, Charlotte Area Transit System (CATS). Gerald Fox MPA Conference, November 2, 2012.

Vi Lyles, Director of Community Partnerships, Charlotte in 2012 Host Committee. POLS 3010, June 13, 2012.

Bill McMillan, Senior Director of Sales, Charlotte Regional Visitors Authority. Interview by Eric Heberlig, May 28, 2013.

Kimberly McMillian, Corporate Communications and Marketing, City of Charlotte. Interview by Karen Smith, November 13, 2012, and Gerald Fox MPA Conference, November 2, 2012.

Harold Medlock, Deputy Chief, Charlotte-Mecklenburg Police Department. Interview by Haley Rader, November 15, 2012, and Gerald Fox MPA Conference, November 2, 2012.

Will Miller, President (2009–11), Charlotte in 2012 Committee. Interviews by Eric Heberlig, January 22, 2013 and July 25, 2013.

Kevin Monroe, Deputy Director of Intergovernmental Affairs and Outreach, Democratic National Convention Committee, and former Chief of Staff to the Mayor of Charlotte. POLS 3010, May 22, 2012; The Washington Center convention seminars, August 27, 2012; interview with Eric Heberlig, February 14, 2012; and Southeastern Conference of Public Administrators, September 26, 2013.

Tracy Montross, Chief of Staff to the Mayor of Charlotte. POLS 3010, June 21, 2012, and interview by Cicily Hampton, November 8, 2012.

Cameron Moody, Senior Advisor, Democratic National Convention Committee. POLS 3010, June 14, 2012.

Bob Morgan, President, Charlotte Chamber of Commerce. Interview by Cicily Hampton, December 7, 2012.

Jim Morrill, Charlotte Observer. POLS 3010, June 6, 2012.

Dan Murrey, President, Charlotte in 2012 Host Committee. The Washington Center convention seminars, August 26, 2012.

Tim Newman, CEO, Charlotte Regional Visitors Authority. Interview by Eric Heberlig, January 24, 2013.

Rob Phocus, Energy and Sustainability Manager, City of Charlotte. POLS 3010, May 31, 2012.

Patty Richbourg, Charlotte Regional Visitors Authority Liaison to Carolinas 2000. Interview by Eric Heberlig, May 23, 2013.

Karen Ruppe, Commodities Supervisor, City of Charlotte. Gerald Fox MPA Conference, November 2, 2012.

Deb Ryan, Charlotte Planning Commission. POLS 3010, May 30, 2012.

Michael Smith, President, Center City Partners. Interview by Eric Heberlig, January 29, 2013.

Kevin Staley, Mecklenburg County EMS. Interview by Bo Fitzgerald, November 15, 2012.

Blair Stanford, Chief Operating Officer, Charlotte Chamber of Commerce. POLS 3010, May 29, 2012.

Lee Teague, former Chair, Mecklenburg County Republican Party. POLS 3010, June 7, 2012.

Mary Tribble, Executive Director of Hospitality and Events, Charlotte in 2012 Host Committee. POLS 3010, June 14, 2012.

Karen Whichard, Community Relations Manager for the Charlotte-Mecklenburg Utility Department. Gerald Fox MPA Conference, November 2, 2012; Southeastern Conference of Public Administrators, September 26, 2013; interview by Michael Boger, November 13, 2012.

Frank Whitney, U.S. District Judge, President of Carolinas 2000. Interview by Eric Heberlig, May 25, 2013.

Appendix 2

Measurements of City Attributes

Airport hub. 1 = city's airport is a hub for a major U.S. commercial carrier (American, America West, Continental, Delta, Northwest, TWA, United, U.S. Airways); 0 = city has a commercial airport but not a hub; −1 = city does not have its own commercial airport. Some cities lost hub status during our time period due to airline mergers and downsizings (Cleveland, Columbus, Pittsburgh, St. Louis).

Arena seating capacity. We thank Samuel Bassett of the University of Illinois, Chicago, for use of his arena data. The data was gathered by searching "[city name] arena" on the web to identify the name of the venue and then searching "[arena name] seating capacity" in www.newsbank.com. Wherever available, the data includes changes in seating capacities over the 1992–2012 time period due to renovations or new construction. If the city itself did not have an arena for civic or sporting events, a university venue is included if available.

Campaign money. Total sum contributed to federal candidates in the previous presidential election by residents and political organizations in the city, 2000–2012. Center for Responsive Politics.

Electoral College. The state's number of Electoral College votes.

Hometown of the national party chair or president. Several of the officials have multiple locations that could be coded as a hometown—one as the predominant location where they were raised, another where they started their professional life. Having no *a priori* expectation as to which hometown should be more important to them, we coded both (e.g., for President Obama, we coded both Honolulu and Chicago). National Party chairs were coded in the years in which bids were submitted and the site selection decisions were made.

Mayor/Council is a form of government in which an independently elected mayor holds power as chief executive (if true, coded 1; other forms, such as manager/council, coded 0). The data is from the International City/County Management Association's *Municipal Yearbook* for the relevant year.

Mayor/governor match. 2 = both mayor and governor are members of the party of the bid; 1 = one in-partisan official, one nonpartisan official; 0 = one official of one party, one official of the other; −1 = one out-partisan official, one nonpartisan official; −2 = both out-partisan officials.

Mayor turnover is counted each time a mayor leaves office during the four-year convention cycle.

Population size. Census Bureau. The natural logarithm is used in statistical models to capture the declining impact of each additional resident on the capacity of the city to host a convention.

Presidential competitiveness is measured as the absolute value of the difference between the Democratic and Republican presidential candidate's popular vote shares in the state in the presidential previous election.

Previous bid. City bid in either of the past two cycles.

Tourism employment. Tourism employment (Census Bureau's Economic Census) divided by its total population (Census Bureau). From the Census Bureau's Economic Census, we measure tourism employment as the sum the number of employees in the arts and entertainment industries and the hotel and restaurant industries for each city. The Economic Census is conducted every five years, so we match the closest census to each convention, and use the average of the two most recent censuses for conventions falling between reports. The 2013 Economic Census is not yet available, so we projected each city's tourism employment for 2012 based on its tourism employment changes between the 2003 and 2008 reports. Likewise, the 1993 Economic Census did not contain comparable employment numbers, so we projected back based on the city's trends from the 1998 to 2003 reports. To capture the curvilinear relationship in the model, we include the linear and the squared term of the city's tourism employment.

Unity. Author's coding of NewsBank articles on convention bid as to whether any organized opposition existed or any major players within the city political or business community opposed the city hosting a convention.

Appendix 3-A

Survey Questions Regarding Paying for Mega-Events, Post-2012
Presidential Election Survey, Mecklenburg County

We would like your views of the ways you think it is best to pay for pursuing
and hosting these mega-events like the presidential convention. Cities elsewhere
have used each of the following options, and on a scale from 1 to 10, with
10 meaning this is the best way to pay for this service, and 1 meaning this
is the worst way to pay, please tell me your preference as to how the city
should raise the funds to pursue and host mega-events.

[Questions asked in random order]

• sales tax increase to cover amount needed

• property tax increase to cover the amount needed

• an increase to the county food and beverage tax

• the creation of a special sales tax district just around the event locations

• an increase in the taxes on hotels and rental cars

Appendix 3-B

Measurements of Attributes of
Donors to Host Committees

Both conventions. Donor contributed to host committees of both cities in same election cycle = 1; otherwise = 0.

DC. Donor is from Washington, D.C. = 1; otherwise = 0.

Electoral spending. Natural logarithm of the sum the donors' hard and soft money donations and independent expenditures in the previous presidential election cycle (Center for Responsive Politics).

Foundation. Donor is identified as a foundation or a trust = 1; otherwise = 0.

GOP convention. Host committee is raising funds to support the Republican National Convention = 1; Democratic National Convention = 0.

Individual. Individual donor = 1; institutional donor = 0.

In-kind. Host committee identifies the contribution as in-kind donation of a good or service in its Federal Election Commission report = 1; otherwise = 0.

Local. Donor is from the home state of the convention host city = 1; out-of-state = 0.

Partisanship. Percentage of funds given to the party hosting the convention and its candidates in the previous presidential election cycle. New donors were placed at the midpoint (50).

Same party convention. Donor contributed to host committees in two or more cycles for the conventions of the same political party = 1; otherwise = 0.

Union. Donor is a labor union = 1; 0 = otherwise.

Appendix 4

Enforcement of
Extraordinary Event Ordinance

Purpose of Ordinance

The purpose of the Extraordinary Event Ordinance is to allow law enforcement to identify risks or individuals intent on doing harm at a large-scale event of national or international significance and/or an event expected to attract a significant number of people to a certain portion of the city. The ordinance should not affect the normal way of life for law-abiding citizens.

Law-abiding citizens going about their daily business will not be subject to arrest for simply possessing a prohibited item during and within the boundary of an Extraordinary Event.

Prohibited Items

Below is a list of items prohibited during an Extraordinary Event. Many of these items are not in and of themselves a weapon. Also there may be times when a person is in possession of these items for a legitimate purpose. Officers will not immediately arrest/cite someone simply because they are in possession of an item. Instead officers will determine whether the person is in possession of an item while going to or from an activity in which that device is used for a legitimate purpose. If so, then the ordinance would not apply and no enforcement action should be taken unless the person actually attempts to use the device as a weapon to injure another person or to damage property.

- Bars, chains, shafts, cables, or plastic pipe capable of inflicting serious injury

- A container or object of sufficient weight that may be used as a projectile, or that contains objects that may be used as a projectile that could inflict serious injury to a person or damage property

- An aerosol container, spray gun, or soaker device

- A paint gun, etching materials, spray paint container, liquid paint or marker containing a fluid that is not water soluble

- A backpack, duffle bag, satchel, cooler, or other item carried with the intent to conceal weapons or other prohibited items

- A glass or breakable container capable of being filled with a flammable or dangerous substance carried with the intent to inflict serious injury to a person or damage to property

- A sharp or bladed object such as a box cutter, utility knife, ice pick, or axe

- A hammer or crowbar

- Pepper spray, mace, or any other irritant carried with the intent to delay, obstruct, or resist the lawful orders of a lawful orders of a law enforcement officer

- Body armor, shield, helmet, protective pads, or gas masks carried or worn with the intent to delay, obstruct, or resist the lawful orders of a law enforcement officer

- A mask or scarf worn with the intent to hide one's identity while committing a crime

- A police scanner

- Rocks, bottles, objects, bricks, or pieces thereof that are of sufficient weight or design as to cause serious injury to a person if thrown at or struck upon another

- A device used to shoot, hurl, or project a missile of any description capable of inflicting serious injury to a person

- A "sock" or "pocket" containing material of sufficient weight as to cause serious injury to a person if thrown or struck upon another

- Fireworks, smoke bombs, sparklers, and stink bombs

- An animal unless specifically allowed as a service animal used to assist a person with a disability. However residents will be able to walk their dog within the Extraordinary Event boundaries without fear of arrest.

To review the complete ordinance (No. 4814), visit cmpd.org.

For questions about Extraordinary Events contact the CMPD Attorney's Office at 704-336-2406.

Appendix 5-A

Survey Methodology

The survey includes responses from 964 residents of Mecklenburg County, North Carolina. After weighting the data for age, sex, and race (based on U.S. Census—American Community Survey numbers), reported results using all data will have a margin of error of approximately 3.5% at the 95% confidence level. Any results that use a subset of the entire sample will naturally have a higher margin of error.

Phone calls were made during weekday evenings, all day Saturday, and Sunday afternoon and evening. Weekday daytime calls are generally not made to avoid oversampling those who are more likely to be at home during the day (e.g., retirees, stay-at-home-moms, etc.). Conducting weekend calls is important to avoid systematically excluding certain populations (such as those who may work second or third shift during the week). Calling occurred November 10–19, December 3–6, 8, and 10, 2012.

The survey used (1) Random Digit Dialing (RDD), and (2) wireless phone number sampling. Both RDD and wireless samples are crucial to ensure no adult in the geographical area of interest is systematically excluded from the sample. Both the RDD sample and the wireless sample were purchased from Survey Sampling International (SSI). A further explanation of RDD methodology, with descriptions taken from SSI's website, may be found below.

Phone numbers selected for the survey were redialed five or more times in an attempt to reach a respondent. Once a household was reached, we also employed procedures to *randomize within households* for RDD sample. Additionally, we screened the wireless sample for **wireless-only** status since individuals who have a cell phone and a land line already have an established probability of appearing in the RDD and weighed responses based on **sex**,

age, and **race** according to the known population of residents of Mecklenburg County, North Carolina, age eighteen and older. Computerized autodialers were not used in order to ensure the survey of wireless phones complied with the Telephone Consumers Protection Act and all FCC rules regarding contacting wireless telephones.

Samples are generated using a database of "working blocks." A block (also known as a 100-bank or a bank) is a set of 100 contiguous numbers identified by the first two digits of the last four digits of a telephone number. For example, in the telephone number 203-567-7200, "72" is the block. A block is termed to be working if some specified number of listed telephone numbers is found in that block.

Samples of random numbers distributed across all eligible blocks in proportion to their density of listed telephone households are selected. All blocks within a county are organized in ascending order by area code, exchange, and block number. Once the quota has been allocated to all counties in the frame, a sampling interval is calculated by summing the number of listed residential numbers in eligible blocks within the county and dividing that sum by the number of sampling points assigned to the county. From a random start between zero and the sampling interval, blocks are systematically selected in proportion to their density of listed households. Once a block has been selected, a two-digit number is systematically selected in the range 00–99 and is appended to the exchange and block to form a 10-digit telephone number.

Appendix 5-B

Survey Measurements, Post-2012 Presidential Election Survey, Mecklenburg County

City Ratings

Competence. Overall, would you describe the local government in Charlotte as *competent* or *incompetent*? 1–5 scale: very competent to very incompetent.

Responsiveness. Would you say the local government in Charlotte is responsive or unresponsive to the needs of its residents? 1–5 scale: very responsive to very unresponsive.

Effectiveness. We'd like your opinion of how effective the city of Charlotte is when it spends its money to accomplish key goals. How much of the money spent by the local government in Charlotte do you think is spent effectively? 1–5 scale: nearly all to almost none.

Attachment. How attached do you feel to the Charlotte region? Would you say your feeling of attachment to the Charlotte region is very strong, somewhat strong, somewhat weak, or very weak? 1–5 scale.

Satisfaction. Would you say that you are satisfied or unsatisfied with the Charlotte region as a place to live? 1–5 scale: very satisfied to very unsatisfied

Mayor rating. How would you rate the performance of the mayor of Charlotte? As excellent, good, only fair, or poor?

DNC Measures

Convention success. Over all, how would you describe Charlotte's performance as a host for the Democratic National Convention? 1–5 scale: very successful to very unsuccessful.

Convention media usage. Combined three questions on media usage to create a 0–6 scale (0 = did not follow any coverage of the DNC; 6 = daily following of multiple news sources): 1) Did you watch any events or speeches of the Democratic National Convention live while it was happening on TV or web? 2) [If yes,] All or almost all of it EACH day, at least party of the convention EACH day, or parts on one or two days? 3) Other than watching LIVE coverage, did you follow reporting on events of the convention in the news? [If yes,] Every day or one or two days?

Convention participation. 1 = participated in either activity; 0 = participated in neither activity. 1) Did you attend the Carolina Fest street festival in uptown Charlotte on Labor Day? Yes/no. 2) Did you volunteer to assist with any of the events during the 2012 Democratic National Convention? Yes/no.

Mad at ticket loss. 1 = if yes (1) to question A and no (0) to question B; 0 = otherwise. A) Did you have tickets to attend President Obama's acceptance speech in Bank of America Stadium on Thursday, September 6? 1 = yes; 0 = no. B) In your opinion, did convention organizers make the right decision to move the President's acceptance speech from outside in the Bank of America Stadium to inside in the Time Warner arena or should the speech have remained in the stadium? 1 = right decision to move; 0 = should have remained in Bank of America.

Participation

2008

I'd like for you to think back to the **2008** presidential election between **John McCain** and **Barack Obama**, *NOT* the most recent presidential election, but the *previous* one in **2008**.

Did you volunteer for a *presidential* campaign in **2008**? Yes = 1; no = 0.

Did you try to persuade someone to vote for a particular *presidential* candidate in **2008**? Yes = 1; no = 0.

Not everyone can get to the polls to vote even if they want to. Were you able to vote in the **2008** *presidential* election?

Which presidential candidate did you vote for in the ***2008*** presidential election? Did you vote for: [Obama and McCain rotated] Obama = 1; other = 0.

2012

Did you *volunteer* for a **2012** presidential campaign? Yes = 1; no = 0.

Did you try to persuade someone to *vote for a particular presidential candidate* in **2012**? Yes = 1; no = 0.

Turnout. 1 = yes if three questions were all answered with the most positive response; 0 = otherwise. 1) Are you currently registered to vote in North Carolina? 2) How certain are you that your North Carolina voter registration status is up to date, would you say you are **absolutely certain**, **pretty sure**, or **believe that it probably is**. 3) Not everyone can get to the polls to vote even if they want to. Were you able to vote in the **2012** *presidential* election?

Obama Vote. Which *presidential candidate* did you vote for in the **2012** Presidential Election? Obama = 1; other = 0.

POLITICAL DEMOGRAPHY

Education. What is the highest level of education you have completed? 1 = less than high school; 2 = high school/GED; 3 = some college; 4 = two-year tech college grad; 5 = four-year college degree; 6 = post-graduate degree

Efficacy. How much influence would you say someone like you could have over *local government* decisions? A lot, some, very little, or none at all.

Gender. Caller's coding of the gender of the respondent. 1 = female; 0 = male.

Ideology. Regardless of your political party affiliation, would you describe yourself as Very Liberal, Somewhat Liberal, Exactly in the Middle, Somewhat Conservative, or Very Conservative?

Interest in politics: Some people seem to follow what's going on in government and public affairs most of the time, whether there's an election or not.

Others aren't that interested. How often would you say that you follow what is going on in government and public affairs: Most of the time, Some of the time, Only now and then, or Hardly at all?

Length of residence. (natural logarithm) Rounding to the nearest year, how long have you lived in Mecklenburg county?

Minority [recoded from list of options given to respondent] Any minority = 1; white = 0.

Party identification. Traditional 7-point measure of strength of partisanship (including independent "leaners") from strong Democrats to strong Republicans. Third-party and non-identifiers were recoded as pure independents.

Religious attendance. How often do you attend religious services? 1–9 scale: More than once per week to never.

Appendix 5-C

Mayoral Career Measurements

Age. Mayor's age at the time of each presidential election (from local news reports or calculated from online biographies).

Career choice (dependent variable). 1 = sought other office; 0 = sought reelection; −1 = retired.

Convention host. City hosted a presidential nominating convention during the mayor's tenure.

Convention bid. City bid unsuccessfully for a presidential nominating convention during the mayor's tenure.

Crime. Change in the city's rate of violent crime since the last presidential election (calculated with data from the FBI's Uniform Crime Statistics and population data from the Census Bureau). Violent crimes include murder, rape, robbery, and aggravated assault.

Income growth. Change in per capita income in the city since the last presidential election (calculated with data from the Census Bureau, 1998–2012).

Mega-events. Cumulative number of mega-events (excluding presidential nominating conventions) hosted by the city during the incumbent mayor's tenure up to and including the current president cycle. We count the following as mega-events because cities must bid for them and because the security requirements are similar to presidential nominating conventions: G-8 Summits,

NATO Summits, NCAA Final Four, Super Bowl, World Cup tournaments, and the Olympics.

Open seat. 2 = both governor and U.S. Senate contests have no incumbent during mayoral election cycle; 1 = either governor or U.S. Senate contest has no incumbent during mayoral election cycle; 0 = both governor and U.S. Senate contest have incumbents during mayoral election cycle.

Population growth. Change in city's population since the last presidential election (calculated with data from the Census Bureau, 1988–2012).

Population ratio: Ratio of city population to state's population (calculated with data from the Census Bureau, 1999–2012).

Tenure. Incumbent's number of years in office at the time of the mayoral election for elections between 1992 and 2012.

Term limit. 1 = mayor reached term limit; 0 = mayor did not reach term limit or city does not restrict mayor's service (calculated based on online lists of local term limits or city web page).

Appendix 7-A

Support Mega-Events Survey Measurements

City evaluation. Factor score based on the respondent's answers to the following seven questions on city government:

Competence. Overall, would you describe the local government in Charlotte as *competent* or *incompetent*? 1–5 scale: very competent to very incompetent.

Responsiveness. Would you say the local government in Charlotte is responsive or unresponsive to the needs of its residents? 1–5 scale: very responsive to very unresponsive.

Effectiveness. We'd like your opinion of how effective the city of Charlotte is when it spends its money to accomplish key goals. How much of the money spent by the local government in Charlotte do you think is spent effectively? 1–5 scale: nearly all to almost none.

Attachment. How attached do you feel to the Charlotte region? Would you say your feeling of attachment to the Charlotte region is very strong, somewhat strong, somewhat weak, or very weak? 1–5 scale.

Satisfaction. Would you say that you are satisfied or unsatisfied with the Charlotte region as a place to live? 1–5 scale: very satisfied to very unsatisfied.

Mayor rating. How would you rate the performance of the mayor of Charlotte? As excellent, good, only fair, or poor?

DNC Measures

Convention success (dependent variable). Overall, how would you describe Charlotte's performance as a host for the Democratic National Convention? 1–5 scale: very successful to very unsuccessful.

Convention media usage. Combined three questions on media usage to create a 0–6 scale (0 = did not follow any coverage of the DNC; 6 = daily following of multiple news sources): 1) Did you watch any events or speeches of the Democratic National Convention live while it was happening on TV or web? 2) [If yes,] All or almost all of it EACH day, at least party of the convention EACH day, or parts on one or two days? 3) Other than watching LIVE coverage, did you follow reporting on events of the convention in the news? [If yes,] Every day or one or two days?

Economic impact (dependent variable). Overall, do you think hosting the 2012 Democratic National Convention had a positive economic impact, a negative economic impact, or not real economic impact on Charlotte? [If they said a positive or negative impact], Would you say that the impact was very large, somewhat large, somewhat small or very small? Responses were recoded into an 8-point scale from very large positive to very large negative impact.

Left town. Did you leave town during the Democratic National Convention in order to avoid the convention? 1 = yes; 0 = no.

Mad at ticket loss. 1 = if yes (1) to question A and no (0) to question B; 0 = otherwise. A) Did you have tickets to attend President Obama's acceptance speech in Bank of America Stadium on Thursday, September 6? 1 = yes; 0 = no. B) In your opinion, did convention organizers make the right decision to move the president's acceptance speech from outside in the Bank of America Stadium to inside in the Time Warner arena or should the speech have remained in the stadium? 1 = right decision to move; 0 = should have remained in Bank of America.

Participated. 1 = participated in either activity; 0 = participated in neither activity. 1) Did you attend the Carolina Fest street festival in uptown Charlotte on Labor Day? Yes/no. 2) Did you volunteer to assist with any of the events during the 2012 Democratic National Convention? Yes/no.

Reputation (dependent variable). We want you to focus on any satisfaction you feel from being a citizen of the Charlotte area. How important do you believe each of the following is in establishing Charlotte's **national** reputation. Are these events or organizations very important, somewhat important, somewhat unimportant, or very unimportant in building the city's image, or are you not familiar enough with the event or organization to form an option? [In random order:] the Panthers; the Bobcats; NASCAR; Arts, music, and museums; the 2012 Democratic National Convention; Bank of America; Duke Energy. The measure subtracts the DNC response from the respondent's average for the other six responses.

Work disrupted. Was your work disrupted by the Democratic National Convention? 5 = a lot; 4 = a little; 3 = not really; 2 = no; 1 = not working.

Political Demography

Center city. Lived a zip code in or adjacent to Charlotte's center-city district.

Education. What is the highest level of education you have completed? 1 = less than high school; 2 = high school/GED; 3 = some college; 4 = two-year tech college grad; 5 = four-year college degree; 6 = post-graduate degree.

Efficacy. How much influence would you say someone like you could have over *local government* decisions? A lot, some, very little, or none at all.

Gender. Caller's coding of the gender of the respondent. 1 = female; 0 = male. In the Willingness to Pay equation, 1 = male; 0 = female.

Ideology. Regardless of your political party affiliation, would you describe yourself as Very Liberal, Somewhat Liberal, Exactly in the Middle, Somewhat Conservative, or Very Conservative?

Interest in politics. Some people seem to follow what's going on in government and public affairs most of the time, whether there's an election or not. Others aren't that interested. How often would you say that you follow what is going on in government and public affairs: most of the time, some of the time, only now and then, or hardly at all?

Income. Which of the following categories best describes your total household yearly income? Please stop me when I reach the correct category: under $15,000; $15–20,000; $20–30,000; $30–40,000; $40–50,000; $50–75,000; $75–100,000; $100–125,000; $125–150,000; $150–175,000; $175–250,000; over $250,000.

Length of residence. (natural logarithm) Rounding to the nearest year, how long have you lived in Mecklenburg county?

Minority [recoded from list of options given to respondent]. Any minority = 1; white = 0.

Party identification. Traditional 7-point measure of strength of partisanship (including independent "leaners") from strong Democrats to strong Republicans. Third-party and non-identifiers were recoded as pure independents. In the Willingness to Pay equation, we enter two dummy variables for Democrats (Democrats = 1; others = 0) and Republicans (Republicans = 1; others = 0) with independents as the excluded categories.

Related industry. Do you or any members of your household work for any of the following: local government, Center City Partners, Chamber of Commerce, the media, the entertainment industry, the tourism industry? 1 = yes to any of the above; 0 = else.

Support for mega-events **(dependent variable).** 8-point scale based on the following questions:

We would like to see if people can put a dollar value on any civic pride they may feel when their region hosts a large event. In other words, we are interested in understanding the value citizen place on large events like the presidential convention as an amenity that generates civic pride.

Do you think that hosting large events in this region is worth $4 per month to you? [If yes,] Worth $8 per month? [If no,] Worth $2 per month?

Recently, there has been talk of the Charlotte region pursuing large events such as a future Republican National Convention, the Super Bowl, or the Olympics. Would your household be willing to pay $40 per year to fund city efforts to pursue and host events like these? [If yes,] $80 per year? [If no,] $20 per year? [If no,] What amount per year would you be willing to pay to attract and host these events?

Notes

Chapter 1

1. Considerable attention has been given to assessing the effects of the 1970s reforms—who has gained power and who has lost power compared to before the reforms (e.g., Ceaser 1982; Cohen et al. 2008; Kamarck 2009; Polsby 1983; Shafer 1983, 1988). Studies of the activities of the conventions themselves are now quite dated (Bibby and Alexander 1968; Cotter and Hennessy 1964; David, Goldman, and Bain 1960; Davis 1972, 1983) and these focus on the arcane decision-making processes of an era in which these processes actually decided the identities of party presidential nominees.

2. Convention planners are a key constituency for presidential nominating conventions since many Washington, D.C.–based trade associations send representatives to the party conventions. Bill McMillan, senior director of sales, Charlotte Regional Visitors Authority. Interview by Eric Heberlig, May 28, 2013.

3. Nielson ratings for Democratic National Conventions were obtained from Shaffer (2010); ratings for Republican National Conventions were collected by the authors from the Nielson company (2008–2012) and from media reports (1984–2004). Nielson ratings of the conventions correlate between the parties (Pearson's $r = .887$, $p < .01$) and the ratings have declined over time (Pearson's $r = -.61$). Since the elections of the 1980s were less competitive, ratings were actually higher for less competitive contests. Open seat contests and the population size of the host city are unrelated to the Nielson ratings.

4. Bob Morgan, president, Charlotte Chamber of Commerce. "Charlotte Talks with Mike Collins," WFAE. September 3, 2012.

5. Bob Morgan, president, Charlotte Chamber of Commerce. Interview by Cicily Hampton, December 7, 2012.

6. For a similar perspective on Indianapolis, see Rosentraub (2003).

7. Tracy Montross, chief of staff to Mayor Anthony Foxx. Interview by Cicily Hampton, November 8, 2012.

8. Bill McMillan, senior director of sales, Charlotte Regional Visitors Association. Interview with Eric Heberlig, May 28, 2013.

9. To be sure, much of the public assessment is likely based on their reaction to Trump's speech, which was the lowest rated ever with only 35% calling it good or excellent in the Gallup poll (Jones 2016), rather than their evaluations of the management of convention per se. Other polls produced a mixed verdict on the extent to which the convention snafus mattered to the public. Some polls showed a post-convention bump of up to 6 points for Trump—about the historical average—while other polls showed no change (e.g., Nelson 2016).

10. Lee Teague, former chair, Mecklenburg County Republican Party. POLS 3110A Political Conventions, June 7, 2012.

11. Ricky Kirschner, executive producer, DNC 2012. The Washington Center 2012 National Convention Seminars, August 28, 2012. Also see Smith (1989, 410–11).

12. Kirschner, August 28, 2012.

13. Carol Jennings, assistant to the Charlotte city manager. Southeastern Conference of Public Administrators, September. 26, 2013.

14. Kevin Monroe, deputy director of intergovernmental affairs and outreach, Democratic National Convention Committee. Presentation to the 2012 Washington Center Convention Seminar, August 27, 2012; Cameron Moody, senior advisor, Democratic National Convention Committee. POLS 3110A Political Conventions, June 14, 2012.

15. Kevin Monroe, chief of staff to Charlotte mayor Anthony Foxx. Interview with Eric Heberlig, February 14, 2013.

16. Robyn Hamilton, senior advisor, Charlotte in 2012 Host Committee. Gerald Fox MPA Conference: Public Administration and Mega Events: Lessons Learned from Hosting the DNC in Charlotte, November 2, 2012.

17. Murrey, August 26, 2012.

18. Moody, June 14, 2012; Kirschner, August 28, 2012.

19. Carol Jennings, special assistant to the city manager (Charlotte), and Kevin Monroe, 2012 Democratic National Convention Committee. Southeastern Conference of Public Administrators: "What Every Public Administrator Should Know About Planning a Mega-Event: Lessons from the 2012 Democratic National Convention," Sept. 26, 2013; Murrey, August 26, 2012.

20. Lenskyj (2000; 2008) has studied local opposition movements.

Chapter 2

1. Dallas also lost the 1980 RNC to Detroit in part because it would not make its facilities available in July, when desired by the Republican National Committee (Alexander 1983).

2. Burgess passed away in June 2010. The story of her activities is based on several interviews. The primary source is her daughter and DNC traveling companion Gillian Burgess, interviewed by Eric Heberlig, June 18, 2013. Other key contributors were close friend Mary Hopper, director, University City Partners, interview with Eric

Heberlig, June 5, 2013; Tim Newman, former CEO of the Charlotte Regional Visitors Authority, interview with Eric Heberlig, January 24, 2013; Kevin Monroe, chief of staff to Charlotte mayor Anthony Foxx, interview with Eric Heberlig, February 14, 2013.

3. U.S. District Court Judge Frank Whitney, president of Carolinas 2000. Interview with Eric Heberlig, May 25, 2013.

4. As a tax-exempt organization, donations and expenditures must be publicly reported. See chapter 3.

5. Monroe, February 14, 2013.

6. Whitney, May 25, 2013.

7. Bill McMillan, senior director of sales, Charlotte Regional Visitors Authority Interview with Eric Heberlig, May 28, 2013.

8. Patty Richbourg, Charlotte Regional Visitors Authority Liaison to Carolinas 2000. Interview with Eric Heberlig, May 23, 2013.

9. Monroe, February 14, 2013.

10. Ibid.

11. Ibid.

12. Newman, January 24, 2013.

13. Monroe, February 14, 2013.

14. Will Miller, Director, Charlotte in 2012, interview with Eric Heberlig, July 25, 2013; Tracy Montross, chief of staff to Charlotte mayor Anthony Foxx, interview with Cicily Hampton, November 8, 2012.

15. Miller, July 25, 2013.

16. Monroe, February 14, 2013.

17. Miller, January 22, 2013 and July 25, 2013.

18. This section is based on interviews with people involved in the site selection process, Charlotte's 2000 and 2012 bid documents, and newspaper coverage of the process in numerous cities.

19. Warren Cooksey, treasurer, Carolinas 2000. Interview with Eric Heberlig, Jan. 28, 2013.

20. Interestingly, the key contemporary requirements do not differ dramatically from the RFPs of the 1960s (See Cotter and Hennessy 1964, 110–11; Bibby and Alexander 1968, 41–45).

21. Steve Kerrigan, chair of the 2012 DNC's Technical Advisory Group and director of the DNCC, interview with Eric Heberlig, April 23, 2013; Cameron Moody, senior advisor, 2012 Democratic National Convention Committee, presentation to POLS 3010 Political Conventions, June 14, 2012.

22. See the Measurement Appendix for information on the measurement of airline hubs and median income. Airline passenger data is from the Federal Aviation Administration: http://www.faa.gov/airports/planning_capacity/passenger_allcargo_stats/passenger/media/CY12AllEnplanements.pdf. Last accessed: April 23, 2014. Fortune 500 companies: http://fortune.com/fortune500/2010/. Last accessed September 8, 2014. Campaign donations: www.opensecrets.org, then search by "state," "year," and "geography." Last accessed: September 10, 2014.

23. Moody, June 14, 2012.

24. For example, in 1990, Salt Lake's population was 159,936; by 2012, it was 186,440. We use cities rather than metropolitan areas because parties have invited multiple cities within the same metropolitan area to bid (e.g., Los Angeles/Anaheim, Baltimore/Washington) and multiple cities within a metropolitan area may have the ability to host a convention but have chosen not to bid.

25. These articles were found using the search string "[party name] national convention bid" AND "[city name]" for each convention cycle from 1992 through 2012. Prior to 1992, fewer sources are available on NewsBank, making the reliability of search results suspect.

26. In thirty-five instances, we found no news reports on a city receiving an invitation in a particular cycle, but it received an invitation in the preceding and subsequent cycles. (The NewsBank data produce 147 cities that received invitations, 21.1% of cases; the extrapolated data produce 182 cities that received invitations, or 26.1% of cases.) It seems unlikely that both parties would disinvite a city for a single cycle. Typically, the party does not invite the city that hosted its previous convention but the other party does. In the statistical analysis (table 2.3), we ran the model with our NewsBank-generated list, and the list with invitations extrapolated from the adjacent convention cycles. The variables that attain statistical significance are the same in both models; the adjusted R^2 and the size of the coefficients are larger using the extrapolated data. The counts presented in table 2.5 use the extrapolated data.

27. Because we are using panel data—cities in each convention cycle—many cases are included multiple times in the data set. This violates the standard statistically assumption that the cases are independent. We adjust by estimating the model using robust standard errors clustered by city. Estimating the model as panel data set with random fixed effects produces the same results.

28. Whitney, May 25, 2013; Brosnan (1998).

29. McMillan, May 28, 2013; Richbourg, May 23, 2013.

30. Ibid.

31. The dynamics of 9/11 disruption costs also affects the relationship between tourism employment and bidding (Heberlig, Leland, Shields, and Swindell 2016). Prior to 9/11, the hypothesized curvilinear relationship between tourism and bids is significant. Cities with medium-size tourism industries were more likely to bid. After 9/11 and the drop in the number of bids, the relationship no longer attains statistical significance.

32. When governors and mayors are entered as separate variables, governors are statistically significant and mayors fall just short at $p < .13$.

33. In the past, the Democrats' site selection team often surpassed fifty people. Smith and Nimmo (1991: 83) note sardonically: "If a city can afford to wine and dine the Democrats' site visitation team, it is deemed capable of handling the convention." Cities increasingly pushed back against this expensive "boondoggle" for party donors and didn't like the perception that site selection was based on "schmoozing" more than their capabilities (Monroe, May 22, 2012).

34. Kerrigan, April 23, 2013.

35. Ibid.

36. Ibid.

37. Former Republican National Committee member Bryan Wagner (Associated Press 1987). Cooksey, January 28, 2013.

38. Kerrigan, April 23, 2013; Miller, July 25, 2013.

39. Similarly, in the case of the Olympics, Christopher Hill (1996, 73) observes: "The IOC [International Olympic Committee] will not look seriously at a candidate city unless it is able to demonstrate that it has the backing of all levels of government, and that arrangements have been made to cover any eventual loss."

40. When we include CRP measure in a model of advancement through the site selection process 2000–2012, it is unrelated to advancement. Population size and campaign contributions are highly correlated (.75) so population still captures their influence. We also attempted to use the city's number of Fortune 500 companies as a measure of prospective fundraising. It too is highly correlated with population size (.82) and does not significantly predict fundraising when population size is controlled.

41. We found instances of conflict between the city and local or state party organizations, but these cities decided not to bid.

42. The Republicans select their city first, so in cases in which the RNC host city also bid for the DNC, we remove it from the rankings for Democratic bid cities. In years in which Minneapolis/St. Paul and Tampa/St. Petersburg bid jointly (all but Minneapolis in 2012), we combined their attributes.

43. We combined the populations of Minneapolis/St. Paul and Tampa/St. Petersburg since they bid jointly. All host cities since 1992—except Cleveland in 2016—have been larger than 550,000. We use the lower threshold to include New Orleans, which hosted in 1988.

44. Cleveland scores lower than some of its competitors for the 2016 GOP convention on *either* the Reliable Agent or the Electoral criteria primarily because its size is lower than the threshold. Its small size had been a problem in past bids but it has increased the number of downtown hotel rooms (but its population size has not increased). So using population size as a proxy for hotel rooms generally works well but not for Cleveland in 2016. Likewise, Dallas and Denver met the population size and fundraising thresholds, but Dallas's arena was not available at the right time, and Denver was less successful than Cleveland in getting funds committed (Murray 2014 a, b).

45. Moody, June 14, 2012.

Chapter 3

1. Federal Election Commission. http://www.fec.gov/disclosurehs/hsnational.do;jsessionid=388AFA322E5B4BF8C93A69F7C7C67C00.worker4. Accessed February 2, 2015.

2. In 1968, Democrats expected President Lyndon Johnson to be re-nominated, so planned a late convention and made no fundraising preparations (Alexander, 1976a: 210). When Johnson withdrew after a close call in the New Hampshire primary and

big donors abandoned them, the Democratic National Committee and Vice President Hubert Humphrey were forced to borrow the money for the convention and much of the 1968 campaign.

3. Our data start in 1980 because host committees were first required to report their financing and spending under the Federal Election Commission's 1979 regulations.

4. San Diego's case is based on a series of stories by Gerry Braun of the *San Diego Union-Tribune*, especially Braun, 1996a; Braun, 1996b; Braun, 1997; and Crabtree, 1995.

5. Frank Whitney, President of Carolinas 2000. Interviewed by Eric Heberlig, May 25, 2013.

6. The federal security grant goes to the host city, not the host committee or the Party Convention Committee, so is not counted by the FEC as a convention disbursement.

7. The grants are not the totality of federal security spending during party conventions. It does not cover the expenses of Secret Service protection for the candidates, or the personnel and operational costs of other federal security agencies involved in the conventions (Garrett and Reese, 2014: 6).

8. The order of each of the financing options was randomized across respondents.

9. Contribution files from earlier host committees are unavailable on the Federal Election Commission's website.

10. The data on the donor's record was obtained from the Center for Responsive Politics (www.opensecrets.org). For organizations, we gathered data on contributions to candidates from their political action committee.

11. Quoted in Henderson (2011).

12. On the importance of access contributions generally, see Fouirnaies and Hall (2014).

13. Only two individuals gave to more than two host committees.

14. Steve Kerrigan, chair of the Democratic National Committee's Technical Advisory Group and director of the Democratic National Convention Committee. Interview with Eric Heberlig, April 23, 2013.

15. Will Miller, president, Charlotte in 2012. Interview with Eric Heberlig, July 25, 2013.

16. It is not unprecedented for cities to establish multiple fundraising organizations for conventions, with each organization having different implementation responsibilities and fundraising/reporting requirements. For the 1984 conventions, for example, Dallas had three different committees and San Francisco had two committees (Alexander and Haggerty, 1987: 296–308). The Dallas Convention Fund raised money for underwriting the Republican National Committee's convention activities and security; the Dallas Welcoming Committee contracted with the city to provide hospitality for the media and other nonofficial visitors; the Republican Host Committee was established by the county party to provide hospitality for GOP party officials and convention delegates. As a local party committee, it raised money under Texas law and did not file reports with the FEC.

17. Mary Tribble, executive director of hospitality and events, Charlotte in 2012 Host Committee. Presentation to POLS 3010, June 14, 2012.

18. Duke could claim the line of credit as a business expense so shareholders had to pay $6 million of the total cost. Despite this loss, Duke's 2012 earnings were $1.7 billion. (Henderson, 2013).

19. "Out-party" donors are evenly split between local and nonlocal contributors. Nonlocal out-party givers provide larger checks ($240,931 on average vs. $155,775), suggesting that large out-party donors have connections to fundraiser and/or contribute for access rather than to promote the host city.

20. We also estimated the models in several other ways. We used fixed effects models by cities. The GOP convention variable is excluded from these models. The results are extremely similar to those we present. We also estimated linear regression models with robust standard errors clustered on 1) the host city, and 2) the donor. Again, the results are extremely similar. We also estimated the total amount model with a logged dependent variable and produced very similar results. The only variables that produced results that depended on the estimation method were the foundation and the local donor variables in the timing models, as we note in the text.

21. For example, Denver raised funds for 900 days while St. Paul raised funds for 490 days prior to their respective conventions.

22. Excluding late contributions does not change the results presented here.

23. Local contributions are statistically significant in the random effects model (p. < .01) and marginally significant (p < .07) in an OLS model with robust standard errors clustered on the host city. Local contributions not significantly related to donation size when the logarithmic value of the dependent variable is used.

24. The results for foundations are not consistently significant across models. It is not significant by narrow margins in the fixed effects and cluster models.

25. It passed 295–103 in the House (113th Congress roll call 632). An earlier version that used the convention money to reduce the deficit passed by a smaller margin (239–160, roll call 25). Sixty-two House Democrats switched when the bill was framed as supporting pediatric research (ten Democrats joined a nearly united GOP in roll call 25). In the 112th Congress, the Senate agreed to an amendment eliminating convention funding 95–4 (roll call 162).

Chapter 4

1. Quoted in Morrill, 2011.

2. Committee organization and membership documents provided by Tracy Montross, chief of staff, mayor of Charlotte during the 2012 Convention.

3. The subcommittees' responsibilities speak to the wide variety of tasks facing a city in implementing a convention: airport, airport security, civil disturbance, consequence management, counter-surveillance, credentialing, crisis management, critical infrastructure protection, dignitary/VIP protection, explosive device response, fire/life safety/HAZMAT, health/medical, intelligence and counterterrorism, interagency

communication, legal/civil liberties, public affairs, tactical, training, transportation/traffic, venue security, logistic/asset identification, technology, and staffing and housing for law enforcement.

4. Karen Whichard, community relations manager for the Charlotte-Mecklenburg Utility Department. Gerald Fox MPA Conference, November 2, 2012.

5. Jon Hannan, Charlotte fire chief. Presentation at the Southeastern Conference of Public Administrators: "What Every Public Administrator Should Know About Planning a Mega-Event: Lessons from the 2012 Democratic National Convention," September 26, 2013.

6. Dr. David Callaway, director, Med-one Mobile Emergency Unit, Carolinas Medical Center. "Charlotte Talks with Mike Collins," WFAE, August 31, 2012.

7. Larry Kopf, chief operations planning officer, Charlotte Area Transit System. "Lessons Learned from Hosting the DNC in Charlotte." Gerald G. Fox Master of Public Administration Alumni and Student Conference. University of North Carolina Center City Building, Charlotte, North Carolina, November 2, 2012.

8. Harold Medlock, deputy chief, Charlotte-Mecklenburg Police Department. Interview with Haley Rader, November 15, 2012.

9. Medlock, November 15, 2015.

10. Kevin Staley, Mecklenburg County Emergency Management Services. Interview by Bo Fitzgerald, November 15, 2012.

11. Kimberly McMillan, director of corporate communications and marketing, City of Charlotte. Interview with Karen Smith, November 13, 2012; and "Lessons Learned from Hosting the DNC in Charlotte. Gerald G. Fox Master of Public Administration Alumni and Student Conference. University of North Carolina Center City Building, Charlotte, North Carolina, November 2, 2012.

12. Robert Hagemann, city attorney, Charlotte. Class Presentation to POLS 3010A, June 4, 2012.

13. Hagemann, June 4, 2012. Also see Wootson, 2012.

14. Ibid.

15. Ibid.

16. Hagemann. Southeastern Conference of Public Administrators, September 26, 2013.

17. Jennings. Southeastern Conference of Public Administrators, September 26, 2013.

18. McMillan, November 2 and 13, 2012.

19. Medlock, November 15, 2012.

20. Hannan, September 26, 2013.

21. Whichard, September 26, 2013.

22. Jennings, September 26, 2013; McMillan, November 13, 2012.

Chapter 5

1. Quoted in Funk and Morrill (2012b).

2. Warren Cooksey, Charlotte city councilman and treasurer for Carolinas 2000. Interview with Eric Heberlig, January 28, 2013.

3. Cameron Moody, senior advisor, 2012 Democratic National Convention Committee, Presentation to POLS 3010, June 14, 2012; Cooksey, January 28, 2013.

4. Cooksey, January 28, 2013.

5. Kevin Monroe, 2008 DNCC deputy director of security. Interview with Eric Heberlig, February 14, 2013. The Obama campaign used this technique at other rallies during the 2008 campaign (McDonald and Schaller, 2011: 95–96).

6. Bruce Clark, 2011 campaign manager, Anthony Foxx. Presentation to POLS 3010A, June 6, 2012.

7. Monroe, February 14, 2013.

8. All analyses conducted below are weighted by census category.

9. The turnout decline documented in the survey is larger than the actual decline in turnout according to the Mecklenburg County Board of Elections. In 2008, we only asked respondents whether they voted. (For the precise wording, please see the Participation Questions in Appendix 5-B.) In 2012, we asked whether they are currently registered, how certain they are that their registration is up to date, and if they were absolutely certain that their registration was up to date. Only if they passed all three screens did we ask them about voting in the 2012 presidential election. Respondents who did not pass the screens or who admitted that they did not vote were coded as not voting.

10. Only one-third of total volunteers participated in both presidential election years. In contrast, 60% of the persuaders were active in both elections.

11. The American National Election Study shows the opposite patterns nationally: Democrats reported a slight decrease in turnout from 2008 to 2012 (80.8% to 79.6%), while non-Democrats increased from 69.0% to 74.4%.

12. Participation in convention activities and consuming convention news are significantly correlated, but the magnitude of the correlation, .168, is weak.

13. Due to an error in the skip pattern of the survey, the convention participation and media usage questions were not asked to 186 respondents, so we should be cautious with the results. We filled in the missing cases as follows. For the participation variables, the cases were entered at the means. For the media usage questions, they were estimated with the respondent's interest in politics, knowledge about politics, following the 2008 campaign, and difference in feeling thermometers between the Democratic and Republican parties.

14. Harold Medlock, deputy chief, Charlotte-Mecklenburg Police Department. Interview with Haley Rader, November 15, 2012.

15. The order of the seven questions of the series was randomized during each administration of the survey. All of the local government evaluations questions were asked at the beginning of the survey (questions 2–8) so respondents' answers to them were not primed by the questions on the DNC, the 2012 election, or their own political attitudes.

16. Analyzing each city evaluation separately shows that partisanship strongly affects evaluations of partisan offices (mayor, city council), the interactive effects are

strong in process evaluations (competence, responsiveness, effectiveness), and the effects of the interaction are weaker for end-state evaluations (satisfaction, attachment).

17. Using the full convention success scale produces very similar results.

18. The questions were 4-point scales, but numerous respondents volunteered a middle option.

19. We will model the respondents' rating of the city's success as convention host in chapter 7.

20. We also estimated two alternative measures. The first adds the responses to all seven evaluation questions and divides by the total number of questions to produce a percentage score. The key variables (partisanship, convention evaluation, and their interaction) perform in the same way as the factor score, though some of the controls (specifically, gender and race) differ. Second, we used the additive scale and estimated the model with tobit accounting for right- and left-censored observations. It produces the same substantive results as those presented in the text.

21. Modeling the local government evaluation model separately by party shows that the magnitude of the impact of ratings of the success of the convention varies by party. As predicted, it has the strongest impact among out-party Republicans (b = .25, B = .31, p < .001). But the effect of convention success ratings are actually weakest, though still positive and significant, among independents (b = .15, B = .14, p < .02). Among in-party Democrats, the effect is slightly stronger than independents but about half the magnitude (according to the Beta value) of the success rating on Republicans (b = .21, B = .17, p < .01).

22. Future research should demonstrate that the obverse is the case—that in-partisans are willing to fault their party when the evidence indicates that is has performed poorly.

23. For an expanded statement of the theory and evidence on the political advancement of convention host mayors, see Heberlig, McCoy, Leland, and Swindell (Forthcoming 2017).

Chapter 6

1. Quoted in DePriest, Bell, and Johnson (2012).

2. While every state has access to the legislative referendum tool, many times elected officials will try to avoid allowing public votes on such measures if possible. Also, only twenty-three states (and the U.S. Virgin Islands) have access to the popular referendum tool whereby citizens can petition a piece of legislation already passed be put up for a popular vote for potential repeal (National Conference of State Legislature, 2015).

3. We include co-host cities Minneapolis and St. Petersburg. Their inclusion does not affect the statistical results or our conclusions.

4. Adding controls and using fixed effects for year and city does not change the null result.

5. Bob Morgan, Charlotte Chamber of Commerce. Interview by Cicily Hampton. December 7, 2012.

6. https://www.google.com/trends.

7. Specifically, searches on the city as a municipality, using its name alone, not just a generic word or associated with its sports teams or airports, etc. Searches on "city name" and "Republican" or "Democratic National Convention" obviously produce very short-term spikes only around the time of the convention.

8. Convention months were the highest months for New York City and Cleveland. Boston's DNC in 2004 would have been first except for the Boston Marathon bombing.

9. Searches for New York City show a similar decline.

10. Tracy Montross, chief of staff to Charlotte mayor Anthony Foxx. Presentation to POLS 3010A, June 21, 2012.

11. Vi Lyles, director of community partnerships, Charlotte in 2012 Host Committee. Presentation to POLS 3010A, June 13, 2012; Montross, June 21, 2012.

12. Lyles, June 13, 2012.

13. Scola (2015); Montross, June 21, 2012.

14. Bill McMillan, senior director of sales, Charlotte Regional Visitors Association. Interview with Eric Heberlig, May 28, 2013.

15. Blair Stanford, chief operating officer, Charlotte Chamber of Commerce. Presentation to POLS 3010A, May 29, 2012.

16. Stanford, May 29, 2012.

17. Dunn (2012a); Stanford, May 29, 2016.

18. Bob Morgan, Charlotte Chamber of Commerce. Interview by Cicily Hampton, December 7, 2012.

Chapter 7

1. Frank, John. 2012. "Heady week of politics." *Charlotte Observer*, September 7, 12A.

2. Brad Krantz, WBT-AM. Quoted in "Talk of the town is radio row." *Charlotte Observer*, September 7, 2012, 14A.

3. Carol Jennings, assistant to the Charlotte city manager. Southeastern Conference of Public Administrators, September 26, 2013.

4. The mega-event valuation questions were 17–23 in the survey, after city government evaluation and Charlotte organizations reputations questions, and before DNC evaluation questions or 2008 or 2012 political questions. Responses, therefore, were not primed by questions on the DNC or on partisan political activities during the 2012 election.

5. Because the "worth it per month" question had four response options and the "willing to pay per year" question had five options, we recoded the per month question so that the three values in which the respondent was willing to give something

aligned with the three highest categories of the "per year" question. Respondents who did not want to contribute anything per month retained a value of 0. So the values for the "per month" question were 4, 3, 2, and 0.

6. This question specifically asks about individual level of value one feels for the intangibles. But we take a conservative approach by using the results as household estimates instead of individual estimates.

7. Using the lowest value of each valuation category applied to the proportion of households presented in that category yields a conservative estimate of that group's aggregate value. In keeping with this conservative approach, there is no entry in the calculation for the lowest category (the $0-$2 group). Thus, the estimate provided here is conservative and represents the low end of the value households have of the intangible aspects of hosting mega-events, such as civic pride and national reputation.

8. Analyzing the respondent's intangible valuation and willingness to pay separately produces results that are extremely similar to results of the combined scale (the two scales are correlated at .63). The only difference is the respondent's income is significantly related only to willingness to pay and his or her assessment of the reputational benefits of the convention is significantly related only to their assessment of the intangible benefits of the convention.

9. The traditional 7-point strength of party identification scale is unrelated to support for mega-events funding. Entering Democrats and Republicans separately allows us to show that independents are actually the most generous partisan group in contributing toward mega-events.

10. We lose 196 cases when income is included in the model. None of the key theoretical variables, however, are affected by the inclusion of income in the model and the resultant loss of cases. Local efficacy is positively and significantly related to willingness to pay when income is not included the model.

11. Jennings, September 26, 2013.

Bibliography

Agranoff, R., and M. McGuire. 2003. "Inside the matrix: Integrating the paradigms of intergovernmental and network management." *International Journal of Public Administration* 26, no. 12: 1401–22.

Alexander, Herbert E. 1976a. *Financing Politics*. Washington, DC: CQ Press.

Alexander, Herbert E. 1976b. *Financing the 1972 Election*. Lexington, MA: Lexington.

Alexander, Herbert E. 1979. *Financing the 1976 Election*. Washington, DC: CQ Press.

Alexander, Herbert E., and Brian A. Haggerty. 1987. *Financing the 1984 Election*. Lexington, MA: Lexington.

Anderson, Kendall. 2008. "Minneapolis St. Paul RNC host committee is out-fundraising its Denver counterpart." *Finance & Commerce* (Minneapolis), May 29.

Andranovich, Greg, Matthew J. Burbank, and Charles H. Heying. 2001. "Olympic Cities: Lessons Learned from Mega-Event Politics." *Journal of Urban Affairs* 23, no. 2: 113–31.

Appleman, Eric M. 2004. "Dallas Rules Out Bidding for 2004 Conventions." *Conventions*. Democracy in Action.

Arceneaux, Kevin, and Robert M. Stein. 2006. "Who is Held Responsible When Disaster Strikes? The Attribution of Responsibility for a Natural Disaster in an Urban Election." *Journal of Urban Affairs* 28, no. 1: 43–53.

Arnold, R. Douglas, and Nicholas Carnes. 2012. "Holding Mayors Accountable: New York's Executives from Koch to Bloomberg." *American Journal of Political Science* 56, no. 4: 949–63.

Arrow, Kenneth, Robert Solow, Paul R. Portney, Edward E. Leamer, Roy Radner, Howard Shuman. 1993. "Report of the NOAA Panel on Contingent Valuation." *Federal Register* 58: 4601–14.

Asher, Herbert, Eric S. Heberlig, Randall B. Ripley, and Karen C. Snyder. 2001. *American Labor Unions in the Electoral Arena*. Lanham, MD: Rowman & Littlefield.

Associated Press. 1987. "Atlanta, New Orleans Differ in Convention Funding." *Dallas Morning News*, March 3.

Atkeson, Lonna Rae, and Cherie D. Maestas. 2012. *Catastrophic Politics: How Extraordinary Events Redefine Perceptions of Government*. New York: Cambridge University Press.

Atkinson, Matthew D., Christopher B. Mann, Santiago Olivella, Arthur M. Simon, and Joseph E. Uscinski. 2014. "(Where) Do Campaigns Matter: The Impact of National Party Convention Location." *Journal of Politics* 76, no. 4: 1045–58.

Axon, Rachel. 2015. "Boston sours on '24 Olympic Bid." *USA Today* 1C, 10C.

Baade, Robert A., Robert Baumann, and Victor A. Matheson. 2008. "Selling the Game: Estimating the Economic Impact of Professional Sports through Taxable Sales." *Southern Economic Journal* 74, no. 3: 794–810.

Baade, Robert A., Robert Baumann, and Victor A. Matheson. 2009. "Rejecting 'Conventional' Wisdom: Estimating the Economic Impact of National Political Conventions." *Eastern Economic Journal* 35: 520–30.

Baade, Robert A., Robert Baumann, and Victor A. Matheson. 2010. "Slippery Slope: Assessing the Economic Impact of the 2002 Winter Olympic Games in Salt Lake City, Utah." *Région et Développement* 31: 81–91.

Baca, Maria Elena. 2008. "Local companies gave big to host RNC." *Star Tribune*, October 17.

Barron, Alicia E. 2010. "Grijalva calls for boycott of Arizona over proposed immigration bill." *KTVK/KASW*, April 21. http://www.azfamily.com/news/Grijalva-calls-for-boycott-91671599.html. Accessed June 20, 2014.

Beacon Hill Institute. 2004. The Real Effects of the National Political Conventions on the Boston and New York Metropolitan Areas. http://www.beaconhill.org/FaxSheets/RNCDNCConventionupdate6290.pdf. Accessed May 20, 2015.

Berry, Michael J., and Kenneth N. Bickers. 2012. "Forecasting the 2012 Presidential election with State-Level Economic Indicators." *PS: Political Science & Politics* 45, no. 4: 669–74.

Bialik, Carl. 2012. "The Economic Oomph from Big Events." *Wall Street Journal*. August 17. http://blogs.wsj.com/numbers/the-economic-oomph-from-big-events-1159/. Accessed July 27, 2015.

Bianco, William T., and Robert H. Bates. 1990. "Cooperation by Design: Leadership, Structure, and Collective Dilemmas." *American Political Science Review* 84: 133–47.

Bibby, John F., and Herbert E. Alexander. 1968. *The Politics of National Convention Finances and Arrangements*. Princeton, NJ: Citizens' Research Foundation.

Box-Steffensmeier, Janet M., Peter M. Radcliffe, and Brandon L. Bartels. 2005. "The Incidence and Timing of PAC Contributions to Incumbent U.S. House Members, 1993–94." *Legislative Studies Quarterly* 30, no. 4: 549–79.

Braun, Gerry. 1996a. "Convention disarray dismissed by GOP." *San Diego Union-Tribune*, August 1.

Braun, Gerry. 1996b. "GOP, city at odds over convention costs." *San Diego Union-Tribune*, July 12.

Braun, Gerry. 1996b. "Republican convention here was a $45 million production San Diego, host committee spending put at $31 million." *San Diego Union-Tribune*, October 23.

Braun, Gerry. 1997. "Tobacco firm gave richly to convention." *San Diego Union-Tribune*, February 11.

Bridges, Tyler. 2002. "Democrats Pick Boston for 2004," *The Miami Herald*, November 14.

Brosnan, James W. 1998. "Memphis, Nashville Forgo Convention." *The Commercial Appeal*. April 28.

Brown, Clifford W., Jr., Lynda W. Powell, and Clyde Wilcox. 1995. *Serious Money: Fundraising and Contributing in Presidential Nomination Campaigns*. New York: Cambridge University Press.

Bryce, James. 1959. *The American Commonwealth*. New York: G. P. Putnam.

Burbank, Matthew J., Greg Andranovich, and Charles H. Heying. 2001. *Olympic Dreams: The Impact of Mega-Events on Local Politics*. Boulder, CO: Lynne Rienner Publishers.

Burbank, Matthew J., Greg Andranovich, and Charles H. Heying. 2002. "Mega-Events, Urban Development, and Public Policy." *Review of Policy Research* 19, no. 3: 179–202.

Bureau of Justice Assistance. 2013. *Managing Large Scale Security Events: A Planning Primer for Local Law Enforcement Agencies*. U.S. Department of Justice. Washington, DC

Burden, Barry C. 2002. "United States Senators as Presidential Candidates." *Political Science Quarterly* 117, no. 1: 81–102.

Burns, Nancy. 1994. *The Formation of American Local Governments: Private Values in Public Institutions*. New York: Oxford University Press.

Campbell, James E. 2001. "When have presidential campaigns decided election outcomes?" *American Politics Research* 29: 437–60.

Campbell, J. E., L. Cherry, and K. Wink. 1992. "The convention bump." *American Politics Research* 20: 287–307.

Carney, Eliza Newlin. 2012. "'People Power' May Lead to Low-Wattage Event." *CQ Weekly*, September 3: 1736–57. http://library.cqpress.com/cqweekly/weeklyreport112-000004146206.

Caywood, Thomas. 2004. "DNC Mess: I-93 closure will take toll." *Boston Herald*, June 16.

Ceaser, James W. 1982. *Reforming the Reforms: A Critical Analysis of the Presidential Selection Process*. Cambridge, MA: Ballinger.

Cera, Joseph, and Aaron Weinschenk. 2012. "The Individual-Level Effects of Presidential Conventions on Candidate Evaluations." *American Politics Research* 40, no. 1: 3–18.

Chacon, Daniel J. 2008a. "Auditor wants mayor's assurance that tax funds won't go to host DNC." *Rocky Mountain News*, June 13.

Chacon, Daniel J. 2008b. "Denver neglects fundraising duty for DNC, Dem Committee charges." *Rocky Mountain News*, May 13.

Chacon, Daniel J., and David Montero. "Funding for DNC Dicey Local Panel Needs to Raise Millions by Middle of June." *Rocky Mountain News*. May 14.

Cheney, Kyle. 2014. "Columbus mayor to DNC: Pick us or lose Ohio." *Politico*, July 22. Accessed July 22, 2014 at http://www.politico.com/story/2014/07/columbus-ohio-democratic-national-convention-2016-109245.html?hp=r1.

Cheney, "Dems Pick Philadelphia for 2016 Convention."

Cherkis, Jason, and Rhainnon Fionn. 2012. "Host City for Sale: Did Uptown Boosters Sell a Sanitized Charlotte for the DNC?" *Creative Loafing*, April 10.

Chesto, John. 2004. "LNG will skip shipment." *Boston Herald*, May 12.

City and County of Denver. 2008. 2008 Democratic National Convention Impact Report. http://www.gwu.edu/~action/2008/chrnconv08/denverimpact.pdf. Accessed May 19, 2014.

City of Charlotte. 2012. Enforcement of Extraordinary Event Ordinance. http://charmeck.org/city/charlotte/newsroom/newsarchive/documents/enforcement%20of%20extraordinary%20events.pdf.

Clarke, Susan E., and Martin Saiz. 2003. "From Waterhole to World City: Place-Luck and Public Agendas in Denver." In *The Infrastructure of Play: Building the Tourist City*, edited by Dennis R. Judd. Armonk, NY: M. E. Sharpe, 168–201.

Coates, Dennis, and Craig Depken. 2006. "Mega-Events: Is the Texas-Baylor Game to Waco What the Superbowl Is to Houston?" International Association of Sports Economists Working Paper Series, no. 06-06.

Cohen, Marty, David Karol, Hans Noel, and John Zaller. 2008. *The Party Decides: Presidential Nominations Before and After Reform*. Chicago: University of Chicago Press.

Confessore, Nicholas. 2014. "GOP Angst Over 2016 Led to Provision on Funding." *New York Times* Dec. 13, 2014. Accessed December 17, 2014: http://www.nytimes.com/2014/12/14/us/politics/gop-angst-over-2016-convention-led-to-funding-provision.html.

Cooke, Meghan, and Ames Alexander. 2012. "Monroe: Flexibility, open dialogue helped keep
peace." *Charlotte Observer*, Sept. 8, 1A, 11A.

Cotter, Cornelius P., and Bernard C. Hennessy. 1964. *Politics Without Power: The National Party Committees*. New York: Atherton.

Cover, Albert D. 1986. "Party Competence Evaluations and Voting for Congress." *Western Political Quarterly* 39, no. 2: 304–12.

Crabtree, Penny. 1995. "Is the Republican National Convention worth the price?" *San Diego Union-Tribune*, August 20.

Crompton, John. 2006. "Economic Impact Studies: Instruments for Political Shenanigans?" *Journal of Travel Research* 45, no. 1: 67–82.

Daily Breeze. 2000. "Convention funding draws hostility." *Daily Breeze* (Torrence, CA), June 21.

Danielson, Richard, John Martin, and Darla Cameron. 2012. "Fundraising Success for RNC Host Committee Came from Small Number of Big Checkbooks." *Tampa Bay Times*, October 18.

David, Paul T., Ralph M. Goldman, and Richard C. Bain. 1960. *The Politics of National Party Conventions*. Washington, DC: The Brookings Institution.

Davis, James W. 1972. *National Conventions: Nominations Under the Big Top*. Woodbury, NY: Barron's.

Davis, James W. 1983. *National Party Conventions in an Age of Reform*. Westport, CT: Greenwood.

DeBlasio, Allan J., Terrance J. Regan, Margaret E. Zirker, Joshua Hassol, and Craig Austin. 2005. Transportation Management and Security during the 2004 Democratic National Convention. Washington, DC: U.S. Department of Transportation Research and Special Services Administration.

Denver 2008 Convention Host Committee. 2008. *Greening the Democratic National Convention.* https://www.sanjoseca.gov/DocumentCenter/View/987. Accessed November 16, 2015.

DePriest, Joe, Adam Bell, and Lukas Johnson. 2012. "GOP-tinged Towns Bask in DNC's Afterglow." *Charlotte Observer*, Sept. 9, 1B, 3B.

Diaz, Kevin, and Richard Meryhew. 2011. "Dems to go south for 2012 confab." *Star Tribune*, February 2.

Doren, Jenny, and Demond Fernandez. 2014. "Cleveland beats Dallas in bid to host Republican Convention." *WFAA* (Dallas). July 8. Accessed via Newsbank July 11, 2014.

Eisinger, Peter K. 1988. *The Rise of the Entrepreneurial State: State and Local Economic Development Policy.* Madison: University of Wisconsin Press.

Eisinger, Peter K. 2000. "The Politics of Bread and Circuses: Building the City of the Visitor Class." *Urban Affairs Review* 35, no. 3: 316–33.

Elliot, Philip, and Steve Peoples. 2014. "Cleveland Tops Dallas in Bid to Host RNC in 2016." July 8. http://www.denverpost.com/editorials/ci_26107589/rnc-panel recommend-site-2016-convention. Accessed July 11, 2014.

Erickson, Robert S., and Christopher Wlezian. 2012. *The Timeline of Presidential Elections: How Campaigns Do (And Do Not) Matter.* Chicago: University of Chicago Press.

Eskow, Richard. 2012. "Will Democrats Speak for the People?" Huff Post Politics. Retrieved December 14, 2015. http://www.huffingtonpost.com/rj-eskow/will-the-democrats-speak_b_1853255.html.

Eysberg, Cees D. 1989. "The Origins of the American Urban System: Historical Accident and Initial Advantage." *Journal of Urban History* 15, no. 2: 185–95.

Fainstein, Susan S., and Dennis R. Judd. 1999. "Cities as Places to Play." In Dennis R. Judd and Susan S. Fainstein. *The Tourist City.* New Haven, CT: Yale University Press.

Federal Election Commission. 2014. Advisory Opinion 2014-12. Accessed October 16, 2014: http://saos.fec.gov/saos/searchao;jsessionid=293645E47322087458B 5BAEA1B3839DAjsessionid=91F53F2380C45ADA6D07E78E90E28DD8?SUB MIT=continue&PAGE_O=0.

Federal Election Commission. 2003. Public Financing of Presidential Candidates and Nominating Conventions. Federal Register Volume 68, No. 153. Accessed October 16, 2014: http://www.gpo.gov/fdsys/pkg/FR-2003-08-08/pdf/03-19893.pdf.

Federal Election Commission. 1994. Presidential Election Campaign Fund and Federal Financing of Presidential Nominating Conventions; Federal Register Volume 59, Number 124 (Wednesday, June 29, 1994)]. Accessed October 16, 2014: http://www.gpo.gov/fdsys/pkg/FR-1994-06-29/html/94-15710.htm.

Feeney, Susan, and Carl P. Leubsdorf. 1991. "GOP picks Houston for '92 convention city chosen over New Orleans, San Diego." *Dallas Morning News.* January 9.

Fenno, Richard F. 1978. *Home Style.* New York: Harper Collins.

Flammang, R. 1979. "Economic Growth and Economic Development: Counterparts or Competitors." *Economic Development and Cultural Change* 28: 47–62.

Florida, Richard. 2002. *The Rise of the Creative Class.* New York: Basic Books.

Fouirnaies, Alexander, and Andrew B. Hall. 2014. "The Financial Incumbency Advantage: Causes and Consequences." *Journal of Politics* 76, no. 3: 711–24.

Francia, Peter L., John C. Green, Paul S. Herrnson, Lynda Powell, and Clyde Wilcox. 2003. *The Financiers of Congressional Elections: Investors, Ideologues, and Intimates.* New York: Columbia University Press.

Francia, Peter. 2006. *The Future of Organized Labor in American Politics.* New York: Columbia University Press.

Frieden, Bernard J., and Lynne B. Sagalyn. 1989. *Downtown, Inc.: How America Rebuilds Cities.* Cambridge, MA: MIT Press.

Funk, Tim. 2012. "This jobs needs surgeon's touch." *Charlotte Observer,* June 10, 1A, 10A.

Funk, Tim, and Jim Morrill. Sept 3. "Convention is Obama camp's not-so-secret weapon in NC." *Charlotte Observer,* 1A., 9A.

Gansen, Kristyn. 2010. "Group hopes to discourage DNC from hosting convention in Minneapolis." *Minneapolis Examiner,* July 18.

Garrett, R. Sam. 2007. "Lights, Camera, Chaos? The Evolution of Convention 'Crisis.'" In *Rewiring Politics: Presidential Nominating Conventions in the Media Age,* edited by C. Panagopoulos. Baton Rouge: Louisiana State University Press, 113–32.

Gatlin, Greg. 2003. "DNC planners sure of funding." *Boston Herald,* May 8.

Gelman, A., and G. King. 1993. "Why Are American Presidential Election Polls So Variable When Votes Are So Predictable?" *British Journal of Political Science* 23: 409–51.

Gillman, Todd J. 2014. "It's pretty hard for cities to raise money for political conventions." McClatchy News, March 18. http://www.governing.com/news/headlines/its-pretty-hard-for-cities-to-raise-money-for-political-conventions-.html.

Goldstein, Josh, and Jan M. Von Bergen. 2000. "Companies Flock to Contribute to GOP Convention." *Philadelphia Inquirer,* January 20.

Goldstein, Scott. 2014. "Arena official: American Airlines Center won't need required 6 weeks to prepare 2016 Republican National Convention." *Dallas Morning News.* Accessed July 11, 204.

Gomez, Brad T., and J. Matthew Wilson. 2001. "Political Sophistication and Economic Voting in the American Electorate: A Theory of Heterogeneous Attribution." *American Journal of Political Science* 45: 899–914.

Grant, J. Tobin, and Thomas J. Rudolph. 2002. "To Give or Not to Give: Modeling Individuals' Contribution Decisions." *Political Behavior* 24: 31–54.

Green, Donald, Bradley Palmquist, Eric Schickler. 2002. *Partisan Hearts and Minds: Political Parties and the Social Identities of Voters.* New Haven, CT: Yale University Press.

Green, Donald P., and Alan S. Gerber. 2008. *Get Out the Vote: How to Increase Voter Turnout.* Washington, DC: Brookings Institution.

Green, John C., et al. 2003. "Participation, Competition, Engagement: How to Revive and Improve Public Funding For Presidential Nomination Politics." Washington, DC: Campaign Finance Institute. Accessed January 15, 2015: http://cfinst.org/president/pdf/fullreport.pdf.

Grier, Kevin B., Michael C. Munger, and Brian E. Roberts. 1994. "The Determinates of Industry Political Activity, 1978–1986." *American Political Science Review* 88: 911–26.

Grim, Ryan. 2012. "Money talks during political conventions—Why different rules still make for the same game." *Creative Loafing*, August 30.

Guerra, Carlos. 1998. "Not all those invited will bid—wonder why?" *San Antonio Express News*. April 23.

Hamburger, Tom, and P. J. Hufstutter. 2008. "Hard Fundraising Times Send GOP Scrambling." *St. Paul Pioneer Press*, August 11.

Harrison, Steve. 2011. "Inside the convention's $42 million wish list." *Charlotte Observer*, February 3.

Hatcher, W., M. Oyer, and R. Gallardo. 2011. The Creative Class and Economic Development as Practiced in the Rural U.S. South: An Exploratory Survey of Economic Development Professionals. *The Review of Regional Studies* 41: 139–59.

Hagen, Michael G., and Richard Johnston. 2007. "Conventions and Campaign Dynamics." In *Rewiring Politics: Presidential Nominating Conventions in the Media Age*, edited by C. Panagopoulos. Baton Rouge: Louisiana State University Press.

Hayes, Stan M. 2012. *The First American Political Conventions: Transforming Presidential Nominations, 1832–1872.* Jefferson, NC: McFarland.

Heberlig, Eric S., Suzanne M. Leland, Mark Shields, and David Swindell. 2016. "The Disruption Costs of Post-911 Security Measures and Cities' Bids for Presidential Nominating Conventions." *Journal of Urban Affairs.*

Heberlig, Eric, Justin McCoy, Suzanne Leland, and David Swindell. Forthcoming, 2017. "Mayors, Accomplishments, and Advancement." *Urban Affairs Review.*

Henderson, Bruce. 2011. "Committed to raising money." *Charlotte Observer*, February 3.

Henderson, Bruce. 2012. "The Pitfalls of Preparation." *Charlotte Observer*, February 12, 1A, 9A.

Henderson, Bruce. 2013. "Duke won't be repaid from DNC." *Charlotte Observer*, March 1, 1A, 4A.

Henneberger, Melinda. 2016. "Chaotic Convention Puts Trump's Managerial Brilliance in Question." Roll Call, July 21. Last accessed August 1, 2016. http://www.rollcall.com/news/opinion/chaotic-convention-puts-trumps-managerial-brilliance.

Herrnson, Paul S. 2009. "The Roles of Party Organizations, Party-Connected Committees, and Party Allies in Elections." *Journal of Politics* 71: 1207–24.

Hibbing, John R., and Elizabeth Theiss-Morse. 2002. *Stealth Democracy*. New York: Cambridge University Press.

Hill, Christopher R. 1996. *Olympic Politics*, 2nd ed. New York: Manchester University Press.

Hillygus, D. S., and S. Jackman. 2003. "Voter Decision Making in Election 2000: Campaign Effects, Partisan Activation, and the Clinton Legacy." *American Journal of Political Science* 47: 583–96.

Holman, Craig, Angela Canterbury, and Zoe Bridges-Curry. 2008. "Party Conventions Are Free-For-All for Influence Peddling." *Public Citizen*. Last accessed October 14, 2014. http://www.citizen.org/documents/Party%20Conventions2.pdf.

Hoppin, Jason. 2010. "Another convention already? It could happen." *St. Paul Pioneer Press*, July 2.

Hosenball, Mark. 2008. "Assessing the Obama Assassination Plot." Newsweek. August 26. Last accessed on August 16, 2016. http://www.newsweek.com/assessing-obama-assassination-plot-88253.

Howell, Susan E., and Huey L. Perry. 2004. "Black Mayors/White Mayors: Explaining Their Approval." *Public Opinion Quarterly* 68, no. 1: 32–56.

Hudson, Ian. 2001. "The Use and Misuse of Economic Impact Analysis: The Case of Professional Sports." *Journal of Sport and Social Issues* 25, no. 1, 20–39.

Hunter, Walt. 2015. "Experts Optimistic About Security and Economic Impact of 2016 Democratic National Convention in Philadelphia." *CBS Philly.* February 12. http://philadelphia.cbslocal.com/2015/02/12/experts-optimistic-about-security-economic-impact-of-2016-democratic-national-convention-in-philadelphia/. Accessed July 27, 2015.

International City/County Management Association. 1990–2012 editions. "Directory: Officials in U.S. Municipalities." In *The Municipal Yearbook.* Washington, DC: ICMA.

Isenstadt, Alex, and Shane Goldmacher. 2016. "GOP Cleveland organizers beg Adelson for $6 million." *Politico.* July 14. Last accessed: July 16, 2016 http://www.politico.com/story/2016/07/rnc-begs-adelson-for-6-million-to-cover-convention-shortfall-225571.

Jobling, Ian. 2000. "Bidding for the Olympics: Site Selection and Sydney 2000." In *The Olympics at the Millennium; Power, Politics, and the Games,* edited by Kay Schaffer and Sidonie Smith. New Brunswick, NJ: Rutgers University Press, 258–71.

Johnson, Bruce, Michael Mondello, and John Whitehead. 2007. "The Value of Public Goods Generated by a National Football League Team." *Journal of Sport Management* 21, no. 1: 123–36.

Jones, Jeffrey M. 2016. "Americans More Positive About Democratic Than GOP Convention."

Gallup. August 1. Last accessed August 1, 2016. http://www.gallup.com/poll/194084/americans-positive-democratic-gop-convention.aspx.

Judd, Dennis R., ed. 2003. *The Infrastructure of Play: Building the Tourist City.* Armonk, NY: M. E. Sharpe.

Judd, Dennis R., and Susan S. Fainstein, eds. 1999. *The Tourist City.* New Haven, CT: Yale University Press.

Judd, D., and Swanstrom, T. 2012. *City Politics* (8th Ed.). Boston: Longman.

Kamarck, Elaine C. 2009. *Primary Politics: How Presidential Candidates Have Shaped the Modern Nominating System.* Washington: Brookings Institution.

Keith, Bruce E., David B. Magleby, Candice J. Nelson, Elizabeth Orr, Mark C. Westlye, and Raymond E. Wolfinger, 1992. *The Myth of the Independent Voter.* Berkeley: University of California Press.

Kersten, Katherine. 2008. "RNC anarchists had friends in 'peaceful' protest groups." *Star Tribune,* September 28.

Kettl, D. 2007. Homeland Security: The Federalism Challenge. In *American Intergovernmental Relations,* edited by Laurence J. O'Toole. Washington, DC: CQ Press, 322–44.

Kiewiet, Roderick D., and Langche Zeng. 1993. "An Analysis of Congressional Career Decisions, 1947–1986." *American Political Science Review* 87, no. 4: 928–41.

Koff, Stephen. 2011. "Cleveland loses its bid for Dems' convention." *Plain Dealer*, February 2.

Kunda, Ziva. 1990. "The Case for Motivated Political Reasoning." *Psychological Bulletin* 108, no. 3: 480–98.

La Torre, David. 2000. "State Taxpayers Footing $7 Million Gift to Convention" *Morning Call* (Allentown), July 30.

Lauermann, John. 2015. "Boston's Olympic bid and the evolving urban politics of event-led development." *Urban Geography*: 1–9.

Leland, Elizabeth. 2012. "Charlotte chief faces biggest test." *Charlotte Observer*, May 20, 1A, 4A.

Lelyveld, Nita. 2000. "A GOP Resource for Democrats Fund." *Philadelphia Inquirer*, April 3.

Lenskyj, Helen. 2000. *Inside the Olympic Industry Resistance: Power, Politics, and Activism.* Albany: State University of New York Press.

Lenskyj, Helen. 2008. *Olympic Industry Resistance: Challenging Olympic Power and Propaganda.* Albany: State University of New York Press.

Levine, Marc V. 2003. "Tourism Infrastructure and Urban Redevelopment in Montreal." In *The Infrastructure of Play: Building the Tourist City*, edited by Dennis R. Judd. Armonk, NY: M. E. Sharpe.

Logan, J., and H. Molotch. 1987. *Urban Fortunes: The Political Economy of Place.* Berkeley: University of California Press.

Los Angeles Police Department. 2000. "2000 Democratic National Convention." Last accessed November 14, 2015. http://www.lapdonline.org/history_of_the_lapd/content_basic_view/1135.

Lowe, Frederick H. 1994. "Corporate Funding Expected To Handle One-Third of Cost." *Chicago Sun-Times*, July 21.

Lucey, Catherine. 2010. "Return of the Democrats in '12?" *Philadelphia Daily News*, January 14.

MacAloon, John J. 2006. "The Theory of Spectacle: Reviewing Olympic Ethnography." In *National Identity and Global Sports Events: Culture, Politics, and Spectacle in the Olympics and Football World Cup*, edited by Alan Tomlinson and Christopher Young. Albany: State University of New York Press.

Mailer, Norman. 1968. *Miami and the Siege of Chicago.* New York: New York Review Books.

Malbin, Michael J. 1981. "The Conventions, Platforms, and Issue Activists." In *The American Elections of 1980*, edited by Austin Ranney. Washington, DC: American Enterprise Institute.

Martin, Jonathan, and Maggie Haberman. 2016. "Corporations Grow Nervous About Participating in Republican Convention." *New York Times*, March 30. Last accessed: April 7, 2016. http://www.nytimes.com/2016/03/31/us/politics/donald-trump-republican-national-convention.html?_r=1.

Malizia, E., and E. Feser. 1999. *Understanding Local Economic Development.* New Brunswick, NJ: Center for Urban Policy Research, State University of New Jersey.

Malpezzi, S. 2003. "Economic Development and Its Finance." In *Financing Economic Development in the 21st Century*, edited by S. White, R. Bingham, and E. Hill. Armonk, NY: M. E. Sharpe.

Mataconis, Doug. 2012. "Political Conventions Don't Bring Economic Benefits to Host Cities." August 27. http://www.outsidethebeltway.com/political-conventions-dont-bring-economic-benefits-to-host-cities/. Accessed July 27, 2015.

Mayhew, David R. 1974. *Congress: The Electoral Connection*. New Haven: Yale University Press.

McCartney, Scott. 1984. "GOP convention gives Dallas chance to alter image." *Daily Breeze* (Torrance, CA), August 19.

McDonald, Greg. 1991. "Problems with San Diego's bid open door for Houston." *Houston Chronicle*, January 9.

McDonald, Michael P., and Thomas F. Schaller. 2011. "Voter Mobilization in the 2008 Presidential Election." In *The Change Election*, edited by David B. Magelby. Philadelphia: Temple University Press.

McGerr, Michael. 1986. *The Decline of Popular Politics: The American North, 1865–1928*. New York: Oxford University Press.

McNitt, Andrew Douglas. 2010. "Tenure in Office of Big City Mayors." *State and Local Government Review* 42, no. 1: 36–47.

Meyers, Jack. 2004. "Mayor hopes scare tactics prevent road nightmare." *Boston Herald*, April 1.

Mider, Zachary, and Elizabeth Dexheimer. 2016. "More Companies Choose to Sit Out Trump's Coronation in Cleveland." Bloomberg News. June 16. Last accessed: June 17, 2016. http://www.bloomberg.com/politics/articles/2016-06-16/more-companies-opt-to-sit-out-trump-s-coronation-in-cleveland.

Miller, Jay. 2014. "RNC to Spark big digital upgrade downtown." July 20. http://www.crainscleveland.com/article/20140720/SUB1/307209982/rnc-to-spark-big-digital-upgrade-downtown

Mills, Brian M., and Mark S. Rosentraub. 2013. "Hosting Mega-Events: A Guide to the Evaluation of Development Effects in Integrated Metropolitan Regions." *Tourism Management* 34 (February): 238–46.

Mills, Brian M., Mark S. Rosentraub, Jason A. Winfree, and Michael Cantor. 2014. "Fiscal Outcomes and Tax Impacts from Stadium Financing Strategies in Arlington, Texas." *Public Money & Management* 34, no. 2: 145–52.

Minneapolis Saint Paul 2008 Host Committee. 2008. Republican National Convention Impact Report. http://minnesota.publicradio.org/features/2009/09/01_rncimpact/report.pdf. Accessed May 19, 2014.

Minnesota Public Radio. 2008. http://www.mprnews.org/story/2008/09/01/rnc_day1.

Mitchell, Robert, and Richard Carson. 1989. *Using Surveys to Value Public Goods: The Contingent Valuation Method*. Washington, DC: Resources for the Future.

Morrill, Jim. 2010a. "Charlotte a finalist for Dems in 2012." *Charlotte Observer*, July 1.

Morrill, Jim. 2010b. "Politics a wild card in picking convention site." *Charlotte Observer*, August 5.

Morrill, Jim. 2011. "Before the spotlight shines on Charlotte, Tampa Leads off." *Charlotte Observer*, December 18, 1A, 11A.

Morrill, Jim. 2012. "A fix for DNC's red ink?" *Charlotte Observer*, Dec. 8, 1A, 9A.

Morrill, Jim. 2016. "Democrats' fundraising has fewer restrictions." *Charlotte Observer*, May 4, 15A, 16A.

Morrill, Jim, and Tim Funk. 2012. "DNC organizers struggling, but bullish on money." *Charlotte Observer*, July 12, 1A, 9A.

Murray, Jon. 2014a. "Down to 2: Denver out for hosting 2016 event." *Denver Post*, June 26.

Murray, Jon. 2014b. "Money becomes bid drawback." *Denver Post*, June 13.

Musgrave, R., and P. Musgrave. 1989. *Public Finance Theory and Practice* (5th ed.). New York: McGraw-Hill.

National Conference of State Legislatures. 2015. Initiative and Referendum States. http://www.ncsl.org/research/elections-and-campaigns/chart-of-the-initiative-states.aspx. Accessed August 3, 2016.

Nelson, Louis. 2016. "New poll: No convention bounce for Trump." *Politico*, July 26. Last accessed August 1, 2016. http://www.politico.com/story/2016/07/poll-trump-republican-convention-226198.

Nicholas, P. 2000. "For Rendell, GOP Convention Work Is Done as Mayor: He Lobbied Hard to Bring the Gathering Here. As Head of the DNC, He Will Be Keeping His Distance." *Philadelphia Inquirer*, July 7, A01.

Noll, Roger, and Andrew Zimbalist (eds.). 1997. *Sports, Jobs, and Taxes: The Economic Impact of Sports Teams and Stadiums*. Washington, DC: The Brookings Institution Press.

Nunkoo, Robin. 2015. "Tourism Development and Trust in Local Government." *Tourism Management* 46: 623–34.

Oliver, J. Eric. 2012. *Local Elections and the Politics of Small Scale Democracy*. Princeton: Princeton University Press.

Olson, Mancur. 1965. *The Logic of Collective Action*. Cambridge, MA: Harvard University Press.

Oot, Torey Van. 2015. "DNC a Boon to Philly's Stature; Money Impact Likely Mixed." *NECN*. February 12. http://www.necn.com/news/national-international/DNC-Economic-Impact-Convention-Philadelphia-Hotels-Jobs-Money-2016-Democrats-Cost--291741811.html. Accessed July 27, 2015.

O'Sullivan, Feargus. 2014. "Oslo Really Didn't Want the 2022 Olympics." *CityLab*, Oct. 6. Last accessed Oct. 9, 2014. http://www.citylab.com/politics/2014/10/oslo-doesnt-want-the-2022-winter-olympics/381133/.

O'Toole, Jr., L. J. 1988. "Strategies for Intergovernmental Management: Implementing Programs in Interorganizational Networks." *International Journal of Public Administration* 11, no. 4: 417–41.

Ostrogorski, Moisei. 1908. *Democracy and the Organization of Political Parties* (vol. II). London: The MacMillan Company.

Panagopoulos, Costas, ed. 2007. *Rewiring Politics: Presidential Nominating Conventions in the Media Age*. Baton Rouge: Louisiana State University Press.

PBS. 2008. http://www.pbs.org/pov/betterthisworld/photo_gallery_timeline-protests-2008-rnc.php#.Vi_VR36rTcs.

Penland, Brittany. 2012. "DNC volunteers find out flexibility is a big necessity." *Charlotte Observer*, September 6., 7B.

Peffley, Mark, Stanley Feldman, and Lee Sigelman. 1987. "Economic Conditions and Party Competence: Processes of Belief Revision." *Journal of Politics* 49, no. 1: 100–21.

Peoples, Steve, and Jill Colvin. 2016. "Convention missteps renew concerns about Trump and governing." Associated Press. July 22. Last accessed August 1, 2016. http:/ elections.ap.org/content/convention-missteps-renew-concerns-about-trump-and-governing.

Perry, David C. 2003. "Urban Tourism and the Privatizing Discourses of Public Infrastructure." In *The Infrastructure of Play: Building the Tourist City*, edited by Dennis R. Judd.Armonk, NY: M. E. Sharpe, 19–49.

Petrocik, John R. 1996. "Issue Ownership in Presidential Elections, with a 1980 Case Study." *American Journal of Political Science* 40, no. 3: 825–50.

Philpot, Tasha S. 2007. *Race, Republicans, and the Return of the Party of Lincoln*. Ann Arbor: University of Michigan Press.

Politico. 2016. "The Worst Convention in U.S. History?" *Politico*. July 22, 2016. Last accessed August 1, 2016. http://www.politico.com/magazine/story/2016/07/rnc-2016-worst-convention-historians-214091.

Polsby, Nelson W. 1983. *Consequences of Party Reform*. New York: Oxford University Press.

Polsby, Nelson W., Aaron Wildavsky, Steven E. Schier, and David A. Hopkins. 2012. *Presidential Elections: Strategies and Structures of American Politics*, 13th ed. Lanham, MD: Rowman & Littlefield.

Powell, Richard J. 2004. "The Strategic Importance of State-Level Factors in Presidential Elections." *Publius: The Journal of Federalism* 34, no. 3: 115–30.

Preuss, Holger. 2004. *The Economics of Staging the Olympics: A Comparison of the Games 1972–2008*. Northampton, MA: Edward Elgar.

Preuss, H., and C. Alfs. 2011. "Signaling through the 2008 Beijing Olympics-Using Mega Sport Events to Change the Perception and Image of the Host." *European Sport Management Quarterly* 11, no. 1: 55–71.

Read, Dustin, and Suzanne M. Leland. Forthcoming. "A Gendered Perspective on Local Economic Development: Differences in the Perceived Importance of Public Services in the Business Recruitment Process." *Administration & Society*.

Radin, Beryl. 2006. *Challenging the Performance Movement: Accountability, Complexity, and Democratic Values*. Washington, DC: Georgetown University Press.

Reese, Shawn. 2013. "National Special Security Events." *Congressional Research Service*, RS22754.

Reinsch, J. Leonard. 1988. *Getting Elected: From Radio and Roosevelt to Television and Reagan*. New York: Hippocrene Books.

Roche, M. 1994. "Mega-events and Urban Policy." *Annals of Tourism Research* 21, no. 1: 1–19.

Rosentraub, Mark S. 2003. "Indianapolis, A Sports Strategy, and the Definition of Downtown Redevelopment." In *The Infrastructure of Play: Building the Tourist City*, edited by Dennis R. Judd. Armonk, NY: M. E. Sharpe, 104–24.

Rosentraub, Mark S. 2010. *Major League Winners: Using Sports and Cultural Centers as Tools for Economic Development*. Boca Raton, FL: CRC Press.

Rosentraub, Mark. S., and David Swindell. 2009 "Doing Better: Sports, Economic Impact Analysis, and Schools of Public Policy and Administration." *Journal of Public Affairs Education* 15, no. 2: 219–42.

Rosentraub, Mark. S., David Swindell, Michael Przybylski, and Daniel R. Mullins. 1994. "Sport and Downtown Development Strategy: If You Build It, Will Jobs Come?" *Journal of Urban Affairs* 16: 221–39.

Rosentraub, Mark S., and John Brenna. 2011. "Contingent Valuation and Estimates of Residents' Support for Revitalization Plans: A Better Tools for Public Officials?" *American Review of Public Administration* 41, no. 6: 654–69.

Rosinski, Jennifer. 2004. "MBTA to begin screening riders before convention." *Boston Herald*, July 13.

Roth, Bennett. 1991. "Convention warning: No detail too small to ignore." *Houston Chronicle*, August 18.

Rusk, David. 1993. *Cities Without Suburbs*. Washington, DC: Woodrow Wilson Center Press.

Rusk, David. 1999. *Inside game outside game: Winning strategies for saving urban America*. Washington, DC: Brookings Institution Press.

Sack, Kevin. 1987a. "Atlanta In '88: The Democrats Come To Town" *Atlanta Journal and Constitution*, February 11.

Sack, Kevin. 1987b. "The Presidential Campaign-Convention: Down to the nitty-gritty." *Atlanta Journal-Constitution*, July 19.

Salisbury, Robert H. 1969. "An Exchange Theory of Interest Groups." *Midwest Journal of Political Science* 13: 1–32.

Sanders, Heywood. 2005. "Space Available: The Realities of Convention Centers as Economic Development Strategy." *Research Brief*. Washington, DC: The Brookings Institution Press.

Sanders, Heywood. 2014. *Convention Center Follies: Politics, Power, and Public Investment in American Cities*. Philadelphia: The University of Pennsylvania Press.

Sandomir, Richard. 2010. "Madison Square Garden to Slow for Construction." *New York Times*. May 5. Accessed June 20, 2014: http://www.nytimes.com/2010/05/06/sports/06garden.html?partner=rssnyt&emc=rss&_r=0.

Saniszlo, Marie. 2004. "Gridlock Countdown: DNC commuter hell begins in just a week." *Boston Herald*, July 29.

Schlesinger, Joseph A. 1966. *Ambition and Politics: Political Careers in the United States*. Chicago: Rand McNally.

Schneider, Mark, and Paul Teske. 1992. "Toward a Theory of the Political Entrepreneur: Evidence from Local Government." *American Political Science Review* 86: 737–47.

Scola, Nancy. 2015. "Dim Lights, Smart City." *Politico*. Accessed Nov. 27, 2015: http://www.politico.com/magazine/story/2015/11/the-smart-city-that-doesnt-mind-being-a-little-less-bright-213369.

Shafer, Byron E. 1983. *Quiet Revolution: The Struggle for the Democratic Party and the Shaping of Post-Reform Politics*. New York: Russell Sage.

Shafer, Byron E. 1988. *Bifurcated Politics: Evolution and Reform in the National Party Convention*. Cambridge, MA: Harvard University Press.

Sharp, Elaine B. 1990. *Urban Politics and Administration: From Service Delivery to Economic Development*. New York: Longman Group United Kingdom.

Shaw, Daron, and Brian Roberts. 2000. "Campaign Events and the Prospects of Victory: The 1992 and 1996 U.S. Presidential Elections." *British Journal of Political Science* 30: 259–89.

Silberman, Ellen J. 2003a. "Dems Need Cash: Sky-high Costs Dog Convention." *Boston Herald*, December 4.

Silberman, Ellen J. 2003b. "Romney: Taxpayers won't foot DNC bill." *Boston Herald*, December 5.

Smith, A. 2014. "Leveraging Sport Mega-Events: New Model or Convenient Justification?" *Journal of Policy Research in Tourism, Leisure, and Events* 6, no. 1, 15–30.

Smith, Ben. 2004. "Mike's On Phone! Mayor's Specialty: $1 Million Calls." *New York Observer*, July 19.

Smith, Celeste 2013. "Locals Saw 31% of DNC Work." *Charlotte Observer*, February 2.

Smith, Hedrick. 1989. *The Power Game: How Washington Works*. New York: Ballantine Books.

Snyder, James M. 1990. "Campaign Contributions as Investment: The U.S. House of Representatives, 1980–1986." *Journal of Political Economy* 98: 1195–1227.

Spence, A. 1973. "Job Market Signaling." *Quarterly Journal of Economics* 87, no. 3: 355–74.

Spielman, Fran. 1994. "Convention Gets Tax Help." *Chicago Sun-Times*, October 16.

Söderberg, Magnus. 2014. "Willingness to Pay for Nontraditional Attributes Among Participants of a Long-Distance Running Race." *Journal of Sports Economics* 15, no. 3: 285–302.

Stewart, Jocelyn. 1998. "Bid Launched for 2000 Democratic Convention." *Los Angeles Times*. April 18. http://articles.latimes.com/1998/apr/18/local/me-40434. Accessed July 27, 2015.

Stimson, James. 2004. *Tides of Consent: How Public Opinion Shapes American Politics*. New York: Cambridge University Press.

Stokols, Eli. 2016. "Trump's four dysfunctional days in Cleveland." *Politico*, July 22, 2016. Last accessed August 1, 2016. http://www.politico.com/story/2016/07/rnc-2016-donald-trump-dysfunction-226001.

Stone, Clarence N. 1989. *Regime Politics: Governing Atlanta, 1946–1988*. Lawrence: University of Kansas Press.

Strom, Elizabeth. 2008. "Rethinking the Politics of Downtown Development." *Journal of Urban Affairs* 30: 37–61.

Sundquist, Betsy. 2008. "Surreal St. Paul." *St. Paul Legal Ledger Capitol Report*, September 3.

Sweet, Lynn. 1993. "Chicago on the Short List: Wilhelm Gives City Edge for '96 Dem Convention." *Chicago Sun-Times*, December 24.

Sweet, Lynn, and Fran Spielman. 1995. "Convention May Cost City $15 Million." *Chicago Sun-Times*, June 12.

Swindell, David, Mark Rosentraub, and Alexandra Tsvetkova. 2008. "Public Dollars, Sport Facilities, and Intangible Benefits: The Value of a Team to a Region's Residents and Tourists." *Journal of Tourism* 9, no. 2: 133–59.

Taber, Charles S., and Milton Lodge. 2006. "Motivated Skepticism in the Evaluation of Political Beliefs." *American Journal of Political Science* 50: 755–69.

Thomson, C. A. H. 1956. *Television and Presidential Politics: The Experience in 1952 and the Problems Ahead*. Washington, DC: Brookings Institution.

Thomas, Scott E. 2003. "The Presidential Election Public Funding Program—A Commissioner's Perspective." Task Force on Financing Presidential Nominations, The Campaign Finance Institute, Washington, DC, January 31. Accessed October 16, 2014 through www.fec.gov.

Tiebout, Charles M. 1956. "A Pure Theory of Local Expenditures." *Journal of Political Economy* 64, no. 5: 416–24.

Tourism Economics. 2013. Economic Impact of the 2012 Democratic National Convention in Charlotte, North Carolina. http://crva.com/files/docs/DNC%20Economic%20Impact%20Study.pdf. Accessed August 23, 2014.

Trounstine, Jessica. 2008. *Political Monopolies in American Cities*. Chicago: University of Chicago Press.

Vadala, Nick. 2016. "DNC week fun for everyone." *Philadelphia Inquirer*, July 22, W10.

Van Ryzin, Gregg G. 2006. "Testing the Expectancy Disconfirmation Model of Citizen Satisfaction with Local Government." *Journal of Public Administration Research and Theory* 16: 599–611.

Van Ryzin, Gregg G. 2007. "Pieces of a Puzzle: Linking Government Performance, Citizen Satisfaction and Trust." *Public Performance and Management Review* 30: 521–35.

Van Ryzin, Gregg G. 2011. "Outcomes, Process, and Trust of Civil Servants." *Journal of Public Administration Research and Theory* 21, no. 4: 745–60.

Vargas, Claudia. 2016a. "DNC host body lists donors to convention." *Philadelphia Inquirer*, September 28, B1.

Vargas, Claudia. 2016b. "Many Donors to Democratic Convention Remain a Secret." *CQ Magazine*. July 25.

Vargas, Claudia. 2016c. "Turned down by the IRS, Philly's DNC host committee goes for Plan B." *Philadelphia Inquirer*, July 16, B1.

Vaughan, Kevin. 2008. "DNC sponsorships raise questions on motivations." *Rocky Mountain News*, May 12.

Vaughan, Kevin, and Daniel J. Chacon. 2008. "Right on the money, say DNC hosts Speech at stadium helps fundraisers meet obligations." *Rocky Mountain News*, August 20.

Verba, Sidney, Kay Lehman Schlozman, and Henry E. Brady. 1995. *Voice and Equality: Civic Voluntarism in American Politics*. New York: Cambridge University Press.

Wagman, Jake. 2011a. "St. Louis comes up short in bid to host Democrats." *St. Louis Post Dispatch*, February 2.

Wagman, Jake. 2011b. "St. Louis put it all on the line." *St. Louis Post-Dispatch*, February 6.

Walter, Amy. 2016. "What We've Learned from the RNC Thus Far." *The Cook Political Report*. July 20. Last accessed: August 1, 2016. http://cookpolitical.com/story/9766.

Warner, Jr., Sam Bass. 1968. *The Private City: Philadelphia in Three Periods of its Growth*. Philadelphia: The University of Pennsylvania Press.

Wayne, Stephen J. 2011. *Road to the White House 2012*. Cengage.

Webb, Tom. 2008. "Corporate Minnesota Antes up for the RNC." *St. Paul Pioneer Press*, July 11.

Weissman, Steve, with Margaret Sammon and Jennifer Sykes. 2008. Inside Fundraising for the 2008 Party Conventions. Campaign Finance Institute. http://www.cfinst.org/books_reports/conventions/2008Conventions_Rpt1.pdf. Accessed July 23, 2014.

Wilcox, Clyde, Lee Sigelman, and Elizabeth Cook. 1989. "Some Like It Hot: Individual Differences in Responses to Group Feeling Thermometers." *Public Opinion Quarterly* 53, no. 2: 246–57.

Wilmath, Kim. 2012. "Emergency Officials pick RNC as subject of hurricane disaster drill." *Tampa Bay Times*, May 20: Web Edition Articles (FL).

Wootson, Cleve. 2012. "Police: Protest space a concern for DNC." *Charlotte Observer*, May 24, 1A, 9A.

Wright, D. S. 1974. "Intergovernmental Relations: An Analytical Overview. *The Annals of the American Academy of Political and Social Science* 416, no. 1: 1–16.

Wright, John R. 1985. "PACs, Contributions, and Roll Calls: An Organizational Perspective." *American Political Science Review* 79: 400–14.

Yoo, Seung-Hoon and Kyung-Suk Chae. 2001. "Measuring the Economic Benefits of the Ozone Pollution Control Policy in Seoul: Results of a Contingent Valuation Survey." *Urban Studies* 38, no. 1: 49–60.

Zeleny, Jeff. 2011. "Democrats Pick Charlotte for 2012 Convention." *New York Times*. February 1. http://thecaucus.blogs.nytimes.com/2011/02/01/democrats-will-meet-in-charlotte-in-2012/?partner=rss&emc=rss.

Index